D1600314

CICERO

XXX

LCL 556

CICERO

FRAGMENTARY SPEECHES

EDITED AND TRANSLATED BY

JANE W. CRAWFORD
ANDREW R. DYCK

HARVARD UNIVERSITY PRESS
CAMBRIDGE, MASSACHUSETTS
LONDON, ENGLAND
2024

First published 2024

LOEB CLASSICAL LIBRARY® is a registered trademark
of the President and Fellows of Harvard College

Library of Congress Control Number 2023051343
CIP data available from the Library of Congress

ISBN 978-0-674-99762-2

*Composed in ZephGreek and ZephText by
Technologies 'N Typography, Merrimac, Massachusetts.
Printed on acid-free paper and bound by
Maple Press, York, Pennsylvania*

CONTENTS

CONTENTS

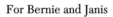

For Bernie and Janis

PREFACE

We are grateful to John Ramsey, who has offered much helpful advice in the course of our work on this edition, especially but not only on the "Asconian" speeches *On Behalf of Cornelius* and *In a White Toga.* We are likewise grateful to General Editor Jeffrey Henderson and Managing Editor Michael B. Sullivan, as well as the Loeb Foundation's Executive Trustee Richard Thomas for their support and encouragement throughout. Our greatest debt, indicated in the dedication, is to our spouses for their unfailing support.

GENERAL INTRODUCTION

CICERO'S FRAGMENTARY SPEECHES

Unlike the other orators collected in *Fragmentary Republican Latin*, Cicero has a number of speeches (fifty-eight) that survive intact or in large part,[1] for during and after his lifetime his orations were keenly read, circulated, and collected, being an object of study for other orators, especially orators in training, as well as for scholars and grammarians.[2] Even so, some of his published speeches failed to survive but left traces in the record that we call "fragments," that is, either verbatim quotations or an indication

---

[1] A brief general introduction to oratory at Rome will be found at *FRLO* 1: xiii–xviii. Greek and Latin authors and works are abbreviated as in *OCD*. All dates are BC unless otherwise indicated. Cicero's letters are cited by the traditional numeration followed by Shackleton Bailey's in brackets; *De republica* is cited according to Powell 2006, with the traditional paragraph number (if different) following in brackets.

[2] Thus Cicero speaks of publishing his consular corpus because he was "stimulated by the enthusiasm of young people" (*adulescentorum studiis excitati*: *Att.* 2.1[21].3; cf. *QFr.* 3.1[21].11); for further testimonia and discussion, see Stroh 1975, 52. On the use of Cicero's speeches in rhetorical schools, cf. Keeline 2018; La Bua 2019. For discussion of the collection and circulation of Cicero's orations in antiquity, cf. Espluga 2016.

of the content.[3] Other speeches known to have been delivered by Cicero apparently remained unpublished; the testimonia for these have been collected and edited, most recently by Crawford 1984,[4] but in this edition we have included only speeches with attested fragments.[5]

[3] Crawford 1994 distinguishes testimonia (marked with "T") from fragments ("F") based on the presence of a verbatim quotation in the latter group. We have generally followed that policy here with the exception of 5 F 51 and 9 F 14 and 17, where Asconius specifically records what Cicero "says" and gives a clear indication of the content of his remarks even if there is no verbatim quotation; cf. also 5 F 40, where Cicero's words are quoted in indirect discourse, and 12 F 1, if Quintilian is paraphrasing rather than quoting directly.

[4] To these can be added the testimonia for the speech *On Behalf of P. Vatinius*, printed with introduction and select comments by Crawford 1994, 301–8 (it is not clear that the quotation of Ter. *Eun.* 440–45 at *Fam.* 1.9[20].19 should be considered a fragment of the speech; Crawford argues against, 1994, 309–10; cf. Čulík-Baird 2022, 106). Crawford 1984 casts her net widely, including court testimony (nos. 24 and 64). Her no. 16 ("On Behalf of Q. Mucius Orestinus") might be queried, as the case was settled out of court and never went to trial (cf. 9 F 27); some other modifications are suggested by Malaspina 2001.

[5] In this respect, this edition differs from *FRLO*, which, following Malcovati 1976, includes speeches for which there are testimonia but no fragments. A similar approach to Malcovati's is taken by Malaspina 1997b. In working up his case, Cicero prepared notebooks (*commentarii*) in which introductory and essential arguments were written out; his notebooks were published by Tiro (Quint. *Inst.* 10.7.30–31); one of them (probably from the defense of Gabinius) was cited by Jerome (*Adv. Rufin.* 1.1); cf. Puccioni 1972, 127–30.

The fragments collected here are, with two exceptions (nos. 14 and 16), from speeches that Cicero polished for publication, so they are generally equal in quality to his fully preserved speeches. Though his oratory is, on the whole, well attested, some of the fragmentary speeches fill gaps in our knowledge. Thus the two speeches *On Behalf of C. Cornelius* (nos. 5–6) show the kind of rhetoric Cicero deployed in defending an ex-tribune against attacks from optimate leaders, an unusual role for him, but one demonstrating his versatility, ingenuity, and tact in managing to do so successfully without endangering his own political ambitions. Significant in a different way is *In a White Toga* (no. 9), which counters electoral propaganda from his opponents for the consulship, L. Sergius Catilina (commonly, "Catiline" in English) and C. Antonius, who coordinated their efforts with the plebeian tribune Orestinus, a speech that adumbrates in some respects the rhetorical approach of the *First Catilinarian*.[6]

Our sixteen orations fall, like Cicero's career in general, into three periods: the preconsular, the consular, and the postconsular. The first group is the most numerous, comprising ten examples. In his youth, Cicero needed to handle as many cases as possible in order to spread his reputation, but as an unknown orator he did not have a wide choice of clients. He took risks, accepting some defenses that he might later have rejected, such as that of the freedman Scamander in 74.[7] He also published many speeches for purposes of self-advertisement, including some that did not win acquittal for his clients (*On Behalf of L. Vare-*

[6] See the introduction to *In a White Toga* (no. 9).

[7] On this case, see further Crawford 1984, 39–42.

nus, no. 1, and probably also *On Behalf of P. Oppius* and *On Behalf of Q. Gallius*, nos. 3 and 10). The loss of these early, more audacious speeches is regrettable, especially the defense of Varenus, which Quintilian singled out for an innovative arrangement of matter (*dispositio*) that served the interests of this particular case (1 T 1 and 3). On the other hand, in the defense of Oppius, Cicero adopts the diffident tone to broach a difficult case that he would later perfect in *On Behalf of Cluentius* (3 T 7).[8]

It is perhaps unsurprising that such unsuccessful defenses, and one for an obscure client like Fundanius (no. 8), though they may interest us, failed to circulate widely enough to pass through the bottleneck in late antiquity when texts destined to survive intact were copied from the roll to the codex (i.e., the modern book) format. Two speeches of this period, those *On Behalf of Cornelius* (nos. 5 and 6), did secure the defendant's acquittal. But their subject matter, *lesé majesté*, made them unique within Cicero's corpus. Moreover, this was a fairly unusual offense, so they would not have been in demand as models for use in rhetorical schools. They were also bulky, comprising four days' pleadings within two volumes (5–6 T 11.7).[9] At a time when writing materials and trained copyists were becoming scarce, these factors may have been sufficient to doom them.

In this period Cicero also began publishing political

---

[8] In this respect his model may have been M. Antonius' defense of Norbanus (*FRLO* 65 F 23 = *De or.* 2.202–3).

[9] Plin. *Ep.* 1.20.8 speaks, however, of "one book, albeit large" (*unum librum grandem quidem*); see on 6 F 9b.

speeches, of which two were delivered in the senate (*On King Ptolemy*, no. 7, and *In a White Toga*, no. 9) and one before a public meeting (*On C. Manilius*, no. 4). Political speeches had, however, somewhat less interest for rhetoricians, whose focus was primarily on the courts, and they resisted grouping in a larger corpus. Of the speech *On King Ptolemy* (no. 7) we have just enough to whet our appetite for more: several fragments give a glimpse of a moralizing posture in international relations that is not prominent in Cicero's later oratory (though it does reappear, notably at *Off.* 2.26b–29).[10] The other oration delivered in the senate, *In a White Toga* (no. 9), had, however, like the Cornelian orations, the good fortune to be the object of a surviving commentary by Asconius and so is relatively well attested. The odd item among the early speeches, neither political nor forensic, is *When He Departed Lilybaeum as Quaestor* (no. 2), essentially a display speech that Cicero may have published to memorialize his activities in his first public office. Unconnected with the courts or high politics, this speech, unsurprisingly, left a light footprint: only one testimonium and one fragment.

Being part of a larger corpus provided a certain amount of protection for an individual speech. To keep the memory of his consulship fresh, Cicero carefully prepared a corpus of his consular speeches, as he reports to Atticus in a letter dated by Shackleton Bailey (2002) circa June 3(?), 60 (*Att.* 2.1[21].3), listing ten speeches and two excerpts.

---

[10] Cf. 7 F 1, 2, 6 (Cicero's first extant mention of a "just cause of war"), 8. Such moralizing in foreign policy is associated above all with Cato Uticensis; cf. Morrell 2017, ch. 3.

In the next century, the elder Pliny shows familiarity with it (*HN* 7.116–17).[11] The corpus had a fairly good success rate: all but two of the complete speeches survive (albeit the defense of Rabirius is mutilated at §19 and at the end). Of the lost speeches we have one fragment each (*On Otho* and *On the Sons of the Proscribed*, nos. 11 and 12). One of the excerpts (*On the Agrarian Law* 4) has, however, perished altogether. As might be expected, the two fragmentary speeches deal with special problems (a riot at the games in honor of Apollo and the demand of the sons of the proscribed for restoration of their political rights) and are unconnected with litigation or major political issues.

From the postconsular period four speeches have survived in fragments alone, three delivered in the senate (nos. 13, 14, 15), one at a trial (no. 16). One of these, *Against Q. Metellus' Speech in a Public Meeting* (13), was an isolated incident, albeit a harbinger of trouble ahead, and so apparently failed to gain purchase. Likewise *Interrogation about Milo's Debt* (no. 15) was on a special problem without political relevance after Milo's exile in 52 (and the speech may have been viewed as redundant beside the defense of Milo that did survive). An unusual case is that of *Against Clodius and Curio* (no. 14), which Cicero did not intend to publish. It was, however, circulated publicly during his exile; possibly it fell into the hands of a member of the mob that sacked and destroyed his house on the

---

[11] See further Cape 2002; Manuwald 2018, xxxv–xxxviii; Berry 2020, 59–82, arguing for the revision for publication of the *Catilinarians*.

Palatine after his departure in March 58 and was leaked to embarrass him (cf. 14 T 2–3). The speech is interesting in that it recycles some of the points Cicero first raised in debate with Clodius in the senate in the aftermath of the Bona Dea trial (*Att.* 1.16[16].10 ~ 14 F 19–20, 26)[12] and anticipates some of his later invective (Clodius' feminine disguise at the goddess's mysteries: 14 F 21–23 ~ *Har. resp.* 44; his "blindness": 14 F 20 ~ *Har. resp.* 26, etc.). We also include here, for the sake of completeness, the fragment of the speech Cicero delivered at Milo's trial for violence (*de vi*) on April 8, 52,[13] which was taken down and circulated by others (no. 16) but replaced by the extant speech *On Behalf of Milo.*

This brief survey shows that the fragmentary speeches have failed to survive intact due to factors contingent on the way Cicero's speeches were read, circulated, and evaluated in antiquity, especially late antiquity, when crucial decisions about survival were made. That does not necessarily reduce their value and interest for readers today: as Crawford points out, "When these [lost and fragmentary] orations are integrated into the body of extant speeches, a clearer view of [Cicero's] development as a politician, statesman, advocate, and orator emerges. The picture is fuller and more nuanced; successes and failures alike play a role. For these reasons we should not ignore this valuable resource, but be glad we have as many of these speeches as we do."[14]

[12] Cf. Malaspina 1997b, 136–37.
[13] For the date, cf. Keeline 2021, 15n70 and 336.
[14] Crawford 2002, 326–27.

THE QUOTING AUTHORS

Our fragments have survived because they attracted the interest of later authors for their content, oratorical strategies, or use of language. As is to be expected, the earlier quoting authors generally provide the most reliable evidence, since they had a better grasp of the underlying historical situations, institutions, and cultural practices.

Our best source in general is Asconius, a careful historian, who wrote commentaries on Cicero's speeches in the mid-first century AD.[15] For three of the speeches (nos. 5, 6, 9) we rely primarily on the evidence of Asconius' surviving commentaries. Asconius is particularly helpful, since his general practice of citing passages in the order of their occurrence in the speeches establishes a framework for reconstructing the whole speech in each case.[16] He sometimes also provides helpful guideposts to orient readers to the place of the individual passage within the speech as a whole (e.g., "a little later"); we have included such indications in our text in small capitals.[17] One problem, however, is that Asconius' text survived the Middle Ages in a single corrupt manuscript, discovered by Poggio at St. Gall in 1416, which has since disappeared, and its

[15] For details on his life and work, see the introduction to Ramsey forthcoming; for his working methods, Keeline 2023.

[16] For an exception to this, cf. on 9 F 22.

[17] As to Asconius' references to numbers of lines, it should be borne in mind that the lines he refers to appear to be about 20 percent shorter than those of an Oxford Classical Text; see further Ramsey forthcoming.

reconstruction from extant copies is fraught with difficulties.[18]

Next in order of importance is Quintilian, a teacher of rhetoric at Rome, whose magnum opus, *The Orator's Education*, dates from the 90s AD. He was a fervent admirer of Cicero, whose name was, for him, not that of a man but of eloquence itself[19] and whom he often cites to illustrate his points. His value as a source is shown, for instance, by the absence, in his quotation from *On Behalf of Q. Gallius* (10 F 1a), of the sentence interpolated by the third-century rhetorician Aquila of Rome (10 F 1c), whose "illustrations from Cicero [are] often misquoted from memory";[20] Quintilian's remark when he cites the same passage elsewhere makes it clear that the point was to give a negative characterization of the prosecutor, not the defendant, as the interpolated sentence implies (10 F 1b). In another instance, however, Quintilian offers a less plausible version of a fragment than another source (cf. 14 F 6). It is not always easy to decide whether points embedded in Quintilian's argument should be taken as direct quotations from Cicero or merely paraphrases, as 12 F 1 shows. To our benefit, the Flavian rhetorician took a particular interest in the early defenses of Varenus and Oppius (nos. 1 and 3): to him we owe more than half of the testimonia and fragments of these two speeches, including perceptive observations on deviations from the norms inculcated by school rhetoric (cf. 1 T 1, 3).

---

[18] See detailed discussion by Welsh 2017.

[19] Quint. *Inst.* 10.1.112: *non hominis nomen, sed eloquentiae.*

[20] So *OCD* s.v. Aquila Romanus.

Quintilian is one of several authors of rhetorical handbooks who searched Cicero's works for examples to illustrate their precepts (or copied those of their predecessors) and to whom we owe a great many of our surviving fragments. The earliest of these is P. Rutilius Lupus, writing late in the Augustan age, who rendered into Latin a handbook on figures of speech by the Athenian rhetorician Gorgias, perhaps to be identified with the teacher of Marcus Cicero, Jr., whom his father dismissed for corrupting the young man (*Fam.* 16.21[337].6; Plut. *Vit. Cic.* 24.8). Rutilius regularly translates Gorgias' Greek examples but adds Latin ones where appropriate; for instance, our Unplaced F 1 is quoted apropos of paronomasia, Rutilius' only Ciceronian example.[21]

Next chronologically is probably the fragment of a rhetorical handbook that is attributed in one branch of the tradition to Augustine but is almost certainly not by the church father; it probably belongs rather to the second or third century.[22] He names a certain Democrites as his teacher (63.11 Giomini) and has evidently, like Rutilius, translated his base text from the Greek, with some of the Greek examples replaced by Ciceronian ones. Here Cicero is cited for his masterly way of beginning his speeches, including the vigorous and confident passage "in which

---

[21] The quotation is unattributed by Rutilius, but its Ciceronian provenance is confirmed by Charisius and Diomedes (*GL* 1.282.2 [= p. 370.18 Barw.] and 446.20). For Gorgias and Rutilius, cf. Münscher, *RE* 7.2:1604.50–1605.40 (identification with the teacher of Cicero, Jr., date of the Latin rendering) and 1609.10–29 (Rutilius' treatment of examples); Stein-Witte, *RE* s.v. Rutilius 28.

[22] So Riesenweber 2023, 91; Giomini 1990, 8–13 argues for Augustine's authorship.

[Cicero] seems to exult" in the discomfiture of his opponent Metellus Nepos (13 F 1).[23]

Examples from Cicero feature prominently in Aquila of Rome, who in the latter half of the third century wrote a handbook *On Figures of Thought and Diction* based on a Greek predecessor, Alexander Numenius (9 ff. Sp.). The treatment consists of a Greek term, followed by Latin translation and definition, then mostly Ciceronian examples replacing those from Demosthenes in his source.[24] This pattern makes it likely that Unplaced F *14 and *15, transmitted by Aquila, are from Cicero. Aquila's work was continued by Iulius Rufinianus (third/fourth century)[25] and was the source for the treatment of figures in Book 5 of Martianus Capella's *On the Marriage of Philology and Mercury* from the last quarter of the fifth century.[26] Martianus offers a version of Aquila's preserved text for 6 F 1 and Unplaced F 13, *14, and *15. Moreover, Martianus used a manuscript of Aquila more nearly complete than our extant ones; hence he alone preserves the remarks on the "artificial arrangement" at 5–6 T 25 and on argument from contradictories at 5 F 40.

[23] See further Riesenweber 2023, 99–100.

[24] Cf. Brzoska, *RE* s.v. Aquila 10; Elice 2007, xl–xliii; Riesenweber 2023, 120n160. A similar pattern appears in the anonymous treatise *Figures of Thought* (*Schemata Dianoeas*), of uncertain date, from which Unplaced F 11 derives. Heavily dependent on Quintilian, it is transmitted in cod. Parisinus 7530 (8th century).

[25] So dated by W.-L. Liebermann, *BNP* s.v. Iulius IV.20. Rufinianus is the source of Unplaced F 16, 17, and 18, as well as part of 14 F 21.

[26] Mart. Cap. 5.523–57; cf. Brzoska, *RE* 2.1:316.39–42; Zetzel 2018, 303–4. For his date, cf. Shanzer 1986, 8–17.

Several other rhetoricians of the fourth and fifth centuries contribute Ciceronian fragments that would not otherwise survive. Marius Victorinus, who was active in the mid-fourth century as a teacher of rhetoric at Rome,[27] was the author of a commentary on Cicero's early treatise *On Invention* but also of a work *On Definitions* that is a source of several fragments.[28] One obvious topic for Marius' work was the concept of *laesa maiestas*, which is addressed in the case of C. Cornelius (5 F 18; cf. F 29 and *30). Less expected is a type of definition "by sketch" ($\kappa\alpha\theta$' $\dot{\upsilon}\pi o\tau\dot{\upsilon}\pi\omega\sigma\iota\nu$), for which he cites from 5 F 44, where Cicero denies that the relevant testimony offers any description of Cornelius' actions; the other example is from the defense of Fundanius, where Cicero describes rather than names a certain competitor of his (in the consular elections: 8 F 5). The fifth-century rhetorician Grillius followed in Victorinus' footsteps with his own commentary for *On Invention*, of which only the beginning survives.[29] Grillius does, however, enrich our picture of *On Behalf of Cornelius I*, especially its diffident opening (5 F 1 and 3, and possibly Unplaced F 22) as well as other aspects of its strategy (5–6 T 22, 5 F 49). Iulius Victor, the author of another roughly contemporary rhetorical handbook, quotes Cicero apropos of Metellus Nepos' hostile attitude and actions (13 F 5).[30]

[27] Cf. Wessner, *RE* s.v. Marius 70; Herzog in Herzog 1989, 343; Zetzel 2018, 259–60 and 301–3.

[28] Riesenweber 2022 announces that he is preparing a new edition and offers samples of his work in progress.

[29] Cf. Zetzel 2018, 259–60.

[30] He is dated to the fourth century with a query by Winterbottom, *OCD* s.v.; cf. Zetzel 2018, 260.

In the mid-fifth century, the Gallic rhetor Iulius Seve-rianus, a friend of Sidonius Apollinaris, wrote a rhetorical handbook that has been described with slight exaggera-tion as a framework for displaying examples from Cicero's speeches.[31] In fact, with the exception of one passage as-cribed to Calvus,[32] he draws his identifiable examples ex-clusively from Cicero. This therefore creates the pre-sumption that Unplaced F *21 is also Ciceronian. Besides offering verbatim fragments (also 1 F 1–2), he sometimes helpfully comments on Ciceronian strategies (1 T 8, 3 T 9, 10 T 5). In the late fifth century Fortunatianus, who au-thored an *Art of Rhetoric* in three books, shows in general far fewer citations from Cicero's speeches than Severia-nus. He does, however, highlight the careful advance preparation ($\pi\rho o\kappa\alpha\tau\alpha\sigma\kappa\epsilon\nu\dot\eta$) in *On Behalf of P. Oppius* (3 T 11). Apropos of *On King Ptolemy*, he notes the use of a "mixed division" of the case and an unusually detailed citation of the opponent in order to expose a contradiction (7 T 2–3). He also calls attention to the fact that Cicero can use humble diction effectively, as in a passage of *On Behalf of Cornelius I* (5 F 10).[33]

Most of the rest of our information about the lost speeches derives from authors whose interests are broadly grammatical or exegetical. Grammatical authors may cast

---

[31] For his date, cf. Schindel 2000, 416; the characterization is that of Riesenweber 2023, 121.

[32] *FRLO* 165 F 26 (19, p. 109.23 Castelli Montanari = *RLM* 366.2).

[33] For his date and number of citations, cf. Riesenweber 2023, 94 and the table at 122–25; for a different view, placing him in the late fourth or early fifth century, cf. Calboli Montefusco 1979, 4–5.

their nets more widely than the rhetoricians and preserve unique fragments of special kinds of speeches, such as 2 F 1 (*When He Departed Lilybaeum as Quaestor*) or 11 F 1 (*On Otho*), both quoted by Arusianus Messius, the late fourth-century author of a list of words admitting variable syntactic constructions, which he illustrates from four "school authors" of the time, including Cicero.[34] Arusianus is also remarkable for offering seventeen fragments of the speeches *On Behalf of Cornelius*, accounting for 77 percent of his total Ciceronian quotations. By contrast, Priscian (fifth/sixth century), author of what remained for centuries the authoritative Latin grammar and also fond of the Cornelian speeches, cites them for only 53 percent of his Ciceronian total.[35]

Some grammatical authors could be content with elucidating the meaning of a single word, such as Aulus Gellius (second century), who discusses the oration *Against Q. Metellus' Speech in a Public Meeting* in order to elucidate the word *contio* (13 T 2 and F 4). Such citations do not usually lead us very far (cf., e.g., 8 F 3 and 4, single words quoted, respectively, by Servius on the *Aeneid* and Pseudo-Acro on the *Ars Poetica*). The exegesis of an idea may yield a bit more insight, such as the claim of the Arcadians to be older than the moon, cited in both the commentary on Statius' *Thebaid*, falsely attributed to Lactantius Placidus, and in Servius on the *Georgics* (8 T 4

---

34 For his date, cf. Di Stefano 2011, xxx–xxxvi; for brief discussion see Zetzel 2018, 281–82.

35 On Priscian, see Zetzel 2018, 309–11.

and 5).[36] Scholia to Cicero's speeches are, of course, in a different category. Thus the Bobbio Scholia, a collection of the late third or early fourth century, explicate in detail the speeches *On King Ptolemy*, *Against Clodius and Curio*, and *Interrogation about Milo's Debt* (nos. 7, 14, 15); hence almost all the fragments of these three speeches derive from the Bobbio Scholia.[37] To the early fifth century also belongs the Pseudo-Asconian commentary on the *Divination against Caecilius* and the *Verrines*, the source of testimonia for three of our speeches.[38]

An outlier is **13 F 2, which is transmitted by a medieval source.[39] In the Middle Ages, schoolmasters wrote commentaries on the authors in the curriculum, with background provided in an introductory section called an *accessus* (approach). This type of literature reached its zenith in the twelfth century. In an *accessus* to Lucan, an example is cited that Broscius 1988 has conjecturally assigned to Cicero's speech *Against Metellus*, since it

---

[36] On the former, cf. Jakobi 2004, analyzing the strata in the preserved commentary on the *Thebaid* and concluding that the oldest stratum shows knowledge of Donatus but not yet of Servius. In addition, Servius' citation of Statius at 8 T 5 suggests that he owes his knowledge of *On Behalf of Fundanius* to a commentary on Statius.

[37] On the Bobbio scholiast, see Schmidt in Herzog 1989, 140–42; Zetzel 2018, 258.

[38] 2 T 1, 3 T 10, and 10 T 4; for the dates, cf. La Bua 2019, 159 and 164.

[39] In the edition of this fragment, we have retained the twelfth-century Latin orthography.

contains a derogatory remark about Caecilius, the gentile name of Cicero's target.[40] The fragment is, however, marked with double asterisk as dubious, since it is not clear how this information could have reached the author and it is not attributed to Cicero, let alone to the specific work. It is not excluded that the example was simply invented by the schoolmaster.[41]

But perhaps the most interesting fragments are quoted by two authors who can be described as neither rhetoricians nor grammarians. One is a maxim about statesmanship quoted appreciatively by the historian Ammianus Marcellinus (ca. AD 330–395) in criticizing the cruelty and rapaciousness of the emperor Valentinian in the aftermath of his failed Parthian campaign. He not only aptly quotes and applies Cicero's words but traces them back to their Greek source (see on 3 F 5).[42] If Cicero was a ma-

---

[40] On this type of literature, cf. Olsen 2013; Wheeler 2015, 1–5 and 14–16 for strictures on Huygens' edition, from which this passage derives (the *accessus* edited by Wheeler, in Codex latinus monacensis 19475 of the twelfth century, includes only the first sentence: §20.58).

[41] Further grounds for doubt: the phrase *altera vice* does not occur in Classical Latin, and Cicero might have been expected to express the matter more specifically, e.g., "by the same Greek" or the like, rather than simply "by a Greek."

[42] Amm Marc. 19.12.18 is sometimes also claimed as a fragment of an unknown speech (Orelli-Baiter-Halm 6:1055 no. 3): *Imitandus sit Tullius cum parcere vel laedere potuisset, ut ipse adfirmat, ignoscendi quaerens causas, non puniendi occasiones, quod iudicis lenti et considerati est proprium* (Tullius should be imitated in seeking reasons to pardon, not opportunities to pun-

jor literary influence on the pagan Ammianus, so he was also on his younger Christian contemporary, Jerome (ca. AD 347–420), who once dreamed of being accused at the Last Judgment of being not a Christian but a Ciceronian (*Ep.* 22.30). Jerome offers a lengthy quotation, aptly cited in a letter on a clergyman's duties addressed in 394 to Nepotian, Bishop of Altinum, to illustrate the hollowness of applause bestowed on empty words (*Ep.* 52.8 = 10 F 2). One wishes there were more examples of such thoughtful reading and deployment of Cicero's ideas.

PROBLEMATIC CASES

In his *Orthography* (s.v. *clamo*), Bede attributes to *Cicero, De Prasio* (sic), the words "the innocent man was punished by shouts alone" (*solis innocens acclamationibus punitus est*). Piacente 1986–1987 wants to insert this text into *Pro Rabirio perduellionis reo* 18, but it is unclear how it could be accommodated (there is no apparent lacuna in the text). If this is a genuine Ciceronian fragment, perhaps it might rather come from the speech *De (rege) Ptolemaeo* (*On King Ptolemy*), a speech in which Cicero argued that Ptolemy XII Auletes was unjustly deprived of his throne by a mob at Alexandria; see further on no. 7 below. If that is so, the words *solis . . . acclamationibus* will be

---

ish, when, as he asserts, he could either have spared or harmed another, and this is the proper role of the mild and thoughtful judge). But perhaps this is a paraphrase of a plea such as that at *Sul.* 92–93; cf. fr. ex inc. scriptis no. 40 Garbarino with note.

causal ablative: "on the basis of" or "because of shouts alone," that is, he [Ptolemy] was merely punished (by loss of his throne) on this basis, not because of evidence of wrongdoing.

Puccioni 1972, 117, and Crawford 1994, 289–93, recognize as an additional speech one they designate *Against P. Servilius Isauricus (In P. Servilium Isauricum)*.[43] This is based on the text transmitted at Quint. *Inst.* 6.3.48: "Therefore Cicero's remark directed at the aforementioned Isauricus: 'I am surprised that your father, a man of great constancy, left us someone like you, so mottled [i.e., black and blue from whipping]' is not only thus [i.e., having a double meaning] but almost scurrilous" (*quare non hoc modo <sed> paene et ipsum scurrile Ciceronis est in eundem de quo supra dixi Isauricum: "miror quid sit quod pater tuus, homo constantissimus, te nobis varium reliquit"*). However, Winterbottom at Russell 2001 ad loc. deletes the attribution to Cicero, whose words Quintilian is unlikely to have characterized so negatively. The sentence might more plausibly be attributed to M. Caelius as a quip accompanying his substitution of a chair strung with leather straps for the curule chair broken by Servilius as consul in 48, the leather thongs serving as a reminder of the whipping to which Servilius' father had once subjected him (Quint. *Inst.* 6.3.25). Quintilian not only narrated the incident a short while previously but cross-refers here to the earlier mention of Isauricus, and his comment in this context, that such remarks are rarely apt unless helped

---

[43] Schoell 1918, 467.8–9, lists this as no. 3 among the "fragments of uncertain speeches."

by the actual facts (*nisi rebus ipsis adiuvantur*), invites the reader to think of the previously narrated incident of the chair with leather straps. That speech is therefore excluded from this edition.

In addition, several of the Unplaced Fragments (*Fragmenta incertae sedis*) listed at Crawford 1994, 295–300, should be deleted:

1. As pointed out by Keeline, her Unplaced Fragment 5 (= Quint. *Inst.* 9.2.41) is explicitly a paraphrase of *Mil.* 79.[44]

2. Fragments *6 and *7, quoted by Quintilian, *Inst.* 9.2.47, are both from the *Pro Cluentio*: *6: "I pass over that first crime of passion" (*mitto illam primam libidinis iniuriam*) from *Clu.* 188; *7: "I do not even read out the testimonies that were given about the 600,000 sesterces" (*ne illa quidem testimonia recito quae dicta sunt de sestertiis sescentis milibus*) from *Clu.* 99.

3. Fragment *8: "What is left?" ("*Quid relicum est?*") is from Pers. *Sat.* 6.58.

4. Fragment 18, attributed by Arusianus Messius (34.14 Di Stefano = *GL* 7.470.1–2) to "Cicero *On Punishments*," i.e., *Verr.* 2.5, is probably a corruption of *Verr.* 2.4.21; certainly it appears nowhere in *Verr.* 2.5. The quoted words are: "when the pirates depart from Sicily" (*ut exeunt e Sicilia praedones*). At *Verr.* 2.4.21 there is a description of Phaselis, a town on the coast of Lycia, that reads: "its location was

[44] Keeline 2021, 298.

such and it extended so far into the sea that pirates departing from Cilicia often necessarily landed there" (*erat eius modi loco atque ita proiecta in altum ut et exeuntes e Cilicia praedones saepe ad eam necessario devenirent*). The corruption of *Cilicia* to *Sicilia* in a text from the *Verrines* is an easy one; and the phrase *ut . . . praedones*, quoted separately, would easily be taken as an independent clause and the "correction" made of *exeuntes* (departing) to *exeunt* (depart). In view of the extensive treatment of pirates in *Verr.* 2.5.59–95, Arusianus or his source wrongly connected the passage with *On Punishments*.

5. Fragment 20: "And allow me to keep to my order of argument" (*meque meum dicendi ordinem servare patiamini*) is from *Clu.* 6.

6. Fragment 21 is cited from Isidore, *On Propriety of Language* (*De proprietate sermonum*) I 507 (= *PL* 83.61): "Among *sceleratum*, *scelestum*, and *scelerosum*. Grammarians say that that man is *sceleratus* (accursed) on whom a wicked act is done, as Cicero (says): 'O you accursed one, who were massaged and prostituted!'"[45] There are several problems. Isidore's authorship of the surviving treatise *On Propriety of Language* can no longer be sustained; it dates, rather, from the fourth to fifth century. The recension produced by the most recent editor contains no

---

[45] *Inter "sceleratum," "scelestum," et "scelerosum." Grammatici dicunt sceleratum illum esse in quo fit scelus, ut Cicero: "O te scelerate, qui subactus et prostitutus es."*

reference to Cicero and omits the purported quotation. This material thus seems to have been interpolated.[46] It might be added that Cicero does not use the interjection *o* with *scelerate*, only Ovid does so in extant classical Latin;[47] nor does Cicero otherwise use *o te* in combination or *subigo* in the sense "massage."

7. Fragment 22 is quoted by Pompeius Iulianus (*GL* 5.304.8) in this form: "Therefore you inflicted no punishment on him, but you abandoned your guestfriend" (*itaque in illum non animadvertisti, sed hospitem reliquisti*). This is a condensed and/or garbled version of *Pro rege Deiotaro* 10: "Therefore you not only did not inflict punishment on him but freed him of all fear, recognized him as your guestfriend and left him as king" (*itaque non solum in eum non animadvertisti, sed omni metu liberavisti, hospitem agnovisti, regem reliquisti*).

8. Fragment 31, quoted by Iulius Victor 42.6 Giomini-Celentano, deals with slaves gathering and committing murder, the subject matter of the *Pro Tullio*, and was rightly included by Clark 1911 as fragment 4 of that speech.

[46] Cf. Uhlfelder 1954, 24–25 (on authorship and the poor quality of previous texts, Migne reprinting Arevalo 1803, based in turn on Du Breul 1601) and §62 of her edition.

[47] *Met.* 9.577–78: *dum licet, o vetitae scelerate libidinis auctor, / effuge!* ("Flee while you may, wicked sponsor of forbidden lust!": Caunus to the slave who delivered the love letter from his sister Byblis).

PLAN OF THIS EDITION

The speeches are arranged chronologically and numbered continuously. Each speech receives a brief introduction in italics. Then follows the relevant evidence, with testimonia (T) preceding fragments (F). Within the latter, enough of the quoting author is included to make the reason for citation clear (except when the fragments are transmitted as lemmata in commentaries), and Cicero's own words are enclosed in quotation marks, as in *FRLO*. The testimonia are arranged chronologically by quoting author. The fragments are arranged, insofar as possible, in the order in which they would have occurred in the given speech, with unplaceable fragments relegated to the end of the series. Occasionally, different versions of the same fragment are printed separately and distinguished as "a," "b," "c," etc. The "Unplaced Fragments" are arranged chronologically by quoting author. Deviations from the order of items in Crawford (1994) are indicated by references in square brackets after the testimonium or fragment number on the English side and are registered in the concordances at the back. For repeated items the source is followed by "=" and the reference to the previous passage; they are ordinarily printed once only.

According to Loeb Classical Library norms, there is no full critical apparatus. Rather, select variants are indicated in footnotes to the Latin text. If the correct reading appears in a part of the transmission, this generally stands without citation of variants. Peculiar readings of individual witnesses and orthographical variants are excluded. The witnesses are usually cited as *cod.* or *codd.*, the latter in-

dicating the transmitted text, whether or not it is in all witnesses. Readers should seek details in the relevant editions of the source texts (listed in part 1 of the General Bibliography). Where the reading seems fairly secure, we have been parsimonious in citing conjectures. We have cited the evidence more generously for Asconius, whose text is often corrupt; for full citation of readings in Asconius' text, see Ramsey (forthcoming).

The text of Asconius, one of the principal sources, does not, like most classical texts, have agreed chapter divisions but is conventionally cited by reference to page and line number in standard editions. This is usually not a problem, since the testimonia and fragments are generally not more than a few lines and can be located easily. However, rather lengthy portions of Asconius' commentary are required as background for the speeches *On Behalf of Cornelius* (5–6 T 11), *In a White Toga* (9 T 2), and *Against Clodius and Curio* (14 T 6); therefore, to aid the reader, we have introduced our own numbered paragraph divisions for these items and cross-referred to these.

This edition is based on the predecessor work Crawford 1994. Fragments of speeches that are extant in whole or substantial part are excluded, since these feature in the editions of the respective speeches in the Loeb series.[48] The version of the defense of Milo taken down by stenographers and circulated is included here (no. 16), since, though this is a fragment, it is not a fragment of the preserved *Pro Milone*, which is intact; the case is similar to

---

[48] Except *On Behalf of Tullius*, a Loeb edition of which is currently in preparation, including its fragments.

Against Clodius and Curio (no. 14), another speech circulated by others, rather than by Cicero himself. The sources have been examined afresh, and newer source editions substituted where appropriate. Apart from the items listed in the previous section, the revision of the chronology of the speeches, and the rearrangement of testimonia in chronological order, the major changes from 1994 can be summarized as follows (most involve elimination of matter which, though providing background information, is not strictly a testimonium for the speech itself; an exception is 5–6 T 11, where Asconius' full introduction is essential to interpreting the fragments):

1. No. 4: "On Behalf of [*Pro*] C. Manilius" is eliminated as a possible title.
2. Nos. 5–6: new testimonia T 13, 14, 23, and 24 are added; T 19 becomes 6 F 9b; T 22 is eliminated; *6 F 4 becomes 5 F 49; new fragments 5 F 51 and 6 F 9a are added (the latter = T 21.83 in Crawford 1994).
3. No. 7: the earlier attested title, *On King Ptolemy*, is substituted for *On the Alexandrian King*; of the "uncertain testimonies" (*testimonia incerta*), 1 is eliminated; 2 becomes T 4; 3 becomes *T 1.
4. *On Behalf of C. Fundanius* is redated to the second half of 65 or the first half of 64 (see introduction to that speech) and thus becomes no. 8.
5. The order of the speeches *On Behalf of Q. Gallius* and *In a White Toga* is reversed in view of the chronological indication at 10 T 3 (see the introduction to no. 10).
6. No. 9: previous T 5 is eliminated (= *FRLO* 112 F 2

and 113 F 1A) and replaced with new content; new F 14 and 17 are added.

7. No. 10: previous T 4 and F 7 are eliminated as dependent on T 2 and F 6 (*Brut.* 277–78); T 4 is added.

8. The order of *On the Sons of the Proscribed* and *On Otho* is reversed, to match the list at *Att.* 2.1[21].3.

9. No. 11: the title cited by Cicero, *On Otho*, is used; there is a new interpretation of the background, after Ramsey 2021.

10. No. 12: T 4 is eliminated.

11. No. 13: new fragment **F 2 is added.

12. No. 14: previous T 1 and 8 are reduced in scope; T 2 and 6 are eliminated; F 6b is eliminated.

13. No. 15: T 1 and 2 are eliminated; T 3 is reduced in scope.

Concordances at the end indicate all changes that have been made in the inclusion and ordering of the fragments vis-à-vis the 1994 edition and the other commonly used editions of Schoell and Puccioni.[49]

A NOTE ON THE TRANSLATION

A fresh translation has been prepared for this volume, for which some help has been obtained from previous Loeb translations, with thanks to the respective authors. The aim has been to capture the sense of the Latin in idiomatic English that can be read as an independent text but remains in recognizable contact with the Latin version on the facing page for readers who wish to compare.

[49] For these we have added our own numeration of their unnumbered testimonia.

BRACKETS AND SYMBOLS

In Latin Text

[ ]   deletions by modern scholars (unless introduced with
      sc., in which case, editors' insertion)
⟨ ⟩   additions by modern scholars

In English Text

[ ]   editors' insertions

Before Fragment Number

*   conjectural attribution (we do not use if the frag-
      ment is securely attributed in a part of the tradition
      or attributed beyond reasonable doubt)
**   doubtful fragment

ABBREVIATIONS

Barw.	See Bibliography 1.10.
BNP	Cancik, H., and H. Schneider, eds. *Brill's New Pauly*. 30 vols. Leiden-Boston, 2002–2017.
C	See Bibliography 1.7.
Calboli Montefusco	See Bibliography 1.15.
Castelli Montanari	See Bibliography 1.43.
D.–K.	Diels, H., ed. *Die Fragmente der Vorsokratiker.* 3 vols. 11th ed., ed. W. Kranz. Zurich-Berlin, 1964.
FRH	Cornell, T. J., ed. *The Fragments of the Roman Historians*. 3 vols. Oxford, 2013.
FRLO	Manuwald, G., ed. and trans. *Fragmentary Republican Latin: Oratory*. 3 vols. Cambridge, MA, 2019.
G.	Grilli, A., ed. *M. Tulli Ciceronis Hortensius*. Milan, 1962.
Garbarino	Garbarino, I., ed. *M. Tulli Ciceronis fragmenta ex libris philosophicis, ex aliis libris deperditis, ex scriptis incertis*. Milan, 1984.

ABBREVIATIONS

GL	Keil, H., ed. *Grammatici Latini*. 7 vols. Leipzig, 1857–1880.
GRF	Funaioli, H., ed. *Grammaticae Romanae fragmenta*. Vol. 1. Leipzig, 1907.
Huschke	Huschke, P. E., ed. *Iurisprudentiae anteiustinianae quae supersunt*. 4th ed. Leipzig, 1879.
Huygens	See Bibliography 1.3.
Jakobi	See Bibliography 1.17.
L	See Bibliography 1.25.
LPPR	Rotondi, G. *Leges publicae populi Romani*. Milan, 1912. Reprint with supplement, Hildesheim, 1966.
LSJ	Liddell, H. G., and R. Scott. *A Greek-English Lexicon*. 9th ed. Edited by H. S. Jones. Oxford, 1940.
LTUR	Steinby, E. M., ed. *Lexicon topographicum urbis Romae*. 6 vols. Rome, 1993–2000.
Marshall	See Bibliography 1.24.
Marx	Marx, F., ed. *A. Cornelii Celsi quae supersunt*. Leipzig, 1915. Reprint, Hildesheim, 2002.
MRR	Broughton, T. R. S. *Magistrates of the Roman Republic*. 3 vols. New York, 1951–Atlanta, 1986.
Nisbet	See Bibliography 1.11.
OCD	Hornblower, S., A. Spawforth, and E. Eidinow, eds. *The Oxford*

	Classical Dictionary. 4th ed. Oxford, 2012.
OLD	Glare, P. G. W., ed. *Oxford Latin Dictionary*. Oxford, 1982.
Olechowska	Olechowska, E., ed. *M. Tullius Cicero: Pro M. Scauro oratio*. Leipzig, 1984.
Orelli-Baiter-Halm	Orelli, J. C., J. G. Baiter, and C. Halm, eds. *M. Tulli Ciceronis Opera quae supersunt omnia*. 2nd ed. 8 vols. Zurich, 1845–1861.
Peyron	See Bibliography 1.47.
PL	Migne, J.-P., ed. *Patrologia Latina*. Paris, 1841–1902.
R	See Bibliography 1.38.
RE	Wissowa, G., K. Mittelhaus, W. Kroll, and K. Ziegler, eds. *Paulys Realencyclopädie der classischen Altertumswissenschaft*. 83 vols. Stuttgart, 1893–1995.
RLM	Halm, C., ed. *Rhetores Latini minores*. Leipzig, 1863.
Rose	Rose, V., ed. *Aristotelis qui ferebantur librorum fragmenta*. Leipzig, 1886.
RP	Syme, R. *Roman Papers*. Edited by E. Badian and A. R. Birley. 7 vols. Oxford, 1979–1991.
S.B.	See Bibliography 1.11: D. R. Shackleton Bailey 2002.
Schol. Bob.	See Bibliography 1.32.

ABBREVIATIONS

Sp.	Spengel, L., ed. *Rhetores Graeci.* Vol. 3. Leipzig, 1856.
St	See Bibliography 1.32, 50.
TLRR	Alexander, M. C. *Trials of the Late Roman Republic, 149 BC to 50 BC.* Toronto, 1990.
Watt	Watt, W. S., ed. *M. Tulli Ciceronis Epistulae.* Vol. 3. Oxford, 1958.
Wessner	See Bibliography 1.41.

GENERAL BIBLIOGRAPHY

1. EDITIONS OF TRANSMITTING AUTHORS

1.1. Ammianus Marcellinus

Seyfarth, W., ed. *Ammianus Marcellinus: Res gestae.* Leipzig, 1978.

1.2. Anonymous

Endt, J., ed. *Adnotationes super Lucanum.* Leipzig, 1909.

1.3. Anonymous

Huygens, R. B. C., ed. *Accessus ad auctores, Bernard d'Utrecht, Conrad d'Hirsau, Dialogus super auctores.* 2nd ed. Leiden, 1970.

1.4. Anonymous

Schemata dianoeas. In *RLM* 71–77.

1.5. Aquila Romanus

Elice, M., ed. *Romani Aquilae De figuris.* Hildesheim, Zurich, and New York, 2007. Also *RLM* 22–37.

1.6. Arusianus Messius

Di Stefano, A., ed. *Arusiani Messi Exempla elocutionum*. Hildesheim, 2011.

1.7. Asconius

Clark, A. C., ed. *Q. Asconii Pediani Orationum Ciceronis quinque enarratio*. Oxford, 1907. See also 1.32.

1.8. Augustine (Aurelius Augustinus)

Giomini, R., ed. "A. Augustinus 'De rhetorica.'" *Studi latini e italiani* 4 (1990): 7–82.

1.9. Cassius Dio

Boissevain, U. P., ed. *Cassii Dionis Cocceiani Historiarum Romanarum quae supersunt*. 4 vols. Berlin, 1895–1926.

1.10. Charisius

Barwick, C., ed. *Charisii Artis grammaticae libri V.* 2nd ed. Leipzig, 1964.

1.11. M. Tullius Cicero

Malcovati, E., ed. *M. Tulli Ciceronis Brutus.* Leipzig, 1965.

Maslowski, T., ed. *M. Tulli Ciceronis Orationes in P. Vatinium testem, Pro Caelio*. Stuttgart-Leipzig, 1995.

Nisbet, R. G. M., ed. *M. Tulli Ciceronis In L. Calpurnium Pisonem oratio*. Oxford, 1961.

Shackleton Bailey, D. R., ed. *Cicero. Letters to Atticus*. 4 vols. Cambridge, MA, 1999.

———, ed. *Cicero. Letters to Friends*. 3 vols. Cambridge, MA, 2001.

———, ed. *Cicero. Letters to Quintus and Brutus, Letter Fragments. Letter to Octavian, Invectives, Handbook of Electioneering*. Cambridge, MA, 2002.

Westman, R., ed. *M. Tulli Ciceronis Orator*. Leipzig, 1980.

1.12. Q. Tullius Cicero (?)

See 1.11: Shackleton Bailey 2002.

1.13. Diomedes

Artis grammaticae libri III. In *GL* 1.297–529.

1.14. Eugraphius

Wessner, P., ed. *Aeli Donati quod fertur Commentum Terenti. Accedunt Eugraphi Commentum et Scholia Bembina*. Vol. 3.1. Leipzig, 1908.

1.15. Fortunatianus

Calboli Montefusco, L., ed. *Consulti Fortunatiani Ars rhetorica*. Bologna, 1979.

1.16. Aulus Gellius

Holford-Strevens, L., ed. *Auli Gelli Noctes Atticae*. 2 vols. Oxford, 2020.

1.17. Grillius

Jakobi, R., ed. *Grillius. Commentum in Ciceronis Rhetorica.* Munich-Leipzig, 2002.

1.18. Isidore

Lindsay, W. M., ed. *Isidori Hispalensis episcopi Etymologiarum sive Originum libri XX.* 2 vols. Oxford, 1911.

1.19. Jerome (Hieronymus)

Labourt, J., ed. *Saint-Jérôme. Correspondance.* 8 vols. Paris, 1949–1963.

1.20. Lactantius

Wlosok, A., and E. Heck, eds. *L. Caelius Firmianus Lactantius. Divinarum institutionum libri septem.* 4 fascicles. Munich-Berlin, 2005–2011.

1.21. Lactantius Placidus

Sweeney, R. D., ed. *Lactantii Placidi In Statii Thebaida commentum.* Vol. 1: *Anonymi In Statii Achilleida commentum, Fulgentii ut fingitur Planciadis Super Thebaiden commentariolum.* Stuttgart-Leipzig, 1997.

1.22. Macrobius

Kaster, R. A., ed. *Macrobii Ambrosii Theodosii Saturnalia.* Oxford, 2011.

1.23. Martianus Capella

Willis, J., ed. *Martianus Capella. De nuptiis Philologiae et Mercurii et de septem artibus liberalibus libri novem.* Leipzig, 1983.

1.24. Cornelius Nepos

Marshall, P. K., ed. *Cornelii Nepotis Vitae cum fragmentis.* Stuttgart-Leipzig, 1976.

1.25. Nonius Marcellus

Lindsay, W. M., ed. *Nonii Marcelli De conpendiosa doctrina libri XX.* 3 vols. Leipzig, 1903.

1.26. Pliny the Elder (C. Plinius Secundus)

Mayhoff, L. I., and C. Mayhoff, eds. *C. Plini Secundi Naturalis historiae libri XXXVII.* 6 vols. Leipzig, 1892–1906.

1.27. Pliny the Younger (C. Plinius Caecilius Secundus)

Mynors, R. A. B., ed. *C. Plini Caecili Secundi Epistularum libri decem.* Oxford, 1963.

1.28. Plutarch

Ziegler, K., ed. *Plutarchi Vitae parallelae.* Vol. 1.2. Leipzig, 1964.

1.29. Pompeius Iulianus

Commentum Artis Donati. In *GL* 5.81–312.

1.30. Priscian

Institutiones grammaticae. In *GL* 2–3.

1.31. Pseudo-Acro

Keller, O., ed. *Pseudacronis Scholia in Horatium vetustiora*. Vol. 2: *Scholia in Sermones Epistulas Artemque poeticam*. Leipzig, 1904.

1.32. Pseudo-Asconius

Stangl, T., ed. *Ciceronis orationum scholiastae: Asconius, Scholia Bobiensia, Scholia Pseudasconii Sangallensia, Scholia Cluniacensia et recentiora Ambrosiana ac Vaticana, Scholia Lugdunensia sive Gronoviana et eorum excerpta Lugdunensia. Commentarii*. Vienna, 1912.

1.33. Pseudo-Probus

Passalacqua, M., ed. *Tre testi grammaticali Bobbiesi (GL V 555–566; 634–654; IV 207–216 Keil)*. Rome, 1984.

1.34. Quintilian

Russell, D. A., ed. *Quintilian. The Orator's Education*. 5 vols. Cambridge, MA, 2001.

1.35. Iulius Rufinianus

De figuris. In *RLM* 38–62.

1.36. Rufinus

Versus de compositione et de metris oratorum. In *RLM* 575–84.

1.37. Rutilius Lupus

Schemata Lexeos. In *RLM* 3–21.

1.38. Sallust

Ramsey, J. T., ed. *Sallust. The Fragments of the Histories, Letters to Caesar*. Cambridge, MA, 2015.

1.39. Scholia Bobiensia

See 1.32.

1.40. Scholia Gronoviana

See 1.32.

1.41. Scholia in Iuvenalem

Wessner, P., ed. *Scholia in Iuvenalem vetustiora*. Leipzig, 1931.

1.42. Servius

Murgia, C. E., and R. A. Kaster, eds. *Serviani In Vergili Aeneidos libros IX–XII commentarii*. New York, 2018.

Thilo, G., ed. *Servii grammatici qui feruntur In Vergilii Bucolica et Georgica commentarii*. Leipzig, 1887.

1.43. Iulius Severianus

Castelli Montanari, A. L., ed. *Iulii Severiani Praecepta artis rhetoricae summatim collecta de multis ac syntomata*. Bologna, 1995. Also *RLM* 355–70.

1.44. Strabo

Radt, S., ed. *Strabons Geographie, mit Übersetzung und Kommentar*. 9 vols. Göttingen, 2002–2010.

1.45. Suetonius

Kaster, R. A., ed. *C. Suetoni Tranquilli De vita Caesarum libri VIII et De grammaticis et rhetoribus liber*. Oxford, 2016.

1.46. Tacitus

Winterbottom, M., and R. M. Ogilvie, eds. *Cornelii Taciti Opera minora*. Oxford, 1975.

1.47. Turin Palimpsest

Peyron, A., ed. *M. Tulli Ciceronis Orationum Pro Scauro, Pro Tullio, et in Clodium fragmenta inedita . . . ex membranis palimpsestis Bibliothecae R. Taurinensis Athenaei*. Stuttgart-Tübingen, 1824.

1.48. Valerius Maximus

Briscoe, J., ed. *Valeri Maximi Facta et dicta mirabilia*. 2 vols. Stuttgart-Leipzig, 1998.

Shackleton Bailey, D. R., ed. *Valerius Maximus. Memorable Doings and Sayings*. 2 vols. Cambridge, MA, 2000.

1.49. Iulius Victor

Giomini, R., and M. S. Celentano, eds. *C. Iulii Victoris Ars rhetorica*. Leipzig, 1980.

1.50. Marius Victorinus

Stangl, T., ed. *Tulliana et Mario-Victoriniana*. Munich, 1888.

2. SECONDARY LITERATURE

Adams, J. N. 2003. *Bilingualism and the Latin Language*. Cambridge.

Alexander, M. C. 1985. "*Praemia* in the *quaestiones* of the Late Republic." *Classical Philology* 80:20–32.

Allen, W. S. 1987. *Vox Graeca: The Pronunciation of Classical Greek*. 3rd ed. Cambridge.

Arevalo, F., ed. 1803. *S. Isidori Hispalensis Opera omnia*. Vol. 7: *Opera philosophica et historica cum XXIV appendicibus*. Rev. ed. Rome.

Arweiler, A. 2008. "Frauen vor Kultlandschaft: Kleinasiatische Geographie in den Reden Ciceros." In *Vom Euphrat bis zum Bosporus: Kleinasien in der Antike. Fest-*

schrift für Elmar Schwertheim zum 65. Geburtstag, edited by E. Winter, 19–38. Bonn.

Atkins, J. D. 2022. "Cicero on the Justice of War." In *Power and Persuasion in Cicero's Philosophy,* edited by N. Gilbert, M. Graver, and S. McConnell, 170–204. Cambridge.

Aubert, S. 2010. "La polémique cicéronienne contre Atticistes et Stoïciens autour de la sanité du style." In *Les noms du style dans l'antiquité gréco-latine,* edited by P. Chiron and C. Lévy, 87–111. Louvain-Walpole, MA.

Badian, E. 1964. *Studies in Greek and Roman History.* New York.

———. 1967. "The Testament of Ptolemy Alexander." *Rheinisches Museum* 110:78–92.

———. 1969. "Quaestiones Variae." *Historia* 18:447–91.

———. 1973. "Marius' Villas: The Testimony of a Slave and a Knave." *Journal of Roman Studies* 63:121–32.

Balzarini, M. 1968. "Cicerone Pro Tullio e l'editto di Lucullo." In *Studi in onore di Giuseppe Grosso,* 1:323–82. Turin.

Bauman, R. A. 1967. *The* crimen maiestatis *in the Roman Republic and Augustan Principate.* Johannesburg.

Becker, M. 2017. "Suntoque aediles curatores urbis . . .": *Die Entwicklung der stadtrömischen Aedilität in republikanischer Zeit.* Stuttgart.

Benner, H. 1987. *Die Politik des P. Clodius Pulcher.* Stuttgart.

Berno, F. R. 2007. "La *Furia* di Clodio in Cicerone." *Bollettino di Studi Latini* 37:69–91.

Berno, F. R., A. Cucchiarelli, R. Degl'Innocenti Pierini, Y. Baraz, L. Fezzi, S. Petrucciani, F. Prost. 2019. "Intorno al *Commentariolum petitionis.* Suggestioni inter-

disciplinari a partire dal commento di François Prost."
Bolletino di Studi Latini 49:602–42.

Berry, D. 2020. *Cicero's* Catilinarians. New York.

Bispham, E. 2016. "The Social War." In *A Companion to Roman Italy*, edited by A. E. Cooley, 76–102. Malden, MA-Oxford.

Bloomer, M. W. 1992. *Valerius Maximus and the Rhetoric of the New Nobility.* London.

Bonnet, M. 1906. "Le dilemme de C. Gracchus." *Revue des Études Anciennes* 8:40–46.

Brennan, C. 2000. *The Praetorship in the Roman Republic.* 2 vols. Oxford-New York.

Briscoe, J., ed., comm. 2019. *Valerius Maximus*: Facta et dicta memorabilia, *Book 8.* Berlin.

Broscius, M. 1988. "De novo Metellinae fragmento." *Eos* 76:305–6.

Brouwer, H. H. J. 1989. *Bona Dea: The Sources and Description of the Cult.* Leiden.

Buongiorno, P. 2006. "Gaio Antonio (cos. 63) e l'appellativo *Hybrida*." In *Studi sull'età di Marco Antonio*, edited by G. Traina, 297–309. Lecce.

Bur, C. 2013. "Cic., *Att.* 1, 2, 2, Ascon., p. 93 Cl. et la carrière de Q. Curius (*RE* 7)." *Revue de philologie, de littérature et d'histoire anciennes* 87:37–58.

Butrica, J. L. 2002. "Clodius the *pulcher* in Catullus and Cicero." *Classical Quarterly* 52:507–16.

Cadoux, T. J. 2005. "Catiline and the Vestal Virgins." *Historia* 54: 162–79.

Calboli Montefusco, L. 1979. See 1.15.

Cape, R. W., Jr. 2002. "Cicero's Consular Speeches." In May 2002, 113–58.

Carlà-Uhink, F. 2017. *"Alteram loci patriam, alteram*

iuris: 'Double fatherlands' and the Role of Italy in Cicero's Political Discourse." In *Citizens in the Graeco-Roman World: Aspects of Citizenship from the Archaic Period to AD 212*, edited by L. Cecchet and A. Busetto, 259–82. Leiden-Boston.

Clark, A. C. 1911. *M. Tulli Ciceronis Orationes*. Vol. 6. Oxford.

Classen, C. J. 1979. "Bemerkungen zu Ciceros Äusserungen über die Gesetze." *Rheinisches Museum* 122:278–302.

Cosi, R. 1998. "Le degenerazioni politiche tardorepubblicane: i *divisores*." *Annali della Facoltà di Lettere e Filosofia, Università degli Studi di Bari* 41:335–49.

Coskun, A. 2009. *Bürgerrechtsentzug oder Fremdenausweisung? Studien zu den Rechten von Latinern und weiteren Fremden sowie zum Bürgerrechtswechsel in der Römischen Republik (5. bis frühes 1. Jh. v.Chr.)*. Stuttgart.

Courrier, C. 2014. *La plèbe de Rome et sa culture (fin du IIe siècle av. J.-C.–fin du Ier siècle ap. J.-C.)*. Rome.

Craig, C. P. 1993. *Form as Argument in Cicero's Speeches: A Study of Dilemma*. Atlanta.

Crawford, J. W. 1984. *M. Tullius Cicero: The Lost and Unpublished Orations*. Göttingen.

———, ed., comm. 1994. *M. Tullius Cicero: The Fragmentary Speeches*. 2nd ed. Atlanta.

———. 2002. "The Lost and Fragmentary Speeches." In May 2002, 305–30.

Čulík-Baird, H. 2022. *Cicero and the Early Latin Poets*. Cambridge.

Daguet-Gagey, A. 2013. "L'édilité de Cicéron." *Revue des Études Anciennes* 115:29–49.

———. 2015. Splendor aedilitatum: *l'édilité à Rome (1ᵉʳ s. avant J.-C.-IIIᵉ s. après J.-C.)*. Rome.

Dahlmann, H. 1953. *Varros Schrift 'De poematis' und die hellenistisch-römische Poetik*. Abhandlungen der geistes- und sozialwissenschaftlichen Klasse der Akademie der Wissenschaften und der Literatur, Mainz, No. 3. Wiesbaden.

D'Aloja, C. 2018. *"Cornelius homo non improbus, sed iusto pertinacior.* Per una interpretazione dell' operato del tribuno Gaio Cornelio." *Historika* 8:129–46.

Damon, C., and C. S. MacKay. 1995. "On the Prosecution of C. Antonius in 76 B.C." *Historia* 44:37–55.

David, J. M. 1992. *Le patronat judiciaire au dernier siècle de la République Romaine*. Rome.

———. 1999. "Les procès-verbaux des *judicia publica* de la fin de la République romaine." In *Urkunden und Urkundenformulare im Klassischen Altertum und in den orientalischen Kulturen*, edited by R. G. Khoury, 113–25. Heidelberg.

Di Stefano, A. 2011. See 1.6 above.

Douglas, A. E. 1955. "M. Calidius and the Atticists." *Classical Quarterly* 5:241–47.

Drexler, H. 1988. *Politische Grundbegriffe der Römer*. Darmstadt.

Drumann, W., and P. Groebe. 1899–1929. *Geschichte Roms*. 2nd ed. 7 vols. Berlin. Reprint, Hildesheim, 1964.

Du Breul, J., ed. 1601. *Sancti Isidori Hispaliensis episcopi Opera omnia quae extant*. Paris.

Dyck, A. R. 1996. *A Commentary on Cicero,* De officiis. Ann Arbor.

———. 2002. "The 'Other' *Pro Milone* Reconsidered." *Philologus* 146:182–85.

————. 2004. *A Commentary on Cicero*, De legibus. Ann Arbor.

————, ed., comm. 2008a. *Cicero: Catilinarians.* Cambridge.

————. 2008b. "Rivals into Partners: Hortensius and Cicero." *Historia* 57:142–73.

————. 2010. "Cicero's Abridgement of His Speeches for Publication." In *Condensing Texts—Condensed Texts*, edited by M. Horster and C. Reitz, 369–74. Wiesbaden.

————. Forthcoming. *Cicero: The Man and His Works.*

Elice, M. 2007. See 1.5 above.

Elster, M. 2003. *Die Gesetze der mittleren römischen Republik.* Darmstadt.

Espluga, X. 2016. "Cicero, Speeches: An Overview." In *From the Protohistory to the History of the Text*, edited by J. Velaza, 55–101. Bern.

Fedeli, P. 1980. "Cicerone e Lilibeo." *Ciceroniana* n.s. 4:135–44.

Ferrary, J.-L. 2009. "Les lois et les procès de maiestate dans la Rome républicaine." In Santalucia 2009b, 223–49.

Fotheringham, L. 2013. *Persuasive Language in Cicero's* Pro Milone: *A Close Reading and Commentary.* London.

Franciosi, G. 1961. "Il processo di Virginia." *Labeo* 7:20–35.

Frederiksen, M. W. 1966. "Caesar, Cicero and the Problem of Debt." *Journal of Roman Studies* 56:128–41.

Frier, B. 1983. "Urban Praetors and Rural Violence: The Legal Background of Cicero's *Pro Caecina*." *Transactions of the American Philological Association* 113:221–41.

————. 1985. *The Rise of the Roman Jurists.* Princeton.

Frisch, H. 1948. "The First Catilinarian Conspiracy: A Study in Historical Conjecture." *Classica & Mediaevalia* 9:10–36.

Geffcken, K. 1973. *Comedy in the* Pro Caelio. Leiden.

Gigon, O. 1962. "Die Szenerie des ciceronischen Hortensius." *Philologus* 106:222–45.

Gildenhard, I. 2011. *Creative Eloquence: The Construction of Reality in Cicero's Speeches*. Oxford.

Giomaro, A. M. 1974–1975. "Per lo studio della *Lex Cornelia de edictis* del 67 a.C.: la personalità del tribuno proponente, Gaio Publio [sic] Cornelio." *Studi Urbinati* 27:269–325.

Giomini, R. 1990. See 1.8.

Greenidge, A. H. J. 1901. *The Legal Procedure of Cicero's Time*. Oxford.

Gruen, E. S. 1965. "The *lex Varia*." *Journal of Roman Studies* 55:59–73.

———. 1969. "Notes on the 'First Catilinarian Conspiracy.'" *Classical Philology* 64:20–24.

———. 1974. *The Last Generation of the Roman Republic*. Berkeley-Los Angeles-London.

Guérin, C. 2015. *La voix de la vérité. Témoin et témoignage dans les tribunaux romains du Ier siècle avant J.-C.* Paris.

Gundel, H. G. 1963. "Der Begriff Maiestas im politischen Denken der römischen Republik." *Historia* 12:283–320.

Günther, R. 2000. "Sexuelle Diffamierung und politische Intrigen in der Republik: P. Clodius Pulcher und Clodia." In *Frauenwelten in der Antike: Geschlechterordnung und weibliche Lebenspraxis*, edited by T. Späth and B. Wagner-Hasel, 227–41. Stuttgart-Weimar.

Hall, J. 2009. *Politeness and Politics in Cicero's Letters*. Oxford-New York.

———. 2014. *Cicero's Use of Judicial Theater.* Ann Arbor.

Hall, U. 1964. "Voting Procedure in the Roman Assemblies." *Historia* 13:267–306.

Harders, A.-C. 2008. *Suavissima Soror. Untersuchungen zu den Bruder-Schwester-Beziehungen in der römischen Republik.* Munich.

Hartung, H.-J. 1974. "Religio und sapientia iudicum: Einige grundsätzliche Bemerkungen zu einem Geschworenenspiegel in Ciceros Reden." *Hermes* 102:556–66.

Heinze, R. 1909. *Ciceros politische Anfänge.* Abhandlungen der Königlichen Sächsischen Gesellschaft der Wissenschaften, philosophisch-historische Klasse, 27. Leipzig.

———. 1960. *Vom Geist des Römertums. Ausgewählte Aufsätze.* Edited by E. Burck. 3rd ed. Darmstadt.

Helfberend, M. 2022. *Ciceros Rede Pro L. Cornelio Balbo. Einleitung und Kommentar.* Berlin-Boston.

Herzog, R., ed. 1989. *Restauration und Erneuerung. Die lateinische Literatur von 284 bis 374 n. Chr.* Munich.

Higbie, C. 2017. *Collectors, Scholars and Forgers in the Ancient World: Object Lessons.* Oxford.

Hilberg, I. 1905. "Ein verkanntes Bruchstück von Ciceros Rede pro Q. Gallio." *Wiener Studien* 27:93–94.

Hinard, F. 1976. "Remarques sur les 'praecones' et le 'praeconium' dans la Rome de la fin de la République." *Latomus* 35:730–46.

———. 1980. "*Paternus inimicus.* Sur une expression de Cicéron." *Mélanges de littérature et d'épigraphie latines, d'histoire ancienne et d'archéologie. Hommages à la mémoire de Pierre Wuilleumier,* 197–210. Paris.

———. 1985. *Les proscriptions de la Rome républicaine.* Rome.

Humm, M. 2005. *Appius Claudius Caecus. La république accomplie.* Rome.

Huschke, P. E. 1826. "M. Tullii Ciceronis orationis Pro M. Tullio quae exstant cum commentariis et excursibus." In I. G. Huschke, *Analecta litteraria*, 77 ff. Leipzig (cited in Iulius Victor [above, 1.49], inaccessible to us).

Jakobi, R. 2004. "Textgeschichte als Kulturgeschichte. Der sogenannte Lactantius Placidus-Kommentar zur 'Thebais' des Statius." In *Der Kommentar in Antike und Mittelalter: Neue Beiträge zu seiner Erforschung*, edited by W. Geerlings and C. Schulze, 2:1–16. Leiden.

———. 2005. *Grillius: Überlieferung und Kommentar*. Berlin-New York.

Kaser, M. 1956. "Infamia und ignominia in den römischen Rechtsquellen." *Zeitschrift der Savigny-Stiftung für Rechtsgeschichte, Romanistische Abteilung* 73:220–78.

Kaster, R. A., trans., comm. 2006. Cicero, *Speech on Behalf of Publius Sestius*. Oxford.

Keeline, T. J. 2018. *The Reception of Cicero in the Early Roman Empire: The Rhetorical Schoolroom and the Creation of a Cultural Legend.* Cambridge.

———, ed., comm. 2021. *Cicero: Pro Milone*. Cambridge.

———. 2023. "The Working Methods of Asconius." In Pausch and Pieper 2023, 41–68.

Kenty, J. 2020. *Cicero's Political Personae*. Cambridge.

Khrustalyov, W. K. 2018. *"Sic est (non) iusta causa belli?* Issues of Law and Justice in the Debate Concerning a Roman Annexation of Egypt in 65 B.C." *Hyperboreus* 24:244–64.

———. 2022. "Drei Bemerkungen zu Asconius." *Philologia Classica* 17.1:97–106.

Kumaniecki, K. 1961. "De oratione Tulliana in toga can-

dida habita." In *Atti del I Congresso Internazionale di Studi Ciceroniani*, 1:157–66. Rome.

———. 1970. *Les discours égarés de Cicéron 'Pro Cornelio.'* Mededelingen van de Koninklijke Vlaamse Academie voor Wetenschappen, Letteren en Schone Kunsten van Belgie, Klasse der Letteren, 32.4. Brussels.

Kunkel, W., and R. Wittmann. 1995. *Staatsordnung und Staatspraxis der römischen Republik*. Vol. 2: *Die Magistratur*. Munich.

La Bua, G. 2014. "Cicero's *Pro Milone* and the 'Demosthenic' Style: *De optimo genere oratorum* 10." *Greece and Rome* 61:29–37.

———. 2019. *Cicero and Roman Education: The Reception of the Speeches and Ancient Scholarship*. Cambridge.

Lausberg, H. 1998. *Handbook of Literary Rhetoric: A Foundation for Literary Study*. Translated by M. T. Bliss, A. Jansen, and D. E. Orton. Edited by D. E. Orton and R. D. Anderson [= *Handbuch der literarischen Rhetorik*. 3rd ed. Stuttgart, 1990].

Leach, E. W. 2001. "Gendering Clodius." *Classical World* 94.4:335–59.

Leonhardt, J. 1998–1999. "Senat und Volk in Ciceros Reden *De lege agraria*." *Acta Classica Universitatis Scientiarum Debreceniensis* 34–35:279–92.

Leumann, M. 1977. *Lateinische Laut- und Formenlehre*. Munich.

Levick, B. 2015. *Catiline*. London.

Lévy, C. 1998. "Rhétorique et philosophie: la monstruosité politique chez Cicéron." *Revue des Études Latines* 76:139–57.

———. 2020. "Some Remarks on Cicero's Perception of

the Future of Rome." In *The Future of Rome: Roman, Greek, Jewish and Christian Versions*, edited by J. J. Price and K. Berthelot, 17–31. Cambridge.

Lewis, R. G., trans., comm. 2008. *Asconius: Commentaries on the Speeches of Cicero*. Oxford.

Linke, B. 1997. "Appius Claudius Caecus—ein Leben in Zeiten des Umbruchs." In *Von Romulus zu Augustus. Grosse Gestalten der römischen Republik*, edited by K.-J. Hölkeskamp and E. Stein-Hölkeskamp, 69–78. Munich.

Lintott, A. 1968. "*Nundinae* and the Chronology of the Late Roman Republic." *Classical Quarterly* 18:189–94.

———. 1974. "Cicero and Milo." *Journal of Roman Studies* 64:62–78.

———. 1977. "Cicero on Praetors Who Failed to Abide by their Edicts." *Classical Quarterly* 27:184–86.

———. 1990. "Electoral Bribery in the Roman Republic." *Journal of Roman Studies* 80:1–16.

———. 1999. *The Constitution of the Roman Republic*. Oxford.

———. 2008. *Cicero as Evidence: A Historian's Companion*. Oxford.

———, trans., comm. 2013. *Plutarch: Demosthenes and Cicero*. Oxford.

Liou-Gille, B. 1997. "Les *leges sacratae*: esquisse historique." *Euphrosyne* n.s. 25:61–84.

Lo Monaco, F. 1990. "Lineamenti per una storia delle raccolte antiche di orazioni ciceroniane." *Aevum Antiquum* 3:169-85.

Loposzko, T. 1978–1979. "Gesetzesentwürfe betreffs der Sklaven im Jahre 53 v. u. Z." *Index: Quaderni camerti di studi romanistici* 8:153–66.

————. 1980. *Mouvements sociaux à Rome dans les années 57–52 av. J.-C.* Lublin.

Lucarini, C. M. 2009. "Emendationes Asconianae." *Mnemosyne* 62:635–38.

MacKendrick, P. 1995. *The Speeches of Cicero.* London.

Malaspina, E. 1997a. "Le orazioni in frammenti e *deperditae* di Cicerone. Rassegna 1984–1995." *Bollettino di Studi Latini* 28:565–90.

————. 1997b. "Quattro 'nuovi' frammenti oratorii di Cicerone?" *Quaderni del Dipartimento di Filologia, Linguistica e Tradizione Classica dell' Università di Torino*: 131–47.

————. 2001. "Osservazioni su alcune orazioni in frammenti e perdute di Cicerone." *Quaderni del Dipartimento di Filologia, Linguistica e Tradizione Classica dell' Università di Torino*: 177–86.

Malcovati, H., ed. 1976. *Oratorum Romanorum fragmenta liberae rei publicae.* Vol. 1: *Textus.* 4th ed. Turin.

Manuwald, G., ed., trans., comm. 2018. *Cicero: Agrarian Speeches.* Oxford.

————, ed., trans., comm. 2021. *Cicero: Post reditum Speeches.* Oxford.

Marco Simón, F. and F. Pina Polo. 2000. "Mario Gratidiano, los *compita* y la religiosidad popular a fines de la república." *Klio* 82:154–70.

Marshall, B. A. 1985. *An Historical Commentary on Asconius.* Columbia, MO.

————. 1987. "Pompeius' Fear of Assassination." *Chiron* 17:119–33.

Mastrocinque, A. 2014. *Bona Dea and the Cults of Roman Women.* Stuttgart.

May, J. M. 1988. *Trials of Character: The Eloquence of Ciceronian Ethos*. Chapel Hill-London.

——. 1996. "Cicero and the Beasts." *Syllecta Classica* 7:143–53.

——, ed. 2002. *Brill's Companion to Cicero: Oratory and Rhetoric*. Leiden.

McDermott, W. C. 1977. "*Lex de tribunicia potestate* (70 B.C.)." *Classical Philology* 72:49–52.

Meier, C. 1968. "Die loca intercessionis bei Rogationen." *Museum Helveticum* 25:86–100.

Metro, A. 1969. "La lex Cornelia de iurisdictione alla luce di Dio Cass. 36.40.1–2." *Iura* 20:500–24.

Migne, J.-P. *See* Abbreviations under *PL*.

Mommsen, T. 1887–1888. *Römisches Staatsrecht*. 3rd ed. 3 vols. in 5. Berlin.

——. 1899. *Römisches Strafrecht*. Leipzig.

Monaco, L. 2006. "Lex licinia mucia de civibus redigendis." In *Tradizione romanistica e costituzione*, edited by L. Labruna, M. P. Baccari, and C. Cascione, 1:741–59. Naples.

Moreau, P. 1982. *Clodiana religio: un procès politique en 61 avant J.-C.* Paris.

——. 2012. "La *lex Clodia de capite ciuis* (58 avant J.-C.) a-t-elle comporté une clause de serment?" In *La société romaine et ses élites. Hommages à Élisabeth Deniaux*, edited by R. Baudry and S. Destephen, 35–42. Paris.

Morrell, K. 2017. *Pompey, Cato, and the Governance of the Roman Empire*. Oxford.

——. 2018. "Cato, Pompey's Third Consulship and the Politics of Milo's Trial." In van der Blom et al. 2018, 165–80.

————. 2023. "P. Clodius Pulcher and the Praetorship that Never Was." *Historia* 71:29-57.

Morstein-Marx, R. 2021. *Julius Caesar and the Roman People*. Cambridge.

Mouritsen, H. 2022. *The Roman Elite and the End of the Republic: The* Boni, *the Nobles, and Cicero*. Cambridge.

Mueller, C. F. W., ed. 1898. *M. Tulli Ciceronis Scripta quae manserunt omnia*. Vol. 4, pt. 3. Leipzig.

Nadig, P. 1997. Ardet ambitus*: Untersuchungen zum Phänomen der Wahlbestechungen in der römischen Republik*. Frankfurt am Main.

Narducci, E. 2004. *Cicerone e i suoi interprete: studi sull'opera e la fortuna*. Pisa.

Nicolet, C. 1974. *L'ordre équestre à l'époque républicaine (312–43 av. J.-C.)*. Vol. 2: *Prosopographie des chevaliers Romains*. Paris.

Nisbet, R. G. M. 1961. See 1.11: Nisbet 1961.

Noble, F. M. 2014. "Sulla and the Gods: Religion, Politics and Propaganda in the *Autobiography* of L. Cornelius Sulla." PhD diss., Newcastle.

North, J. A. 2011. "*Lex Domitia* Revisited." In *Priests and State in the Roman World*, edited by J. H. Richardson and F. Santangelo, 39–62. Stuttgart.

Olsen, B. M. 2013. "*Accessus* to Classical Poets in the Twelfth Century." In *The Classics in the Medieval and Renaissance Classroom*, edited by J. F. Ruys, J. O. Ward, and M. Heyworth, 131–41. Turnhout.

Pausch, D., and C. Pieper, eds. 2023. *The Scholia on Cicero's Speeches: Contexts and Perspectives*. Leiden-Boston.

Pellam, G. 2015. "*Sacer, sacrosanctus*, and *leges sacratae*." *Classical Antiquity* 34:322–34.

Piacente, L. 1986–1987. "Un nuovo frammento ciceroniano in Beda." *Romanobarbarica* 9:229–45 = L. Piacente, "Prasio usurpatore di Rabirio: Beda *de orth.* 19, 284–89 J." In *Cicerone a reflettori spenti. Episodi della tradizione testuale di orazioni ed epistole*, 97–108. Bari, 2014.

Pieper, C. 2020. *"Nox rei publicae*? Catiline's and Cicero's Nocturnal Activities in the *Catilinarians."* In *The Values of Nighttime in Classical Antiquity. Between Dusk and Dawn*, edited by J. Ker and A. Wessels, 210–33. Leiden-Boston.

Pina Polo, F. 1989. *Las contiones civiles y militares en Roma.* Zaragoza.

——. 1996. Contra arma verbis. *Der Redner vor dem Volk in der späten römischen Republik.* Stuttgart.

——. 2011. *The Consul at Rome: The Civil Functions of the Consuls in the Roman Republic.* Cambridge.

——. 2016. *"Cupiditas pecuniae*: Wealth and Power in Cicero." In *Money and Power in the Roman Republic*, edited by H. Beck, M. Jehne, and J. Serrati, 165–77. Brussels.

——. 2018. "Political Alliances and Rivalries in *contiones* in the Late Roman Republic." In van der Blom et al. 2018, 107–27.

Pina Polo, F., and A. Díaz Fernández. 2019. *The Quaestorship in the Roman Republic.* Berlin-Boston.

Pinkster, H. 2015–2021. *The Oxford Latin Syntax*. Vol. 1: *The Simple Clause*. Vol. 2: *The Complex Sentence and Discourse*. Oxford.

Powell, J. G. F., ed. 2006. *M. Tulli Ciceronis De re publica, De legibus, Cato maior de senectute, Laelius de amicitia.* Oxford.

Prost, F., ed., trans., comm. 2017. *Quintus Cicéron: Petit*

manuel de la campagne électorale. Marcus Cicéron: Lettres à son frère Quintus I, 1 et 2. Paris.

Puccioni, I., ed. 1972. *M. Tulli Ciceronis Orationum deperditarum fragmenta.* 2nd ed. Milan.

Raaflaub, K. A., ed. 2005. *Social Struggles in Archaic Rome: New Perspectives on the Conflict of the Orders.* Malden, MA.

Ramsey, J. T. 1980. "The Prosecution of C. Manilius in 66 B.C. and Cicero's *Pro Manilio.*" *Phoenix* 34:323–36.

————. 1982. "Cicero, *Pro Sulla* 68 and Catiline's Candidacy in 66." *Harvard Studies in Classical Philology* 86:121–31.

————. 2007. "Roman Senatorial Oratory." In *A Companion to Roman Rhetoric,* edited by W. J. Dominik and J. Hall, 122–35. Malden, MA.

————. 2019. "The Postponement of Elections in 63 and the Inception of Catiline's Conspiracy." *Harvard Studies in Classical Philology* 110:213–69.

————. 2021. "Asconius on Cicero's Son-in-Law Lentulus, His Apprenticeship under Pupius Piso, and the *De Othone.*" *Ciceroniana On Line* 5.1:7–28.

————. Forthcoming. *Asconius: Commentaries on Speeches of Cicero.* Translation and commentary by R. G. Lewis. Revised by J. T. Ramsey.

Raskolnikoff, M. 1977. "La richesse et les riches chez Cicéron." *Ktèma* 2:357–72.

Rawson, B. 1971. "*De Lege Agraria* 2.49." *Classical Philology* 66:26–29.

————. 1978. *The Politics of Friendship: Pompey and Cicero.* Sydney.

Reduzzi Merola, F. 2000. "*abrogare, derogare, obrogare*

in Cicerone." In *Au-delà des frontières. Mélanges de droit romain offerts à Witold Wołodkiewicz*, edited by M. Zabłocka, J. Krzynówek, J. Urbanik, Z. Służewska, 735–42. Warsaw.

Reynolds, L. D., ed. 1983. *Texts and Transmission: A Survey of the Latin Classics*. Oxford.

Richardson, L. J., Jr. 1992. *A New Topographical Dictionary of Ancient Rome*. Baltimore-London.

Rieger, H. 1991. *Das Nachleben des Tiberius Gracchus in der lateinischen Literatur*. Bonn.

Riesenweber, T. 2022. "Critical Remarks on the *De definitionibus* of Marius Victorinus." In *The Philosophy, Theology, and Rhetoric of Marius Victorinus*, edited by S. A. Cooper and Václav Nemec, 141–86. Atlanta.

———. 2023. "Ciceros Reden bei den *Rhetores Latini Minores*." In Pausch and Pieper 2023, 87–128.

Rilinger, R. 1989. "Die 'loca intercessionis' und Legalismus in der späten Republik." *Chiron* 19:481–98.

Robinson, A. 1994. "Avoiding the Responsibility: Cicero and the Suppression of Catiline's Conspiracy." *Syllecta Classica* 5:43–51.

Rosillo-López, C. 2017. "The Role and Influence of the Audience (*corona*) in Trials in the Late Republic." *Athenaeum* 105:106–19.

Rüpke, J. 2008. *Fasti sacerdotum: A Prosopography of Pagan, Jewish, and Christian Religious Officials in the City of Rome, 300 BC to AD 499*. Oxford.

Russell, D. A. 2001. See 1.34.

Ryan, F. X. 1995. "The Consular Candidacy of Catiline in 66." *Museum Helveticum* 52:45–48.

———. 1998. *Rank and Participation in the Republican Senate*. Stuttgart.

————. 2001. "Knappe Mehrheiten bei der Wahl zum Konsul." *Klio* 83:402–24.

————. 2006. "Die Apollinarspiele zur Zeit der Republik." *Aevum* 80:67–104.

————. 2016. "Anent the Ciceronian Speech Title *cum quaestor Lilybaeo decederet*." (https://independent.academia.edu/FXRyan)

Santalucia, B. 1998. *Diritto e processo penale nell'antica Roma*. 2nd ed. Milan.

————. 2009a. "Le formalità introduttive del processo per quaestiones tardo-repubblicano." In Santalucia 2009b, 93–114.

————. 2009b. *La repressione criminale nella Roma repubblicana fra norma e persuasione*. Pavia.

Santangelo, F. 2007. *Sulla, the Elites and the Empire: A Study of Roman Policies in Italy and the Greek East.* Leiden-Boston.

————. 2018. "The Social War." In *The Peoples of Ancient Italy*, edited by G. D. Farney and G. Bradley, 231–53. Boston-Berlin.

Schietinger, G.-P. 2017. "Lucius Sergius Catilina. Karriereperspektiven und Karriere eines *homo paene novus* in der späten Römishen Republik." *Klio* 99:149–91.

Schindel, U. 2000. Review of A. L. Castelli Montanari, *Iulius Severianus*. *Gnomon* 72:414–18.

Schneider, W. C. 2000. "Vom Salz Ciceros. Zum politischen Witz, Schmäh und Sprachspiel bei Cicero." *Gymnasium* 107:497–518.

Schoell, F., ed. 1918. "Fragmenta orationum." *M. Tulli Ciceronis Scripta quae manserunt omnia*, 8:391–493. Leipzig.

Scramuzza, V. 1937. "Publican Societies in Sicily in 73–71 B.C." *Classical Philology* 32:152–55.

Scullard, H. H. 1970. *Scipio Africanus: Soldier and Politician.* Bristol.

Seager, R. 1964. "The First Catilinarian Conspiracy." *Historia* 13:338–47.

———. 1965. "Clodius, Pompeius and the Exile of Cicero." *Latomus* 24:519–31.

———. 1972. "Cicero and the Word *popularis.*" *Classical Quarterly* 22:328–38.

———. 2002. *Pompey the Great, a Political Biography.* 2nd ed. Oxford.

———. 2011. "Cicero and the False Dilemma." In *Praise and Blame in Roman Republican Rhetoric*, edited by C. Smith and R. Covino, 99–109. Swansea.

Settle, J. N. 1963. "The Trial of Milo and the Other *Pro Milone.*" *Transactions and Proceedings of the American Philological Association* 94:268–80.

Shackleton Bailey, D. R., ed., comm. 1977. *Cicero: Epistulae ad familiares.* 2 vols. Cambridge.

———. 1992. *Onomasticon to Cicero's Speeches.* 2nd ed. Stuttgart-Leipzig.

———. 2002. See 1.11: Shackleton Bailey 2002.

———. 2009. *Cicero:* Philippics. Revised by J. T. Ramsey and G. Manuwald. 2 vols. Cambridge, MA.

Shanzer, D. 1986. *A Philosophical Commentary on Martianus Capella's* De Nuptiis Philologiae et Mercurii, *Book 1.* Berkeley-Los Angeles.

Shatzman, I. 1975. *Senatorial Wealth and Roman Politics.* Brussels.

Sidoti, A., and C. Cheminade, ed., trans. 2016. *Q. Tullius*

Cicéron: Petit mémoire pour une campagne électoral, Correspondance, Astronomiques. M. Tullius Cicéron: Discours in toga candida, Correspondance (extraits). Paris.

Staveley, E. S. 1972. *Greek and Roman Voting and Elections.* London.

Steel, C. 2013. *The End of the Roman Republic, 146–44 BC: Conquest and Crisis.* Edinburgh.

Steel, C., and H. van der Blom, eds. 2013. *Community and Communication: Oratory and Politics in Republican Rome.* Oxford.

Stone, A. M. 1993. "Three Men in a Hurry." *Classicum* 19:2–4.

———. 1998. "A House of Notoriety: An Episode in the Campaign for the Consulate in 64 BC." *Classical Quarterly* 48:487–91.

Strasburger, H. 1938. *Caesars Eintritt in die Geschichte.* Munich.

Stroh, W. 1975. *Taxis und Taktik: Die advokatorische Dispositionskunst in Ciceros Gerichtsreden.* Stuttgart.

Sumner, G. V. 1964. "Manius or Mamercus?" *Journal of Roman Studies* 54:41–48.

———. 1973. *The Orators in Cicero's "Brutus": Prosopography and Chronology.* Toronto.

Syme, R. 1963. "Ten Tribunes." *Journal of Roman Studies* 53:55–60.

———. 1964. *Sallust.* Berkeley-Los Angeles.

———. 2016. *Approaching the Roman Revolution: Papers on Republican History.* Edited by F. Santangelo. Oxford.

Tatum, W. J. 1991. "Cicero, the Elder Curio and the Titinia Case." *Mnemosyne* 44:364–71.

————. 1999. *The Patrician Tribune: Publius Clodius Pulcher.* Chapel Hill.

————. 2013. "Campaign Rhetoric." In Steel and van der Blom 2013, 132–50.

————. ed., trans., comm. 2018. *Quintus Cicero: A Brief Handbook on Canvassing for Office: Commentariolum petitionis.* Oxford.

Taylor, L. R. 1939. "Cicero's Aedileship." *American Journal of Philology* 60:194–202.

Thomas, Y. 1991. "L'institution de la majesté." *Revue de synthèse* 112:331–86.

Thurn, A. 2018. *Rufmord in der späten römischen Republik. Charakterbezogene Diffamierungsstrategien in Ciceros Reden und Brefen.* Berlin-Boston.

Timpe, D. 2006. *Römisch-germanische Begegnung.* Munich-Leipzig.

Treggiari, S. 1991. *Roman Marriage: iusti coniuges from the Time of Cicero to the Time of Ulpian.* Oxford.

————. 2007. *Terentia, Tullia and Publilia: The Women of Cicero's Family.* London-New York.

Tweedie, F. C. 2012. "The *lex Licinia Mucia* and the *bellum Italicum.*" In *Processes of Integration and Identity Formation in the Roman Republic*, edited by S. T. Roselaar, 123–39. Leiden-Boston.

Uhlfelder, M. L. 1954. *De proprietate sermonum vel rerum: A Study and Critical Edition of a Set of Verbal Distinctions.* Papers of the American Academy in Rome 15. Rome.

Ungern-Sternberg, J. von. 1975. "Die Einführung spezieller Sitze für die Senatoren bei den Spielen (194 v. Chr.)." *Chiron* 5:157–64.

Urso, G. 2019. *Catilina, le faux populiste.* Bordeaux.

Vainio, R., R. Välimäki, A. Vesanto, A. Hella, F. Ginter, M. Kaartinen, T. Immonen. 2019. "Reconsidering Authorship in the Ciceronian Corpus through Computational Authorship Attribution." *Ciceroniana on Line* 3.1:15–48.

van den Berg, C. S. 2021. *The Politics and Poetics of Cicero's* Brutus. Cambridge.

van der Blom, H., C. Gray, and C. Steel, eds. 2018. *Institutions and Ideology in Republican Rome: Speech, Audience and Decision*. Cambridge.

Vedaldi Iasbez, V. 1981. "I figli dei proscritti." *Labeo* 27:163–213.

Ville, G. 1981. *La gladiature en occident des origines à la mort de Domitien*. Rome.

von Albrecht, M. 1980. "Cicero und die Götter Siziliens (*Verr.* II, 5, 184–189)." *Ciceroniana* 4:49–62.

Ward, A. M. 1970. "Politics in the Trials of Manilius and Cornelius." *Transactions of the American Philological Association* 101:545–56.

———. 1977. *Marcus Crassus and the Late Roman Republic*. Columbia-London.

Watson, A. 1967. *The Law of Persons in the Later Roman Republic*. Oxford.

Weische, A. 1972. *Ciceros Nachahmung der attischen Redner*. Heidelberg.

Welsh, J. 2017. "The Manuscripts of Asconius and Pseudo-Asconius." *Phoenix* 71:321–44.

Wessner, P. 1931. See 1.41.

Wheeler, S. M. 2015. *Accessus ad Auctores: Medieval Introductions to the Authors (Codex latinus monacensis 19475)*. Kalamazoo, MI.

Williams, C. A. 1999. *Roman Homosexuality*. 2nd ed. Oxford-New York.

Williamson, C. 2016. "Crimes against the State." In *The Oxford Handbook of Roman Law and Society*, edited by P. J. Du Plessis, C. Ando, and K. Tuori, 333–44. Oxford.

Woodman, A. J. 2021. "Sallust and Catiline: Conspiracy Theories." *Historia* 70:55–68.

Zetzel, J. E. G. 2018. *Critics, Compilers, and Commentators: An Introduction to Roman Philology, 200 BCE–800 CE*. New York.

———. 2022. *The Lost Republic: Cicero's* De oratore *and* De re publica. New York.

FRAGMENTARY SPEECHES

1 PRO L. VARENO

The defense of L. Varenus on charges of murder seems to have been an early case ("80 or in early 70s": TLRR 368). It is similar to the defense of Sextus Roscius (dated to the year 80) in several respects: both apparently occurred in the aftermath of the civil war and/or Sullan proscriptions (cf. F 2); in both the opposing counsel was C. Erucius, a professional prosecutor (F 10);[1] both involve a cast of characters from Umbria (Ameria and Fulginas [F 3 and 4]); and in both Cicero deployed a strategy of counterac-

[1] *FRLO* 79; David 1992, 762–63.

1 T 1 Quint. *Inst.* 4.2.24–26

Nam cum prohoemium idcirco comparatum sit ut iudex ad rem accipiendam fiat conciliatior docilior intentior, et probatio nisi causa prius cognita non possit adhiberi, protinus iudex notitia rerum instruendus videtur. Sed hoc quoque interim mutat condicio causarum . . . Ergo hae quoque quaestiones vim prohoemii optinebant, cum omnes iudicem praepararent. Sed pro Vareno quoque postea narravit quam obiecta diluit. Quod fiet utiliter quotiens non repellendum tantum erit crimen, sed etiam trans-

1 ON BEHALF OF L. VARENUS
(CA. 80 BC)

cusation against persons associated with the prosecution (in Rosc. Am. *the defendant's relations T. Roscius Magnus and T. Roscius Capito; in this case, the slaves of C. Ancharius Rufus: T 4, F 9) and the cui bono (to whose advantage?) argument (*Rosc. Am. *84–88; F 6). But this time the strategy failed, and Varenus was convicted (T 6). Quintilian admired the speech's unconventional approach, violating norms in order to offer the defense best suited to the case (T 1, 3; cf. T 8).*

1 T 1 [= T 5] Quintilian, *The Orator's Education*

Since an exordium is provided so that the judge may become more inclined to hear the case, readier to learn, and keener to listen, and proof cannot be adduced unless the case has first become known, it seems that the judge must be equipped with a knowledge of the facts right away. But the circumstances of a case sometimes even change this . . . These issues, then, were tantamount to an exordium since all of them prepared the judge in advance. But in *On Behalf of Varenus* he also narrated the facts after he refuted the charges. This will prove to be advantageous whenever a charge must be not merely repelled but also

3

ferendum, ut his prius defensis velut initium sit alium
culpandi narratio . . .

1 T 2 Quint. *Inst.* 6.1.49

Discutiendae tamen oratione eius modi scaenae, egre-
gieque Cicero, qui contra imaginem Saturnini pro Rabirio
graviter, et contra iuvenem cuius subinde vulnus in iudicio
resolvebatur pro Vareno multa dixit urbane.

1 T 3 Quint. *Inst.* 7.1.12

Ante actae vitae crimina plerumque prima purganda sunt,
ut id de quo laturus est sententiam iudex audire propitius
incipiat. Sed hoc quoque pro Vareno Cicero in ultimum
distulit, non quid frequentissime sed quid tum expediret
intuitus.

1 T 4 Quint. *Inst.* 7.2.9–10

Interdum enim substituitur mutua accusatio, quam Graeci
ἀντικατηγορίαν vocant, nostrorum quidam "concertati-
vam": interdum in aliquam personam quae extra discri-
men iudicii est transfertur . . . In quibus similis atque in

transferred, so that when these points have first been warded off, the narrative may be, as it were, the beginning of the incrimination of the other party . . .

1 T 2 [= T 8] Quintilian, *The Orator's Education*

Such theatrics [i.e., visual displays in court] should be dispersed by speaking. Cicero did so outstandingly: he spoke in a solemn manner against Saturninus' image in *On Behalf of Rabirius*[1] and with polished humor in *On Behalf of Varenus* against the young man whose wound was repeatedly unbound in court.[2]

[1] *Rab. perd.* 24.   [2] This was presumably a witness against L. Varenus. Unplaced F 18 may possibly be from this context.

1 T 3 [= T 7] Quintilian, *The Orator's Education*

As a rule one should first clear away charges related to the (defendant's) previous life so that the judge may begin to listen to the case he must decide in a positive frame of mind. But in *On Behalf of Varenus* Cicero even postponed this point to the end, since he was looking not at what is most frequently advantageous but what was so on that occasion.[1]

[1] The procedure is also used in *Sull.*, where the defendant's prior life is taken up only at §69; cf. Stroh 1975, 253–54.

1 T 4 Quintilian, *The Orator's Education*

Occasionally a mutual accusation is substituted, which the Greeks call a counteraccusation but some of our countrymen call a "competitive" accusation. Sometimes this is transferred to a party outside the court's jurisdiction . . . In these cases, there is a similar comparison of persons,

ἀντικατηγορίαι personarum causarum ceterorum comparatio est, ut Cicero pro Vareno in familiam Ancharianam, pro Scauro circa mortem Bostaris in matrem avertens crimen facit.

1 T 5 Quint. *Inst.* 7.2.22

Hae porro actiones constant comparatione: ipsa comparatio non una via ducitur. Aut enim totam causam nostram cum tota adversarii causa componimus aut singula argumenta cum singulis. Quorum utrum sit faciendum non potest nisi ex ipsius litis utilitate cognosci. Cicero singula pro Vareno comparat in primo crimine: est enim superior ⟨. . .⟩[1] [enim][2] persona alieni cum persona matris temere compararetur. Quare optimum est, si fieri poterit, ut singula vincantur a singulis.

[1] *lac. indic. Winterbottom*
[2] *om. recc.*

1 T 6 Quint. *Inst.* 7.2.36

Patronus vero, quotiens poterit, instabit huic loco, ut nihil credibile sit factum esse sine causa. Quod Cicero vehementissime in multis orationibus tractat, praecipue tamen pro Vareno, qui omnibus aliis[1] premebatur (nam et damnatus est). At si proponitur cur factum sit, aut falsam causam aut levem aut ignotam reo dicet.

[1] omnibus aliis: criminibus aliis *Puccioni*: *fort.* criminibus odiosis

motives, and other matters as in a counteraccusation, as Cicero does in diverting the charge in *On Behalf of Varenus* to the slaves of Ancharius and in *On Behalf of Scaurus* apropos of Bostar's death to his mother.[1]

[1] *Scaur.* F 11 Olechowska.

1 T 5 [= T 3] Quintilian, *The Orator's Education*

Moreover, these cases are based on comparison, but the comparison itself is not drawn by a single method. Either we compare our entire case with the whole of our opponent's, or we compare individual arguments with each other. Which of these we should do can only be determined on the basis of what is in the interest of the case itself. In *On Behalf of Varenus* Cicero draws a comparison of individual points on the first charge. The earlier is . . . it would be rash to compare the character of an unrelated person with that of the mother. Therefore, it is best, if possible, for individual arguments to be defeated by individual arguments.

1 T 6 Quintilian, *The Orator's Education*

As often as possible the advocate will insist upon the point that it is by no means credible that anything was done without a motive. Cicero emphasizes this point vigorously in many speeches, but above all on behalf of Varenus, who was hard pressed in all other respects (he was found guilty). But if the question is posed, why it was done, he will argue that the motive was either mistaken or trivial or unknown to the defendant.

1 T 7 Plin. *Ep.* 1.20.6–7

Haec ille [*sc.* quidam doctus homo] multaque alia . . . ita eludit ut contendat hos ipsos quorum orationibus nitar pauciora dixisse quam ediderint. Ego contra puto. Testes sunt multae multorum orationes et Ciceronis pro Murena, pro Vareno, in quibus brevis et nuda quasi subscriptio quorundam criminum solis titulis indicatur: ex his apparet illum permulta dixisse, cum ederet omisisse.

1 T 8 Iul. Sev. *Praec. rhet.* 7, p. 83.8 Castelli Montanari (*RLM* 358.25)

Incidunt causae in quibus quod summam habet quaestionis magna ex parte tractandum sit et sic sit ponenda narratio, ut pro Vareno[1] vel pro Habito.

[1] pro Vareno *Halm*: provocare non *codd.*

1 F 1, 2 Iul. Sev. *Praec. rhet.* 23, p. 121.19 Castelli Montanari (*RLM* 369.19)

Cito tamen principiis aptantur [*sc.* loci communes], ut misericordiam captent, cum aut adversariorum calumnias, factiones, solitudinem suscepti vel cetera eius infortunia memoramus, ut pro Vareno: "Amici deficiunt, cognati deserunt" et reliqua, aut accusatorum calumniam prodimus, ut in eodem loco: "In inimicissima civitate urgent, instant, insecuntur, studio, multitudine, pecunia, periurio pugnant."

1 T 7 [= T 2] Pliny the Younger, *Letters*

He [a certain learned man] evades these arguments and many others . . . by contending that even the orators on whose speeches I rely said less than they published. I think the opposite. Many speeches of many men are my witnesses, including Cicero's *On Behalf of Murena* and *On Behalf of Varenus*, in which a brief and, as it were, naked charge of certain crimes is indicated by rubrics alone: from these it is clear that he said a great many things but omitted them when he published.[1]

[1] On Pliny's (not disinterested) remarks, see Dyck 2010.

1 T 8 [= T 1] Iulius Severianus, *Precepts on the Art of Rhetoric*

Cases crop up in which the essential point at issue must receive the major treatment, and the narrative must be placed accordingly, as in *On Behalf of Varenus* or *On Behalf of (Aulus Cluentius) Habitus*.[1]

[1] On the use of an "artificial order" in *Clu.*, see Stroh 1975, ch. 11, esp. 224–25.

1 F 1, 2 Iulius Severianus, *Precepts on the Art of Rhetoric*

(Standard topics) are nonetheless deployed right away in the exordia in order to try to arouse pity when we either call to mind the adversaries' slanders and cabals and the client's isolation or his other misfortunes, as in *On Behalf of Varenus*: "His friends failed him, his relations deserted him," etc., or we reveal the prosecutors' slander, as in the same passage: "In a hostile community, they exert pressure, threaten, and harass him; they are fighting with partisan spirit, with the mob, with money, with perjury."

1 F 3, 4 Prisc. *GL* 2.348.18

In "as" quoque circumflexa . . . tam in "e" quam in "i" finiunt ablativum. Cicero pro Vareno: "C. Ancharius Rufus fuit e municipio Fulginate." Idem in eadem: "in praefectura Fulginate."

1 F 5 Quint. *Inst.* 7.1.9

Intentio simplex: "Occidit Saturninum Rabirius," coniuncta: "Lege de sicariis commisit L. Varenus: nam et C. Varenum occidendum et Cn. Varenum vulnerandum et Salarium item occidendum curavit"—nam sic diversae propositiones erunt: quod idem de petitionibus dictum sit.

1 F 6 Prisc. *GL* 2.595.11

"Cuia" quoque infiniti possessivum cum supra dictis verbis pro genetivo primitivi ponitur. Cicero pro Vareno: "Ea caedes si crimini datur, detur ei potissimum[1] cuia interfuit, non ei cuia nihil interfuit."

[1] potissimum *post* si *codd.: huc transp. Patricius*

1 F 7 Quint. *Inst.* 5.13.28

Praeterea in contradictionibus interim totum crimen exponitur . . . aut pluribus propositionibus iunctis (ut pro Vareno: "Cum iter per agros et loca sola faceret cum Pom-

1 F 3, 4 Priscian, *Textbook of Grammar*

Circumflexes in *as* . . . also terminate the ablative both in
e and *i*. Cicero, *On Behalf of Varenus*: "C. Ancharius Rufus
hailed from the municipality Fulginas [*Fulginate*]." Likewise in the same speech: "in the prefecture Fulginas
[*Fulginate*]."

1 F 5 Quintilian, *The Orator's Education*

A simple charge: "Rabirius killed Saturninus"; a com-
pound charge: "L. Varenus is guilty of murder: he arranged for the killing of C. Varenus, the wounding of Cn.
Varenus,[1] and likewise the killing of Salarius";[2] in this way
there will be various claims (let it be said that the same
applies to civil suits).

[1] Presumably the young man whose wound was displayed to
the jurors (T 2).   [2] All three of the victims are known only
from this passage; cf. Münzer, *RE* s.v. Salarius 1; Gundel, ibid. s.v.
Varenus 1–2.

1 F 6 Priscian, *Textbook of Grammar*

Cuia, the possessive of the indefinite, is also deployed with
the above-mentioned verbs in place of a genitive of the
primary word. Cicero, *On Behalf of Varenus*: "If a charge
is brought for that murder, let it be charged to that man
in particular in whose interest it was, not the one who had
no interest in it."

1 F 7 Quintilian, *The Orator's Education*

Moreover, in counterargument we sometimes set out the
whole charge . . . or with several of the claims conjoined
(as in *On Behalf of Varenus*: "They asserted that when he

11

puleno, in familiam Ancharianam incidisse dixerunt, deinde Pompulenum occisum esse, ilico Varenum[1] vinctum
adservatum dum hic ostenderet quid de eo fieri vellet"):
quod prodest utique si erit incredibilis rei ordo et ipsa
expositione fidem perditurus.

[1] C. *vel* Cn. Varenum *Russell*

1 F 8 Quint. *Inst.* 5.10.69

Fit etiam ex duobus, quorum necesse est ⟨esse⟩[1] alterum
verum, eligendi adversario potestas, efficiturque ut utrum
elegerit noceat. Facit hoc Cicero . . . pro Vareno: "Optio
vobis datur, utrum velitis casu illo itinere Varenum usum
esse an huius persuasu et inductu": deinde utraque facit
accusatori contraria.

[1] *add. Halm*

1 F 9 Quint. *Inst.* 4.1.73 (= 9.2.56)

Contraque est interim prohoemii vis etiam non exordio;
nam iudices et in narratione nonnumquam et in argumen-

was traveling through the fields and solitary places to-gether with Pompulenus, he came upon the slaves of An-charius; then Pompulenus was killed,[1] and Varenus[2] was instantly bound and detained until he [presumably An-charius] indicated what he wanted done with him"). This is certainly advantageous if the order of events is incred-ible and will lose plausibility by the mere telling.

[1] Pompulenus is otherwise unknown (not in the *RE*).
[2] Russell wants to read "C. Varenus," but it is not clear that he, as well as L. Varenus, was present.

1 F 8 Quintilian, *The Orator's Education*

The opponent is given the opportunity to choose between two options, one of which must be true, and the result is that whichever he has chosen is damaging. Cicero does this . . . in *On Behalf of Varenus*: "You have the choice whether to claim that Varenus undertook that journey by chance or at the urging and inducement of this man [pre-sumably Ancharius]"; then he shows that both are against the prosecutor.[1]

[1] The prosecutor's position was that they met by chance (see F 7: "he came upon the slaves of Ancharius"). If so, Varenus acted without premeditation; the alternative is that he was lured by "this man," i.e., Ancharius, and so led into a trap. Cf. Craig 1993, 17; Crawford 1994, 17.

1 F 9 Quintilian, *The Orator's Education*

On the other hand, sometimes what is tantamount to a proem is not in the beginning, for we sometimes beg the

tis ut attendant et ut faveant rogamus, quo Prodicus velut dormitantes eos excitari putabat, quale est: "Tum C. Varenus, ⟨is⟩[1] qui a familia Anchariana occisus est—hoc quaeso, iudices, diligenter attendite."

[1] *add. edd. ex 9.2.56*

1 F 10 Prisc. *GL* 2.112.20

In "us" desinentia secundae declinationis nomina "e" vel "i" antecedentibus mutant "us" in "o" et accepta "lus" faciunt diminutiva . . . Excipitur "Antonius," quod "Antoniaster" facit diminutivum. Cicero pro Vareno: "Lucius ille Septimius diceret—etenim est ad L. Crassi eloquentiam gravis et vehemens et volubilis: 'Erucius hic noster Antoniaster est.'"

1 F 11 Prisc. *GL* 2.307.17

DE GENETIVO PLURALI SECUNDAE DECLINATIONIS . . . Cicero . . . Idem pro Vareno: "deum fidem," pro "deorum."

judges to pay attention and give a favorable hearing both in the narrative and in the argumentation (Prodicus thought that by this tactic they were being roused up as if they were nodding off [84 A 12 D.-K.]), for instance: "Then C. Varenus, the one who was killed by Ancharius' slaves—jurors, I beg you, listen carefully to this."

1 F 10 Priscian, *Textbook of Grammar*

Nouns of the second declension ending in *us* with *e* or *i* preceding change *us* to *o* and form diminutives by addition of *lus* . . . *Antonius* is an exception, since it forms the diminutive *Antoniaster*. Cicero, *On Behalf of Varenus*: "The famous Lucius Septimius—he is, in fact, by the standard of L. Crassus' eloquence, authoritative, vigorous, and fluent—used to say, 'Our friend Erucius here is a pint-sized Antonius.'"[1]

[1] The quip is also quoted by Quintilian (*Inst.* 8.3.22), but without naming the speech. L. Septimius is otherwise unknown, unless he is the Septimius mentioned at Sall. *Hist.* 1.98R; cf. Münzer, *RE* s.v. Septimius 8. L. Crassus (cos. 95; *FRLO* 66) was the most famous orator of the generation before Cicero. The point is that Erucius was an ineffective imitator of M. Antonius (cos. 99; *FRLO* 65). He is called "one of the new orators" (Schol. Bob. 301.23–24St), i.e., he came to prominence after the Sullan slaughter of prosecutors (*Rosc. Am.* 89–90); cf. Nicolet 1974, 870.

1 F 11 Priscian, *Textbook of Grammar*

ON THE GENITIVE PLURAL OF THE SECOND DECLENSION . . . Cicero . . . Likewise in *On Behalf of Varenus*: "by the faith of the gods [*deum*]" instead of *deorum*.

2 CUM QUAESTOR
LILYBAEO DECEDERET

A speech delivered toward the end of his term of office in 75 (MRR 2:98). Its publication is unusual, since it is neither a forensic nor a senate speech. If it is not a forgery,

2 T 1 Ps.-Asc. *Arg. Div. Caec.* 185.7St

Qui omnes [*sc.* Siculi], praeter Syracusanos ac Mamertinos, M. Tullium, illo tempore florentem defensionibus amicorum, ad accusandum descendere compulerunt, iam pridem illis necessitudine copulatum, quod quaestor in Sicilia fuisset praetore Sex. Peducaeo et quod, cum decederet, in illa oratione quam Lilybaei habuit multa his benigne promisisset.

---

1 Peducaeus was probably praetor in 77 and propraetor in 75 (*MRR* 2:88, 98), but the term is sometimes used loosely in this way; cf. Crawford 1994, 19n1.

2 Unusually, Sicily had two quaestors at this period, one based at Syracuse, the other at Lilybaeum, to which Cicero had been assigned (*MRR* 2:98). It was the administrative center of the west-

2 WHEN HE DEPARTED
LILYBAEUM AS QUAESTOR (75 BC)

like The Day before He Went into Exile,[1] *it may have been circulated to publicize his activities this year, which had fallen on deaf ears at Rome (*Planc. 64–65*).*

[1] See Manuwald 2021, xl–xliii and 304–73 (text, translation, and commentary).

2 T 1 Pseudo-Asconius, Argument to Cicero, *Divinatio in Caecilium*

All of them [sc. the Sicilians], apart from the Syracusans and Mamertines, compelled M. Tullius, who at that time was successfully engaged in the defense of his friends, to undertake the prosecution [sc. of C. Verres, who had governed Sicily from 73 to 71]. He was bound to them by ties of long standing because he had been quaestor in Sicily during Sextus Peducaeus' praetorship[1] and because, on his departure, he had made them many kind promises in the speech he delivered at Lilybaeum.[2]

ern part of the island that had been conquered from the Carthaginians; cf. Scramuzza 1937, 154; Pina Polo and Díaz Fernández 2019, 143–51. On Cicero's continuing interest in the city, cf. Fedeli 1980.

2 F 1 Ar. Mess. *Elocut.* 33.1 Di Stefano (*GL* 7.469.1)

Detrecto hanc rem. Cicero cum quaestor Lilybaeo decederet:[1] "quod non detrectare militiam, sed defendere provinciam iudicata est."

[1] dec(ederet) *expl. edd.*: decessit *Ryan 2016*

2 F 1 Arusianus Messius, *Examples of Expressions*

I refuse (*detrecto*) this thing [i.e., the verb is transitive].
Cicero, *When He Departed Lilybaeum as Quaestor*: "because it [sc. *iuventus*, the youth, i.e., the young men] was
judged not to be refusing military service but to be defending the province."[1]

[1] Perhaps in listing his achievements during his term of office,
he alluded to his defense before the governor of young men accused of military indiscipline (mentioned by Plutarch, *Vit. Cic.*
6.2); see further Crawford 1984, 37–38.

3 PRO P. OPPIO

*While serving as quaestor in 74 under M. Aurelius Cotta,
who, as consul, was waging war in Bithynia-Pontus (MRR
2:101, 103), P. Oppius was charged with crimes committed
during the siege of Heraclea on the Black Sea, including
embezzlement of monies earmarked for troops' rations and
attempting to organize a mutiny (T 3 and 8). At a hearing
before his commander, Oppius pulled out a dagger and
was restrained by Cotta and Vulcius, one of his officers
(T 1, F 1). Thereupon Cotta dismissed him from service
and sent him back to Rome (T 2). His trial was initiated by
a letter sent by Cotta (T 4) and probably occurred either
toward the end of 70, after the equites had been empan-
elled (again) as jurors under the Aurelian Law (LPPR*

3 T 1 Sall. *Hist.* 3.80R (= Non. *Comp. doct.* 889L)

At Oppius, postquam orans nihil proficiebat, timide veste
tectum pugionem expedire conatus a Cotta Vulcioque
inpeditur.

3 ON BEHALF OF P. OPPIUS
(END OF 70/EARLY 69 BC)

369), or early in 69.[1] *If F 7 is correct in attesting two speeches, presumably for two sessions* (actiones), *then the primary charge may have been extortion (see ad. loc.). It is not clear why Cicero took on the case (no ties to Oppius are known). His pleading was notable for the care but also the sarcasm with which he treated Cotta, who was, in effect, the prosecutor (T 4, 6, 7, 9, 11, F 5–6). The outcome is not attested (though the disappearance of Oppius from the subsequent historical record is sometimes taken as an indicator of conviction).*

[1] Stroh 1975, 202n32, would date the trial between 72 and 70 on the grounds that M. Aurelius Cotta had not yet returned to Rome by the date of the trial (T 4) and that Cotta was back in Rome by 69, citing *MRR* 2:128; he would refer T 5 to a different trial; see ad loc. *TLRR* 187 refers the trial to 69 in view of T 5.

3 T 1 [= T 3] Sallust, *Histories*

But when his pleas failed to make an impression, Oppius was nervously trying to remove a dagger concealed in his clothing when he was hindered by Cotta and Vulcius.[1]

[1] Vulcius, who is otherwise unknown (not in the *RE*; cf. *MRR* 3:223), was evidently another officer present at the hearing.

3 T 2 Sall. *Hist.* 3.81R (= Serv. ad *Aen.* 12.844)

Dicit se eius opera non usurum, eumque ab armis dimittit.

3 T 3 Quint. *Inst.* 5.13.17

Sed tamen interim oratoris est efficere ut quid aut contrarium esse aut a causa diversum aut incredibile aut supervacuum aut nostrae potius causae videatur esse coniunctum. Obicitur Oppio quod de militum cibariis detraxerit: asperum crimen, sed id contrarium ostendit Cicero, quia idem accustores obiecerint Oppio quod is voluerit exercitum largiendo corrumpere.

3 T 4 Quint. *Inst.* 5.13.19

Cetera quae proponuntur communis locos habent. Aut enim coniectura excutiuntur, an vera sint, aut finitione, an propria, aut qualitate, an inhonesta iniqua improba inhumana crudelia et cetera quae ei generi accidunt, eaque non modo in propositionibus aut rationibus, sed in toto genere actionis intuenda: an sit . . . superba, ut in Oppium ex epistula Cottae reum factum.

3 T 2 [= T 4] Sallust, *Histories*

He said he would not employ his services and discharged him from the army.

3 T 3 [= T 5] Quintilian, *The Orator's Education*

But sometimes it is the orator's task to make an argument seem either self-contradictory or irrelevant to the case or incredible or redundant or aiding our case instead. Oppius was accused of stealing from the soldiers' rations, a difficult charge, but Cicero shows that it is self-contradictory, since the same prosecutors accused Oppius of wanting to corrupt the army by largesse.

3 T 4 [= T 6] Quintilian, *The Orator's Education*

Other claims that are put forward are met with standard topics. Either they are brushed aside by inference (are they true?) or definition (is the terminology correct?) or quality (are they dishonorable, unjust, wicked, inhumane, cruel, and other points that fall under this category?), and one must keep an eye on this not only in the case of claims or arguments but in the whole character of the pleading: whether it is . . . haughty, as toward Oppius, who was charged on the basis of Cotta's letter.[1]

[1] Cf. the similar attempt at *Quinct.* 28 to incite ill will because action was initiated by a letter. But as in the handling of the censors at *Clu.* 117–18, the criticism will have been carefully tempered so as not to provoke enmity; cf. Heinze 1909, 982–83.

3 T 5 Quint. *Inst.* 5.13.21

. . . fortissime invaseris quod est aut omnibus periculosum
. . . aut ipsis iudicibus, ut pro Oppio monet pluribus ne
illud actionis genus in equestrem ordinem admittant.

3 T 6 (= 5–6 T 16) Quint. *Inst.* 6.5.10

Infinitum est enumerare ut Cottae detraxerit auctoritatem, ut pro Ligario se opposuerit, Cornelium ipsa confes-
sionis fiducia eripuerit.

3 T 7 Quint. *Inst.* 11.1.67

Praestatur hoc aliquando etiam dignationibus, ut libertatis
nostrae ratio reddatur, ne quis nos aut petulantes in lae-
dendis eis aut etiam ambitiosos putet. Itaque Cicero,
quamquam erat in Cottam gravissime dicturus neque aliter agi P. Oppi causa poterat, longa tamen praefatione
excusavit officii sui necessitatem.

3 T 5 [= T 7] Quintilian, *The Orator's Education*

. . . you should attack most strongly what is dangerous either to all . . . or to the judges themselves, as in *On Behalf of Oppius* he warns at length that they should not allow this type of action against the equestrian order.[1]

[1] It is not clear how Oppius' conviction would have been prejudicial to the equestrian order, since he was a quaestor at the time of the offenses alleged. Or did this argument pertain to some subsidiary charge? Cf. similar arguments shielding the equites at *Clu.* 143–60 and *Rab. Post.* 13–19 (Heinze 1960, 117n52, suspected that Quintilian has confused *Opp.* with *Clu.*; cf. also Stroh 1975, 201–2n32).

3 T 6 [= T 8] Quintilian, *The Orator's Education*

It would be an endless task to enumerate how (Cicero) diminished Cotta's authority, how he placed himself in the front line in *On Behalf of Ligarius*,[1] how he rescued Cornelius by the very frankness of his confession.[2]

[1] At the beginning of the speech, he acknowledged that he and Ligarius had both opposed Caesar and made his case depend chiefly on Caesar's clemency.
[2] Cf. 5–6 T 3, 11.6, 15, and 5 F 61.

3 T 7 [= T 9] Quintilian, *The Orator's Education*

On occasion we grant persons in high places a justification for our outspokenness so that no one may suppose that we are either reckless in insulting them or even ambitious. Accordingly, even though he was going to take a strong line against Cotta—and P. Oppius' case could not be pleaded in any other way—nonetheless in a long preamble Cicero excused the need for his performance of duty.

3 T 8 Cass. Dio 36.40.3

τοῦ γοῦν Κόττου τοῦ Μάρκου τὸν μὲν ταμίαν Πού-
πλιον Ὅππιον ἐπί τε δώροις καὶ ἐπὶ ὑποψίαι ἐπιβου-
λῆς ἀποπέμψαντος, αὐτοῦ δὲ πολλὰ ἐκ τῆς Βιθυνίας
χρηματισαμένου, Γάιον Κάρβωνα τὸν κατηγορή-
σαντα αὐτοῦ τιμαῖς ὑπατικαῖς, καίπερ δεδημαρχη-
κότα μόνον, ἐσέμνυναν.

3 T 9 (= 5–6 T 23) Iul. Sev. *Praec. rhet.* 19, p. 109.18
Castelli Montanari (*RLM* 366.2)

Misericordiam movemus, si ab iis nos inpugnari dicimus
quorum auxilio tuti esse deberemus, ut Cicero pro Oppio,
vel cum alicuius calamitates commemoramus, cum mag-
nitudinem periculi ostendimus, sicut pro Cornelio Cicero.

3 T 8 [= T 2] Cassius Dio, *Roman History*

Marcus Cotta dismissed the quaestor Publius Oppius on grounds of bribery and suspicion of plotting mutiny, though he himself had made a great deal of money from his Bithynian campaign. They exalted his accuser C. Carbo with consular honors though he was merely a tribune of the plebs.[1]

[1] M. Aurelius Cotta was governor of Bithynia-Pontus from 73 to 71 (*MRR* 2:111, 117, 123). After his return he was prosecuted for extortion by C. Papirius Carbo, who received consular insignia for his success; cf. *MRR* 2:145, dating Carbo's tribunate of the plebs to 67 with a query; *TLRR* 192 (dating the trial to "67 or after"). Carbo's elevation in status was probably a regular reward for successful prosecution for extortion, i.e., he received the convicted man's consular rank; cf. Alexander 1985, 29–30, where our passage should have been taken into account.

3 T 9 [= T 11] Iulius Severianus, *Precepts on the Art of Rhetoric*

We stir pity if we claim that we are being attacked by those persons by whose aid we ought to be safe, as Cicero does in *On Behalf of Oppius*, or when we mention someone's misfortunes, when we show the scope of the danger, as Cicero does in *On Behalf of Cornelius*.[1]

[1] Cf. 5 F 59.

3 T 10 Ps.-Asc. ad *Verr.* 2.1.50 (236.1St)

NON AD PRAETOREM, SED ROMAM DEFERRI OPORTERE.
Atqui legimus et de Oppio et de Procilio ⟨non⟩[1] apud
populum depositas querellas,[2] sed apud eos sub quibus
agebant aut quaesturam aut legationem.

[1] *add. Danesius*
[2] populum depositas querellas *Baiter*: oppium depositasque
sellas *codd.*

3 T 11 Fortun. 121.16 Calboli Montefusco (*RLM* 110.22)

Procatasceua est qua iudicem nobis praeparamus, cum aut
quaedam nobis obsunt et illis prius occurrendum est, ut
fecit Cicero pro Oppio contra M. Cottae auctoritatem,
aut . . .

3 F 1 Quint. *Inst.* 5.10.69

Fit etiam ex duobus, quorum necesse est ⟨esse⟩[1] alterum
verum, eligendi adversario potestas, efficiturque ut utrum
elegerit noceat. Facit hoc Cicero pro Oppio: "Utrum cum
Cottam adpetisset an cum ipse se conaretur occidere te-
lum e manibus ereptum est?"

[1] *add. Halm*

---

[1] The prosecutor evidently claimed that Oppius was about to
attack Cotta when he was restrained. The alternatives Cicero
poses are therefore deceptive; cf. the notorious use of this tactic

3 T 10 [= T 1] Pseudo-Asconius on Cicero, *Verrine Orations*

MUST NOT BE REPORTED TO THE PRAETOR BUT TO ROME:[1] And yet we read in both *On Oppius* and *On Procilius* that complaints were not placed before the people but before those under whom they exercised either the quaetorship or legateship.[2]

[1] *Verr.* 2.1.50. [2] In 54, Procilius (praenomen unknown) was prosecuted by P. Clodius and convicted of murdering a head of household (*pater familias*); he seems to have been represented by Hortensius (our passage supplements *FRLO* 92 F 47); Cicero did not participate (cf. *Att.* 4.15[90].4); see *TLRR* 284; Dyck 2008b, 164.

3 T 11 [= T 10] Fortunatianus, *Handbook of Rhetoric*

Procatasceua is the means by which we prepare the judge for ourselves when either certain factors are against us and we must first meet them, as Cicero did in *On Behalf of Oppius* against M. Cotta's authority, or . . .

3 F 1 Quintilian, *The Orator's Education*

The opponent is given the opportunity to choose between two options, one of which must be true, and the result is that whichever he has chosen is damaging. Cicero does this in *On Behalf of Oppius*: "Was the weapon snatched from his hands when he had attacked Cotta or when he was trying to commit suicide?"[1]

at *Clu.* 64 (the question whether the Junian tribunal was bribed by Cluentius or Oppianicus) and *Mil.* 23 (the question whether Milo ambushed Clodius or vice versa). On this ploy, characteristic of Cicero's weaker cases, see Craig 1993; Seager 2011.

3 F 2 Quint. *Inst.* 5.10.76

Itaque non dubito haec quoque ⟨vocare⟩[1] consequentia,
quamvis ex prioribus dent argumentum ad ea quae secuntur, quorum duas quidam species esse voluerunt: actionis,
ut pro Oppio: "Quos educere invitos in provinciam non
potuit, eos invitos retinere qui potuit?" temporis, ⟨ut⟩[2] in
Verrem . . . Quod utrumque exemplum tale est ut idem
in diversum, si retro agas, valeat; consequens enim est
eos, qui inviti retineri non potuerint, invitos non potuisse
educi.[3]

[1] *add. Spalding*   [2] *add. Russell*   [3] retineri . . . educi
Russell post Gesner: duci . . . retineri *codd.*

3 F 3 Quint. *Inst.* 5.13.30

Neque enim pigebit, quod saepe monui referre: commune
qui prior dicit, contrarium facit; est enim contrarium quo
adversarius bene uti potest: "At enim non veri simile est
tantum scelus M. Cottam esse commentum. Quid? Hoc
veri simile est, tantum scelus Oppium esse conatum?"

3 F 4 Ar. Mess. *Elocut.* 85.9 Di Stefano (*GL* 7.504.14)

Queror tecum pro "apud te." Cicero pro Oppio: "questus-
que mecum est."

3 F 5 Amm. Marc. 30.8.7

Haec forsitan Valentinianus ignorans minimeque reputans
adflicti solacia status semper esse lenitudinem principum,

3 F 2 Quintilian, *The Orator's Education*

I therefore do not hesitate to call these consequences as well, albeit they argue from antecedents to sequels, of which some persons have claimed there are two types: relating to action, as in *On Behalf of Oppius*: "If he could not induce them to go into the province against their will, how could he hold them back against their will?"; relating to time, as in *Against Verres* . . . Each of the two examples is such that it also works in reverse; for it follows that those who could not be held back against their will could not have been induced to go out against their will.

3 F 3 Quintilian, *The Orator's Education*

I do not mind repeating the warning I have often given. The speaker who first makes a shared point is working against himself, for it is a point that an opponent can use to advantage against him: "But it is improbable that M. Cotta invented so great a crime. Well then, is this probable, that Oppius attempted so great a crime?"

3 F 4 Arusianus Messius, *Examples of Expressions*

I lodge a complaint with you [*tecum*] instead of "before you [*apud te*]." Cicero in *On Behalf of Oppius*: "He lodged a complaint with me [*mecum*]."

3 F 5 Ammianus Marcellinus, *History*

Unaware, perhaps, of these examples and failing to consider that the mildness of rulers is always a comfort for a person in distress, Valentinian increased the number of

poenas per ignes augebat et gladios. Quod ultimum in adversis rebus remedium pietas reperitur animorum, ut Isocratis memorat pulchritudo; cuius vox est perpetua docentis, ignosci debere interdum armis superato rectori quam iustum quid sit ignoranti. Unde motum existimo Tullium praeclare pronuntiasse, cum defenderet Oppium: "Etenim multum posse ad salutem alterius honori multis, parum potuisse ad exitium probro nemini umquam fuit."

3 F 6 Quint. *Inst.* 9.2.51

Nec in personis tantum sed et in rebus versatur haec contraria dicendi quam quae intellegi velis ratio, ut . . . ille pro Oppio locus: "O amorem mirum! O benivolentiam singularem!"

3 F 7 Charis. 181.14 Barw. (*GL* 1.143.15)

Senatuis ut fluctuis . . . Senati . . . ut lauri. Cicero quoque . . . pro Oppio II: "senati."

punishments by fire and sword. A loyal spirit is found to be the ultimate remedy in adversity, as a beautiful passage of Isocrates reminds us: his words are for all time when he teaches that pardon must sometimes be granted to a ruler defeated in war rather than to one who does not know what is just.[1] I think that this was the source of Tullius' splendid statement when he was defending Oppius: "In fact, to have great power to secure another's salvation has lent honor to many; to have had too little power to destroy has never been a reproach to anyone."

[1] Isoc. *Panath.* 185.

3 F 6 Quintilian, *The Orator's Education*

This principle of saying the opposite of what you wish to be understood applies not only in the case of people but also things, as for instance . . . that famous passage in *On Behalf of Oppius*: "O wondrous love! O unparalleled kindness!"[1]

[1] Evidently, a sarcastic description of Cotta's treatment of Oppius.

3 F 7 Charisius, *Handbook of Grammar*

Senatuis as *fluctuis* . . . *Senati* . . . as *lauri*. Cicero also . . . in *On Behalf of Oppius II*: "of the senate" (*senati*).[1]

[1] If, as the text suggests, Cicero published two speeches defending Oppius, the case may have been tried in two sessions (*actiones*); if so, the charge may have been extortion (*res repetundae*), since such cases had to be heard in two sessions. It is, however, also possible that if the jurors were in doubt, they might have called for a repetition of the pleadings (*ampliatio*), as in Caecina's case.

4 DE C. MANILIO

A problematic speech, with only one attested fragment, consisting of a single sentence. As the testimonia make clear, Cicero spoke to a public assembly on the last day of his praetorship (of 66: MRR 2:152) about the arrangements he had made for the trial of C. Manilius, claiming that giving Manilius only one day to prepare his defense was a friendly gesture to ensure that he himself would still be the presiding officer at the trial.[1] Under pressure from the crowd, he agreed to extend the deadline for the trial and take on Manilius' defense himself. On the day the trial was to convene (in 65), it was disrupted by the interference of a mob suborned by Manilius (T 2 and 6). The question arises: did Cicero have a chance to speak at the aborted trial, and, if so, is our fragment from that speech or the assembly speech? It seems doubtful that Cicero spoke at all at the trial or that, even if he did, he would have wanted to publish the speech and so memorialize the event and his

4 ON C. MANILIUS
(END OF 66 BC)

connection with it, which was clearly an embarrassment to him (T 4 = 5 F 17). However, publishing the assembly speech might have helped him repair the damage to his reputation that Dio claims he suffered in its aftermath (T 6). The content of the one fragment, such as it is, also suggests that Cicero was responding to pressure and criticism, as in the assembly speech.[2] Given that almost all of Cicero's nonsenate speeches are designated On Behalf of ___, *it should not surprise us if this one was falsely so designated (F 1); even one senate speech was mistakenly called* On Behalf of Marcellus.[3]

---

[1] Perhaps he feared that violence would erupt at the trial (as indeed it later did) if Manilius were given more time in which to organize it.

[2] Cf. Crawford 1994, 41.

[3] So Ramsey 1980, 335–36; Malaspina 2001, 177–79.

4 T 1 (= 5–6 T 2) Q. Cicero (?), *Comment. pet.* 51

Iam urbanam illam multitudinem et eorum studia qui
contiones tenent adeptus es in Pompeio ornando, Manili
causa recipienda, Cornelio defendendo.

4 T 2 (= 5–6 T 11.5 [part]) Asc. ad *Corn.* 60.9C (49.10St)

Sequente deinde anno L. Cotta L. Torquato coss., quo
haec oratio a Cicerone praetura ‹nuper› peracta[1] dicta
est, cum primum p‹ostulatus esset C.›[2] Manilius, qui iudicium per operarum duces turbaverat, deinde quod ex
S. C. ambo[3] consules ‹cum armatis›[4] praesidebant ei[5]
iudicio, non respondi‹sset absens›que[6] esset damnatus . . .

[1] praetura nuper peracta *Kiessling-Schoell*: pr(a)etura . . .
praetore *S et (sine lac.) P*: . . . pretore *M*   [2] prima pars . . .
codd.: primum *Sigonius, reliqua suppl. Ramsey*   [3] anno: *corr.*
Popma   [4] *suppl. Ramsey*   [5] et: *corr. Kiessling-Schoell*
[6] respondisset absensque *Kiessling-Schoell*: respondi *vel* re-
spondis . . . que *SP*: respondi atque *M*: respondisset atque *π*

4 T 1 [= T 7] Quintus Cicero (?), *Handbook of Election-eering*[1]

You have already won over the urban masses and the backing of those who hold assemblies by your praise of Pompey, by taking on Manilius' defense, and by defending Cornelius.

[1] Whether or not written by Quintus Cicero (the question is controversial), the *Handbook of Electioneering* is treated here as a contemporary source containing historically useful information; see further Tatum 2018, ch. 5, with literature cited. The case for authenticity is argued, with a review of recent scholarship, by Prost 2017, 52–82. Stylistic analysis suggests that the work was, in fact, written by Marcus Cicero, possibly with some input from, or based on a draft by, his brother; hence, the stylistic unevenness: Vainio et al. 2019: 34–37; A. Cucchiarelli in Berno et al. 2019, 615–17.

4 T 2 [= T 1] Asconius on Cicero, *Pro Cornelio*

Then in the following year, in the consulship of L. Cotta and L. Torquatus [sc. 65], when this speech was delivered by Cicero upon the recent completion of his praetorship, as soon as C. Manilius had been indicted, who had disrupted the court by using gang leaders[1] as his tools, then, since as authorized by a senatorial decree both consuls were presiding over that trial with armed guards, he failed to answer the charges and was convicted *in absentia* . . .

[1] For the background, cf. 5 F 17.

4 T 3 = 5 F 15

4 T 4 = 5 F 17

4 T 5 Plut. *Vit. Cic.* 9.4–7

Ἔτι δ' ἡμέρας δύο ἢ τρεῖς ἔχοντι τῆς ἀρχῆς αὐτῶι
προσήγαγέ τις Μανίλιον εὐθύνων κλοπῆς. Ὁ δὲ Μα-
νίλιος οὗτος εὔνοιαν εἶχε καὶ σπουδὴν ὑπὸ τοῦ δήμου,
δοκῶν ἐλαύνεσθαι διὰ Πομπήιον· ἐκείνου γὰρ ἦν φί-
λος. Αἰτουμένου δ' ἡμέρας αὐτοῦ, μίαν ὁ Κικέρων
μόνην τὴν ἐπιοῦσαν ἔδωκε, καὶ ὁ δῆμος ἠγανάκτησεν,
εἰθισμένων τῶν στρατηγῶν δέκα τοὐλάχιστον ἡμέρας
διδόναι τοῖς κινδυνεύουσι. Τῶν δὲ δημάρχων ἀγαγόν-
των αὐτὸν ἐπὶ τὸ βῆμα καὶ κατηγορούντων, ἀκουσθῆ-
ναι δεηθεὶς εἶπεν ὅτι τοῖς κινδυνεύουσιν ἀεί, καθ'
ὅσον οἱ νόμοι παρείκουσι, κεχρημένος ἐπιεικῶς καὶ

4 T 3 [= T 2] = 5 F 15

4 T 4 [= T 3] = 5 F 17

4 T 5 [= T 4] Plutarch, *Life of Cicero*

While he was still holding office for two or three days, someone brought Manilius before him on a charge of theft.[1] Manilius, however, enjoyed the goodwill and support of the people, and it was thought that he was being persecuted because of Pompey, whose friend he was. When he [sc. Manilius] demanded some days [to prepare his defense], Cicero granted one day only, the following day, and the public was annoyed since the praetors customarily granted defendants at least ten days. When the tribunes led him [sc. Cicero] to the rostra and spoke accusingly,[2] he begged to be given a hearing and said that he always treated defendants in a fair and kindly fashion, insofar as the laws allowed; he thought it would be outra-

---

[1] This perhaps refers to a charge under the provision of the extortion law, according to which a trial can be held for recovery of any tainted money received (*quo ea pecunia pervenerit*). Hence, the matter was brought before the extortion court presided over by Cicero; cf. Ramsey 1980, 329–31; for a different view (that Plutarch is simply in error about the charge), cf. Urso 2019, 145n56 (but Cicero states that the initial charge was extortion: 5 F 5). The different charge of treason (*maiestas*), reported at T 7, was presumably lodged later, after Manilius disrupted his extortion trial in 65, and would have been tried in the separate court established for that crime by the relevant Cornelian law (*LPPR* 360; Kübler, *RE* 14.1:548.6; cf. Greenidge 1901, 429).   [2] On this means of exerting pressure, cf. Pina Polo 2018, 108–13.

CICERO

φιλανθρώπως, δεινὸν ἡγεῖτο τῶι Μανιλίωι ταῦτα μὴ
παρασχεῖν· ἧς οὖν ἔτι μόνης κύριος ἦν ἡμέρας στρατηγῶν, ταύτην ἐπίτηδες ὁρίσαι· τὸ γὰρ εἰς ἄλλον ἄρ-
χοντα τὴν κρίσιν ἐκβαλεῖν οὐκ εἶναι βουλομένου βο-
ηθεῖν. Ταῦτα λεχθέντα θαυμαστὴν ἐποίησε τοῦ δήμου
μεταβολήν, καὶ πολλὰ κατευφημοῦντες αὐτόν, ἐδέ-
οντο τὴν ὑπὲρ τοῦ Μανιλίου συνηγορίαν ἀναλαβεῖν.
Ὁ δ᾽ ὑπέστη προθύμως, οὐχ ἥκιστα διὰ Πομπήιον
ἀπόντα, καὶ καταστὰς πάλιν ἐξ ὑπαρχῆς ἐδημηγό-
ρησε, νεανικῶς τῶν ὀλιγαρχικῶν καὶ τῶι Πομπηΐωι
φθονούντων καθαπτόμενος.

4 T 6 Cass. Dio 36.44.1–2

Καὶ μετὰ τοῦτο δίκης τέ τινος τῶι Μαλλίωι πρὸς τῶν
δυνατῶν παρασκευασθείσης, καὶ ἐκείνου χρόνον τινὰ
ἐμποιῆσαι αὐτῆι σπουδάζοντος, τά τε ἄλλα κατ᾽ αὐτοῦ ἔπραττε, καὶ μόλις αὐτόν (ἐστρατήγει γὰρ καὶ
τὴν ἡγεμονίαν τοῦ δικαστηρίου εἶχεν) ἐς τὴν ὑστε-
ραίαν ἀνεβάλετο, πρόφασιν ἐπ᾽ ἐξόδωι τὸ ἔτος εἶναι
ποιησάμενος. Κἂν τούτωι δυσχεράναντος τοῦ ὁμίλου
ἐσῆλθέ τε ἐς τὸν σύλλογον αὐτῶν, ἀναγκασθεὶς δῆθεν

geous not to accord the same treatment to Manilius. Therefore, since there remained only a single day in his power as praetor, he purposely specified that day. To postpone the trial to (the term of) another magistrate was not the behavior of a person who wanted to help. These words produced a remarkable change in the public.[3] Amid great applause, they begged him to take on Manilius' defense, and he readily agreed, not least for the sake of the absent Pompey.[4] Getting up once more before the assembly, he started his speech anew, vigorously attacking the optimates and those envious of Pompey.

[3] For a similar effect, cf. 11 T 3.

[4] Cf. *Leg. agr.* 2.49, alleging that the people "imposed" (*imposuistis*) the role of defending Pompey upon him during his praetorship two years previously, a passage that Rawson 1971, possibly rightly, connects with this incident; but cf. also Manuwald 2018, 299, finding instead a reference to Cicero's speech promoting the Manilian law on Pompey's command in Asia.

4 T 6 [= T 5] Cassius Dio, *Roman History*

After this, when a lawsuit was engineered by the optimates against Manilius[1] and he [Manilius] was keen to gain some time for it [i.e., time in which to prepare for it], he [Cicero] tried to thwart him in various other ways and grudgingly granted a postponement to the following day (since he was praetor and had charge of the court), using as his excuse that the year was at an end. Thereupon, when the crowd was annoyed, he went to their assembly under compulsion

[1] "Mallius" is the spelling in Dio's text, whether by authorial or scribal error.

ὑπὸ τῶν δημάρχων, καὶ κατά τε τῆς βουλῆς κατέ-
δραμε καὶ συναγορεύσειν τῶι Μαλλίωι ὑπέσχετο.
Καὶ ὁ μὲν ἐκ τούτου τά τε ἄλλα κακῶς ἤκουε καὶ
αὐτόμολος ὠνομάζετο, τάραχος δέ τις εὐθὺς ἐπιγενό-
μενος ἐκώλυσε τὸ δικαστήριον συναχθῆναι.

4 T 7 Schol. Bob. ad *Mil.* 119.14St

Nam cum C. Manilius post annum tribunatus sui, quem
turbulentissime gesserat, causam de maiestate dicturus
esset accusante Cn. Minucio, id egit ut per multitudinem
conspiratam obsideret eundem Cn. Minucium[1] accusa-
torem suum. Cui obsesso auxilium tulit adgregata bonorum multitudine L. hic Domitius ad quem loquitur et
quem vult inpraesentiarum [rerum][2] exempla illius pris-
tini vigoris imitari.

[1] Municio . . . Municium *codd.*: *corr. Orelli*
[2] *secl. Orelli*

from the tribunes, and inveighed against the senate and promised to represent Manilius. As a result of this, he was stigmatized and called a traitor, but a disturbance suddenly arose and hindered the court from convening.[2]

[2] Dio collapses the chronology, making it appear that Cicero's speech in the assembly was followed immediately by the disruption of Manilius' trial, which must have occurred later, at the new trial date that Cicero set in 65; for a different view, cf. Urso 2019, 146–47.

4 T 7 [= T 6] Bobbio Scholia on the *Miloniana*

After the year of his tribunate, which he had conducted in a disorderly fashion, C. Manilius was to plead his case on a charge of treason,[1] with Cn. Minucius as prosecutor.[2] By means of a mob he had recruited, he besieged the aforementioned Cn. Minucius, his prosecutor. This L. Domitius whom he [Cicero] addresses,[3] along with an assembled band of loyal citizens, came to his [Minucius'] aid when he was under siege, and he [Cicero] wants him [Domitius] at the present time [sc. at Milo's trial in 52] to imitate examples of that old-time vigor.

[1] Literally, "on majesty" (*maiestas*; sc. of the Roman people), i.e., their majesty as allegedly diminished by Manilius; see on T 5 and (on *maiestas*) the introduction to no. 5.

[2] *TLRR* 210.

[3] Sc. *Mil.* 22.

4 F 1 Non. *Comp. doct.* 700L

CONFITERI et PROFITERI. Hoc distat quod profiteri voluntatis est, confiteri necessitatis et coactus. Quod ita positum saepius legimus. Cicero pro Manilio: "Hoc[1] ego non solum confiteor, verum etiam profiteor." Honestius profiteri quam confiteri.

[1] hic: *corr. Clericus*

4 F 1 Nonius Marcellus, *Compendium of Learning*

CONFESS (*confiteri*) AND PROFESS (*profiteri*). This is the difference, that *profiteri* is voluntary, *confiteri* is necessary and coerced. We quite often read it so used. Cicero, *On Behalf of Manilius*:[1] "I do not only confess this, but even profess it."[2] To profess is more honorable than to confess.

[1] See the introduction to this speech.
[2] Perhaps a reference to his unorthodox grant of less than the usual amount of time for Manilius to prepare his case, since he is going to explain that it was actually an honorable gesture intended to help Manilius (T 5).

5–6 PRO CORNELIO I–II

5–6 T 1 (= 8 T 1, 10 T 1) Q. Cicero (?), *Comment. pet.* 19

Nam hoc biennio quattuor sodalitates hominum ad ambitionem gratiosissimorum tibi obligasti, C. Fundani, Q. Galli, C. Corneli, C. Orchivi; horum in causis ad te deferendis quid tibi eorum sodales receperint et confirmarint scio; nam interfui.

5–6 T 2 = 4 T 1

5–6 ON BEHALF OF CORNELIUS I–II
(EARLY 65 BC)

5–6 T 1 [= T 12] Q. Cicero (?), *Handbook of Electioneering*

In the recent two-year period, you have bound under obligation to yourself four clubs[1] of men influential in electioneering, C. Fundanius, Q. Gallius, C. Cornelius, and C. Orchivius. I know what the members undertook and confirmed to you when they assigned their cases to you, since I was present.

[1] The Latin word *sodalitas* can designate any "close association (in political, social, etc., life)" and more particularly "a religious fraternity" or "an electioneering gang": *OLD* s.v., where our passage is classified under the latter sense (2b); the lexicon is followed by Shackleton Bailey 2002, 418–19n16. This sense would accord with the limitation "of men influential in electioneering" and the fact that C. Cornelius is associated with electoral bribery (as a witness) at *QFr.* 2.3(7).5. The word appears in a more general sense, without the limitation, at Q. Cic. (?) *Comment. pet.* 16. For a different view, cf. Tatum 2018, 224.

5–6 T 2 [= T 13] = 4 T 1

5–6 T 3 Cic. *Vat.* 5

. . . veterem meum amicum, sed tamen tuum familiarem
defenderim, cum in hac civitate oppugnatio soleat, qua tu
nunc uteris, non numquam, defensio numquam vitupe-
rari. Sed quaero a te cur C. Cornelium non defenderem:
num legem aliquam Cornelius contra auspicia tulerit, num
Aeliam, num Fufiam legem neglexerit, num consuli vim
attulerit, num armatis hominibus templum tenuerit, num
intercessorem vi deiecerit, num religiones polluerit, aerarium exhauserit, rem publicam compilarit? Tua sunt, tua
sunt haec omnia; Cornelio eius modi nihil obiectum est.
Codicem legisse dicebatur; defendebat[1] testibus conlegis
suis non se recitandi causa legisse, sed recognoscendi.
Constabat tamen Cornelium concilium illo die dimisisse,
intercessioni paruisse. Tu vero, cui Corneli defensio dis-
plicet, quam causam ad patronos tuos aut quod os adferes?
Quibus iam praescribis quanto illis probro futurum sit si
te defenderint, cum tu mihi Corneli defensionem in male-
dictis obiciendam putaris.

[1] *Madvig*: defendebatur *codd.*

5–6 T 3 [= T 1] Cicero, *Against Vatinius*

. . . I defended an old friend of mine who was, however, also close to you, since in this community an attack, which you are now making, is sometimes criticized, whereas a defense never is. But I ask you, why should I not have defended C. Cornelius? Surely Cornelius enacted no law contrary to auspices, surely he did not flout the Aelian or Fufian Law,[1] surely he did not assault a consul or hold a temple with men under arms or thrust an intercessor aside with violence, contaminate religious rites, drain the treasury, pillage the state, did he? These are your acts, yours, all of them; Cornelius was accused of nothing of the kind. He was said to have read the document [sc. containing his bill]. With his [former] colleagues as witnesses, he offered the defense that he read it not to read it out formally, but to review it.[2] All the same, it was agreed that on that day Cornelius dismissed the assembly and abided by the intercession. But you, who dislike Cornelius' defense, what case will you bring to your advocates, what piece of effrontery? You are now laying down how great a disgrace it will be for them if they defend you, since you think that I should be contumaciously reproached for defending Cornelius.

[1] These laws of the mid-second century regulated the reporting of unfavorable auspices and made the days between the announcement and holding of an election noncomitial (i.e., unavailable for holding public assemblies). See further Tatum 1999, 125–33.

[2] This was, as Kumaniecki 1970, 21, suggests, evidently an excuse devised by Cornelius.

5–6 T 4 Cic. *Brut.* 271

Itaque ne hos quidem equites Romanos amicos nostros qui nuper mortui sunt ⟨omittam⟩:[1] P. Cominium Spoletinum, quo accusante defendi C. Cornelium, in quo et compositum dicendi genus et acre et expeditum fuit . . .

[1] *add. Kayser*

5–6 T 5 Cic. *Orat.* 103

At haec interdum temperanda et varianda sunt. Quod igitur in Accusationis septem libris non reperitur genus, quod in Habiti, quod in Cornelii, quod in plurimis nostris defensionibus?

5–6 T 6 Cic. *Orat.* 108

Ipsa enim illa pro Roscio iuvenilis redundantia multa habet attenuata, quaedam etiam paulo hilariora, ut[1] pro Habito, pro Cornelio compluresque aliae . . .

[1] at: *corr. Lambinus*

5–6 T 7 Nep. F 38 Marshall = *FRH* 45 F 13 (*De vita M. Tulli Ciceronis*) apud Hieron. *Contra Ioann. Ierosol.* 12 (*PL* 23.381)

Refert enim Cornelius Nepos se praesente iisdem paene verbis quibus edita est eam pro Cornelio seditioso tribuno defensionem peroratam.

5–6 T 4 [= T 2] Cicero, *Brutus*

I shall, accordingly, not even pass over our friends, the Roman equites who have recently died: P. Cominius of Spoletium, who was prosecutor when I defended C. Cornelius, who had a polished, keen, and fluent style . . .

5–6 T 5 [= T 7] Cicero, *Orator*

But this [i.e., the grand style] must sometimes be moderated and varied. What style is not found in the seven books of the Accusation [sc. of Verres] or in the case of (Aulus Cluentius) Habitus or in that of Cornelius or in my many defenses?

5–6 T 6 [= T 8] Cicero, *Orator*

Even the youthful superfluity in *On Behalf of (Sextus) Roscius* includes much that is whittled down and even elements that are a bit lighthearted, as does my speech *On Behalf of (Aulus Cluentius) Habitus, On Behalf of Cornelius*, and several others . . .

5–6 T 7 [= T 10] Cornelius Nepos, *Life of Cicero*

Cornelius Nepos reports that in his presence the defense on behalf of the treasonous tribune Cornelius was delivered in virtually the same words as its published version.

5–6 T 8 Val. Max. 8.5.4

Age, Q. Metellus, L. et M. Luculli, Q. Hortensius, M'.[1]
Lepidus C. Cornelii maiestatis rei quam non onerarunt
tantummodo testes salutem, sed etiam, negantes illo in-
columi stare rem publicam posse, depoposcerunt! Quae
decora civitatis, pudet referre, umbone iudiciali repulsa
sunt.

[1] M. *codd.: corr. Sigonius*

5–6 T 9 Asc. ad *Corn.* 57.1C (47.4St)

Hanc orationem dixit L. Cotta L. Torquato coss. post annum quam superiores.

5–6 T 8 [= T 3] Valerius Maximus, *Memorable Doings and Sayings*

Come, how did the witnesses Q. Metellus (Pius), L. and M. Lucullus,[1] Q. Hortensius, and M'. Lepidus[2] not only endanger the safety of C. Cornelius on trial for treason but even demand him for punishment, raising the claim that the republic could not stand if he were set free! These ornaments of the state, it is a shame to report, were rebuffed by the shield of the court.

[1] Only M. Lucullus appeared as a witness (cf. T 11.6); L. Lucullus can be excluded, since he remained outside the boundary of the city (*pomerium*) awaiting his triumph and so could not have witnessed the incident.

[2] Probably a reference to M'. (= Manius) Lepidus (cos. 66), not Mamercus Lepidus (cos. 77), as proposed by Sumner 1964 (the mss. give M. [= Marcus] Lepidus, a common mistake); cf. Briscoe 2019, 119–20.

5–6 T 9 [= T 6] Asconius on Cicero, *Pro Cornelio*

He delivered this speech in the consulship of L. Cotta and L. Torquatus [sc. 65], the year after the previous ones.[1]

[1] The speech is merely dated by year rather than exact date, as Asconius does for the defenses of Scaurus and Milo (18.3–4C and 30.1–2C, respectively). The difference is that for the later speeches he could rely on the *acta diurna*, a public record of acts of the magistrates, the people, the senate, and the courts initiated by Caesar in his first consulship; cf. David 1999, 122–24.

5–6 T 10 Asc. ad *Corn*. 81.9C (63.7St)

Magno numero sententiarum Cornelius absolutus est.

5–6 T 11 Asc. ad *Corn*. 57.4–62.5C (47.6–50.13St)

1. ‹C.›[1] Cornelius homo non improbus vita habitus est.
Fuerat quaestor Cn. Pompeii, dein tribunus plebis C. Pisone ‹M'. Glabrione› coss.[2] biennio ante quam haec dicta
sunt. In eo magistratu ita se gessit ut iusto[3] pertinacior
videretur. Alienatus autem a senatu ‹est›[4] ex hac causa.
Rettulerat ad senatum ut, quoniam exterarum nationum
legatis pecunia magna daretur usura turpiaque et famosa
ex eo lucra fierent, ne quis legatis exterarum nationum
pecuniam expensam ferret.[5] Cuius relationem repudiavit
senatus et decrevit satis cautum[6] videri eo S. C. quod ‹aliquot›[7] ante annos L.[8] Domitio C. Coelio[9] coss. factum
erat, cum senatus ante pauculos annos ‹ex eodem›[10] illo

1 add. *Baiter*
2 M'. Glabrione coss. *Baiter*: cos. *codd.*
3 iustior: *corr. Manutius*
4 suppl. *Clark*
5 ferat: *corr. Manutius*
6 factum *PM (lac. in S)*: *corr. Kiessling-Schoell*
7 quod aliquot *Clark*: quod S: quo *PM*
8 L. *Manutius*: Cn. *P et (cum lacuna seq.)* M: *lac. in S*
9 Caelio: *corr. Kiessling-Schoell*
10 lac. suppl. *Kiessling-Schoell*

5–6 T 10 [= T 20] Asconius on Cicero, *Pro Cornelio*

Cornelius was acquitted by a large number of votes.[1]

---

[1] Asconius is again vaguer than he is on later speeches, for which he quotes precise vote totals (cf. 28.25–27C and 53.19–22C for Scaurus and Milo, respectively); see note on previous fragment.

5–6 T 11 [= T 21] Asconius, Argument to Cicero, *Pro Cornelio*

1. C. Cornelius was considered a respectable man. He had been Cn. Pompey's quaestor,[1] then tribune of the plebs in the consulship of C. Piso and M'. Glabrio [sc. 67], two years before these speeches were delivered. In that magistracy his behavior gave an impression of excessive stubbornness. He was, moreover, estranged from the senate for the following reason. He had made a proposal to the senate that, since money was being paid to ambassadors of foreign nations at high rates of interest and shameful and notorious profits were being made from this, no one should pay money to ambassadors of foreign nations. The senate rejected his proposal and decreed that sufficient safeguards seemed to have been provided by the senatorial decree that had been enacted some years before, in the consulship of L. Domitius and C. Coelius [sc. 94], since only a few years previously, on the basis of the same

---

[1] *MRR* 2:122 places Cornelius' quaestorship in 71 with a query (the latest possible date); if that is right, he will have served with Pompey in Spain and during the crushing of the remnants of Spartacus' rebellion (*MRR* 2:124). Perhaps the defense was undertaken not least to gratify Pompey; cf. Rawson 1978, 79. On Cornelius, see Giomaro 1974–1975; D'Aloja 2018.

S. C. decrevisset ne quis Cretensibus pecuniam mutuam
daret. Cornelius ea re offensus senatui questus est de ea
⟨in contio⟩ne:[11] exhauriri provincias usuris propter id
unum[12] ut haberent legati unde praesentia ⟨munera⟩[13]
darent; promulgavitque legem qua auctoritatem senatus
minuebat, ne quis nisi[14] per populum legibus solveretur.
Quod antiquo quoque iure erat cautum; itaque in omnibus
S. C. quibus aliquem legibus solvi placebat adici erat[15]
solitum ut de ea re ad populum ferretur. Sed paulatim ferri
erat desitum resque iam in eam consuetudinem venerat
ut postremo ne adiceretur quidem in senatus consultis de
rogatione ad populum ferenda; eaque ipsa S. C. per pauculos admodum fiebant.

2. Indigne eam Corneli rogationem tulerant potentis-
simi quique ex senatu,[16] quorum gratia magnopere minue-
batur; itaque P. Servilius Globulus tribunus plebis inven-
tus erat qui C.[17] Cornelio obsisteret. Is, ubi legis ferundae
dies venit et praeco subiciente scriba verba legis recitare
populo coepit, et scribam subicere et praeconem pronun-
tiare passus non est. Tum Cornelius ipse codicem recitavit.
Quod cum improbe fieri C. Piso consul vehementer que-
reretur ⟨tollique⟩[18] tribuniciam intercessionem diceret,
gravi convicio a populo exceptus est; et cum ille eos qui

11 ea . . . ne: *suppl. Sigonius*
12 propter id unum *Stangl*: providendum *PM*: *lac. in S*
13 *lac. suppl. Mommsen*
14 quis nisi *ed. Ald.*: quivis *S, Poggius*: quis *P¹*: qui visui *M*
15 adiecerat: *corr. Lodoicus*
16 ex S. C.: *corr. Sigonius*
17 L.: *corr. Manutius*
18 *add. Hotoman*

senatorial decree, the senate had ruled that no one should make a loan to the Cretans. Resentful of the senate on that account, Cornelius complained about it in a public meeting: the provinces were being drained by usury for the sole purpose that the legates might have a source for financing immediate gifts,[2] and he promulgated a law by which he sought to reduce the senate's authority, namely that no one should be exempted from the laws except by a vote of the people. This stipulation had also been enacted in an ancient law; therefore, in all senatorial decrees by which it was decided that anyone should be exempted from the laws, it was customarily added that the matter should be brought before the people. But this gradually ceased to be done, and by now it had finally become customary for no clause to be added to the senate's decree, about bringing a bill to the people; and those senatorial decrees themselves were being enacted at sparsely attended meetings.

2. All the most powerful men of the senate, whose influence was being greatly reduced, were outraged at Cornelius' bill. Therefore the plebeian tribune P. Servilius Globulus was enlisted to obstruct C. Cornelius. When the day arrived for enacting the law and the herald began to read out to the people the words of the law (supplied by the clerk), he [Globulus] forbade the clerk to supply the document, or the herald to read it out. Then Cornelius himself read out the document. When the consul C. Piso lodged a strong complaint that this was being done improperly and said that the tribune's veto was being flouted,

[2] The text here is uncertain (restored by conjecture).

sibi intentabant manus prendi a lictore iussisset, fracti eius fasces sunt[19] lapidesque etiam ex ultima contione in consulem iacti. Quo tumultu Cornelius perturbatus concilium dimisit ‹actutum›.[20]

3. Actum deinde eadem de re in senatu est magnis contentionibus. Tum Cornelius ita ferre rursus coepit ne quis in senatu legibus solveretur nisi ‹non minus›[21] CC adfuissent, neve quis, cum ‹quis ita› solutus[22] esset, intercederet cum de ea re ad populum ferretur. Haec sine tumultu res acta est. Nemo enim negare poterat pro senatus auctoritate esse eam legem; sed tamen eam tulit invitis optimatibus, qui per[23] paucos ‹amicis›[24] gratificari solebant. Aliam deinde legem Cornelius, etsi nemo repugnare ausus est, multis tamen invitis tulit, ut praetores ex edictis suis perpetuis ius dicerent: quae res cunctam[25] gratiam ambitiosis praetoribus, qui varie ius dicere assueverant, sustulit. Alias quoque complures leges Cornelius promulgavit, quibus plerisque collegae intercesserunt: per quas contentiones totum[26] tribunatus eius tempus[27] peractum est.

4. Sequenti deinde anno M'.[28] Lepido L. Volcacio coss., quo anno praetor Cicero fuit, reum Cornelium duo fratres

---

19 cuncti: *corr. Gronovius*   20 *suppl. in lac. Purser*

21 *post Mommsen* (CC non minus) *lac. in M suppl. Dyck* (*cf. Asc.* 72.26C): *om. P*

22 quis ita solutus *Mommsen*: solutus *PM* (*lac. in S*)

23 vel: *corr. Mommsen*   24 *suppl. in lac. Clark*

25 cunctam *Baiter*: eum aut *codd.*

26 totius: *corr. Dyck*

27 eius tempus *Kiessling-Schoell*: tempore eius *codd.*

28 M.: *corr. Manutius*

he was shouted down by the people. When he ordered the lictor to seize those who were making threatening gestures at him, his fasces were broken and rocks were even hurled at the consul from the fringes of the assembly. Upset by this commotion, Cornelius dismissed the assembly at once.

3. Thereupon the senate deliberated about the matter amid great controversy. Then Cornelius initiated a new proposal, that no one should be immunized from the laws in the senate unless no fewer than two hundred members were present and that, once someone had been so immunized, no one should interpose a veto when the matter was brought to the people. This was enacted without commotion, since no one could deny that this law was in support of the senate's authority.[3] Nonetheless the senate passed it in spite of the opposition of the optimates, who were used to obliging their friends with few members present. Then Cornelius enacted another law—with which many were unhappy, though no one dared to oppose it—that praetors should dispense justice on the basis of their standing edicts.[4] This measure eliminated all the influence of ambitious praetors, who had been in the habit of ruling inconsistently. Cornelius also promulgated a number of other laws, many of which were vetoed by his colleagues. His entire term as tribune was spent amid these struggles.

4. Then in the following year, with M'. Lepidus and L. Volcacius as consuls [sc. 66], the year in which Cicero was praetor, the two Cominii brothers prosecuted Cornelius

[3] See further Ryan 1998, 13–14.

[4] *LPPR* 371; cf. Metro 1969; Lintott 1977; and, for the implications, Frier 1983, 230–31 and 1985, 73–76.

Cominii lege Cornelia de maiestate fecerunt. Detulit nomen Publius, subscripsit Gaius.[29] Et cum L.[30] Cassius
praetor decimo die, ut mos est, adesse iussisset, eoque die
ipse non adfuisset seu avocatus propter publici frumenti
curam seu gratificans reo, circumventi sunt ante tribunal
eius accusatores a notis operarum ducibus ita ut mors in-
tentaretur, si mox non desisterent. Quam perniciem vix
effugerunt interventu consulum, qui advocati reo de-
scenderant. Et cum in scalas quasdam Cominii fugissent,
clauso‹s›[31] in noctem ibi se occultaverunt, deinde per
tecta vicinarum aedium profugerunt ex urbe. Postero die,
cum L.[32] Cassius adsedisset et citati accusatores non adessent, exemptum nomen est de reis Corneli; Cominii autem magna infamia flagraverunt vendidisse silentium
magna pecunia.

5. Sequente deinde anno L. Cotta L. Torquato coss.,

[29] C.: L. *Cic. Clu. 100*
[30] *Comment. pet. 7 et Asc. 82.7C*: P. *codd. hoc loco*
[31] *corr. Dyck*
[32] *Comment. pet. 7 et Asc. 82.7C*: P. *codd. hoc loco*

under the Cornelian Law on Treason. Publius was the prosecutor, Gaius the assistant prosecutor.[5] When the praetor L. Cassius had ordered them to appear on the tenth day, as is customary, and on that day the praetor himself failed to appear, whether called away on account of his oversight of the public grain[6] or as a favor to the defendant, his prosecutors were surrounded in front of the tribunal by known gang leaders, with the threat of mortal danger if they did not immediately desist. They barely escaped this calamity by the intervention of the consuls, who had come to support the defendant. When the Cominii had taken refuge in a certain staircase, they kept themselves confined and hidden there until nightfall. Then they fled headlong from the city via the rooftops of neighboring houses. The following day, when L. Cassius had taken his seat [sc. to preside at trials], and the prose-cutors, though summoned, failed to appear, Cornelius' name was removed from the list of defendants. The Comi-nii, however, were stigmatized with the deep disgrace of having sold their silence for a large price.[7]

5. Then in the following year, in the consulship of L. Cotta and L. Torquatus [sc. 65]—when this speech was

[5] On them, cf. *FRLO* 143 + 144; Nicolet 1974, 2:845–47; David 1992, 827–29.

[6] This function of L. Cassius is not mentioned elsewhere; at this period it was normally exercised by the aediles; cf. Lintott 1999, 131.   [7] The deletion of the charge was standard procedure if the prosecutor defaulted (cf. Greenidge 1901, 466–68), but this did not preclude the charge being revived. The prosecutors' dropping of a case was called *tergiversatio* (literally, "turning one's back") and created the suspicion that the prosecution was frivolous or based on malice, not facts.

quo haec oratio a Cicerone praetura ⟨nuper⟩ peracta[33] dicta est, cum primum p⟨ostulatus esset C.⟩[34] Manilius, qui iudicium per operarum duces turbaverat, deinde quod ex S. C. ambo[35] consules ⟨cum armatis⟩[36] praesidebant ei[37] iudicio, non respondi⟨sset absens⟩que[38] esset damnatus, recreavit se ⟨Cominius, ut infam⟩iam acceptae pecuniae tolleret, ac ⟨repetiit⟩ Cornelium[39] lege maiestatis. Res acta est magna exspectatione. Paucos autem comites[40] Cornelius perterritus Manili exitu ⟨recenti⟩[41] in iudicium adhibuit, ut ne clamor quidem ullus[42] ab advocatis eius oriretur.

6. Dixerunt in eum infesti testimonia principes civitatis qui plurimum in senatu poterant Q. Hortensius, Q. Catulus, Q. Metellus Pius, M. Lucullus, M'.[43] Lepidus. Dixerunt autem hoc: vidisse se cum Cornelius in tribunatu

---

[33] praetura nuper peracta *Kiessling-Schoell*: pr(a)etura . . . praetore *S et (sine lac.)* P: . . . pretore *M*

[34] prima pars . . . *codd.*: primum *Sigonius, reliqua suppl. Ramsey*

[35] anno: *corr. Popma*

[36] *lac. suppl. Ramsey*

[37] et: *corr. Kiessling-Schoell*

[38] respondisset absensque *Kiessling-Schoell*: respondi (-dis *P*) . . . que *SP*: respondi atque *M*: respondisset atque *π*

[39] recreavisset . . . iam accepta pecunia tollere ait . . . Cornelium *codd.*: *suppl. emend. Kiessling-Schoell*

[40] autem comites *Clark*: ante me go . . . *codd.*

[41] *lac. suppl. Kiessling-Schoell*

[42] illius: *corr. Manutius*

[43] *Manutius*: M. *P*: L. *SM*

given by Cicero upon recent completion of his praetorship—as soon as C. Manilius had been indicted, who had disrupted the court using gang leaders as his tools, then, since, as authorized by a senatorial decree, both consuls were presiding over that trial with armed guards, he had failed to answer the charges and been convicted *in absentia*,[8] Cominius took heart that he could blot out the disgrace of bribery, and he prosecuted Cornelius again under the law against treason.[9] The case was tried in an atmosphere of keen anticipation. Frightened by Manilius' recent downfall, Cornelius brought few companions to the court so that his supporters would not even raise any uproar.[10]

6. Leading citizens in the community who were powerbrokers in the senate were hostile and pronounced testimony against him: Q. Hortensius, Q. Catulus, Q. Metellus Pius, M. Lucullus, M'. Lepidus.[11] What they said was this: they were witnesses when Cornelius as tribune

[8] That is, he gave up the case in view of the tightened security and loss of Cicero as his advocate; cf. Ward 1970, 553–54.

[9] Was only Publius involved in this trial (Cicero mentions him alone as prosecutor [*nominis delator*] at *Brut.* 271) or also Gaius as assistant prosecutor (*subscriptor*), as previously (cf. para. 4)? Since the prosecutors are referred to in the plural (5 F 9, 44, 47, and possibly 54; 6 F 4, 17, and possibly 2), that may be the case; see Ramsey forthcoming on Asc. 60C.   [10] That is, let alone disrupt the trial. Cf. *Mil.* 3, where Cicero seeks to use to his client's advantage any shout raised by Clodius' partisans.

[11] Q. Hortensius Hortalus (cos. 69), Q. Lutatius Catulus (cos. 78), Q. Caecilius Metellus Pius (cos. 80), M. Terentius Varro Lucullus (cos. 73), M'. Aemilius Lepidus (cos. 66); for this last identification, see on T 8.

codicem pro rostris ipse recitaret, quod ante Cornelium
nemo fecisse existimaretur. Volebant videri se iudicare
eam rem magnopere ad crimen imminutae maiestatis [tri-
buniciae][44] pertinere; etenim[45] prope tollebatur intercessio,
sio, si id tribunis permitteretur. Non[46] poterat negare id
factum esse ‹Cicero›;[47] is eo confugit ut diceret non ideo
quod[48] lectus sit codex a tribuno imminutam esse tribuniciam potestatem. Qua vero arte et scientia orationis, ita ut
et dignitatem clarissimorum civium contra quos dicebat
non violaret, et tamen auctoritate eorum laedi reum non
pateretur, quantaque moderatione rem tam difficilem
aliis[49] tractaverit lectio ipsa declarabit. Adiumentum autem habuit quod, sicut diximus, Cornelius praeter destric-
tum propositum animi adversus[50] principum voluntatem
cetera vita nihil fecerat quod magnopere improbaretur;
praeterea quod et ipse Globulus qui ‹intercess›erat[51] ade-
rat Cornelio, ‹et›[52]—quod ipsum quoque diximus—quod
Cornelius Pompeii Magni quaestor fuerat, apud duas ‹de-
curias›[53] profuit[54] equitum Romanorum et tribuno‹rum
aerariorum›[55] et ex tertia quoque parte ‹senatorum›[56]

44 *del. Marshall*
45 et cum: *corr. Manutius*
46 *fort.* cum non *vel* quoniam non
47 *add. Baiter*
48 ideo quod *Lodoicus:* video qui *codd.*
49 Tullius *Rinkes: fort.* aliis Tullius
50 animi adversus *Kiessling-Schoell:* animadversus *S:* adversus *PM*   51 *lac. suppl. Manutius*
52 *add. Hotoman*   53 *lac. suppl. Madvig*
54 praeferat: *corr. Clark*   55 *lac. suppl. Baiter*
56 *lac. suppl. Kiessling-Schoell*

read out the document before the rostra himself, a thing
which no one was thought to have done before Cornelius.
They wanted it to seem proper for them to judge that act
to be highly relevant to the charge of diminution of majesty,[12] for the veto was virtually annulled if the tribunes
were allowed this. Cicero could not deny that this had
occurred. He took refuge in the claim that the tribunician
power was not diminished because the document was read
by the tribune. Just reading the speech will show with
what artistry and rhetorical expertise and with how much
tact he managed a matter so difficult for others in such a
way that he both spared the standing of the distinguished
citizens against whom he spoke and still did not allow the
defendant to be damaged by their authority. He was aided
by the fact that, as we said, apart from his uncompromising
stance against the will of the leading citizens, the rest of
Cornelius' life gave no great cause for offense. Moreover,
Globulus himself, the intercessor, was supporting Cornelius, and—as we already said—the fact that Cornelius had
been quaestor of Pompey the Great[13] was to his advantage
with two jury panels, those of Roman equites and *tribuni
aerarii*, as well as among a good many of the third division,

[12] After "majesty," "tribunician" appears in the manuscripts;
but cf. Marshall 1985, 227: "There can have been no such thing
as 'tribunician majesty' in a law of Sulla [cf. on T 12], in view of
his attitude toward the tribunate; 'majesty' attached to the Roman
people . . . The *tribuniciae* would best be deleted here, as an intrusion based on *tribuniciam potestatem* at 61.7."

[13] Both points were made above (para. 1 *init.*).

apud plerosque exceptis iis ⟨qui erant⟩[57] familiares principum civitatis.

7. Res acta est magno conventu, magnaque exspectatione quis eventus iudicii futurus esset, ⟨quoniam et⟩[58] a summis viris dici testimo⟨nia⟩[59] et id quod ei dicerent confiteri ⟨reum⟩[60] animadvertebant. Exstat oratio Comini[61] accusatoris quam sumere in manus est aliquod[62] operae pretium, non solum propter Ciceronis orationes quas pro Cornelio habemus sed etiam propter semet ipsam. Cicero, ⟨ut⟩[63] ipse significat, quadriduo Cornelium defendit; quas[64] actiones contulisse eum[65] in duas orationes apparet.[66] Iudicium id exercuit Q. Gallius[67] praetor.

[57] *lac. suppl. Madvig*   [58] *lac. suppl. Stangl*
[59] dicit extimo . . .: *corr. Manutius*
[60] *lac. suppl. Manutius*   [61] hominis: *corr. Gronovius*
[62] aliquot: *corr. ed. Ven.*   [63] *add. Kiessling-Schoell*
[64] duas: *corr. Lodoicus*   [65] cum: *corr. Beraldus*
[66] appareat: *corr. recc., Beraldus*
[67] Gallus: *corr. Manutius*

5–6 T 12 Asc. ad *Corn* 62.6C (50.14St), locus interpolatus in *SM* post argumentum

In hac causa tres sunt quaestiones: prima, cum sit Cornelius reus maiestatis legis Corneliae, utrum certae aliquae

the senators, except for those who were friends of the leading citizens.[14]

7. The trial was held with a large gathering and keen anticipation of its dénouement since people noticed both that leading citizens were testifying and that the defendant confessed to what they said. The speech of the prosecutor Cominius is extant,[15] and it is worth looking at not only because of Cicero's speeches that we have on Cornelius' behalf but also for its own sake. As he himself indicates, Cicero defended Cornelius for four days; it is clear that he assigned those pleadings to two speeches.[16] The praetor Q. Gallius presided.

[14] A reference to the tripartite division of jury panels in use since the Aurelian Law of 70: *LPPR* 369; *MRR* 2:127; Lintott 1999, 160 and n. 55.   [15] *FRLO* 143 + 144 F 2–6. Tacitus, too, seems to have known it: *Dial.* 39.5.   [16] "Those pleadings" is a conjecture for the transmitted text "two pleadings [*actiones*]," which raises problems because two *actiones* would be required for an extortion case or if the jurors were in doubt and called for a repetition (*ampliatio*) of the pleadings (cf. on 3 F 7); this latter possibility seems unlikely, however, in view of the margin by which Cornelius was acquitted: T 10.

5–6 T 12 [= T 5] Asconius on Cicero, *Pro Cornelio* (interpolated)[1]

There are three questions in this case. First, since Cornelius is being charged under the Cornelian law on Treason,[2] whether some specific matters are covered by that law, by

[1] This item is a marginal note that was included in the archetype of Asconius' text. Whether or not written by Asconius himself, it is likely to be of ancient origin, showing a knowledge both of Cicero's speeches and of rhetoric.   [2] That is, the law *de maiestate* (on treason) enacted by L. Cornelius Sulla in 81: *LPPR* 360.

res sint[1] ea[2] lege comprehensae quibus solis reus maiestatis teneatur, quod patronus defendit; an libera eius inter-
pretatio iudici[3] relicta sit, quod accusator proponit. Secunda est an quod Cornelius fecit n⟨omin⟩e[4] maiestatis
teneatur. Tertia an minuendae maiestatis animum habuerit.

[1] sunt: *corr. Kiessling-Schoell*
[2] ex: *corr. Mommsen*
[3] interpretatione iudicii: *corr. Kiessling-Schoell*
[4] nomine *Purser*: ne ca *S*: ne ea *M*

5–6 T 13 Quint. *Inst.* 4.3.13

Hanc partem παρέκβασιν vocant Graeci, Latini egres-
sum vel egressionem. Sed hae sunt plures, ut dixi, quae
per totam causam varios habent excursus . . . Quo ex genere est . . . pro C. Cornelio popularis illa virtutum Cn.
Pompei commemoratio, in quam divinus orator, veluti nomine ipso ducis cursus dicendi teneretur, abrupto quem
inchoaverat sermone devertit actutum.

which alone a defendant is guilty of treason, which is the position taken by counsel for the defense; or, as the prosecutor proposed, the law is left to the free interpretation of the judge.[3] Second is whether what Cornelius did is covered under treason. Third, whether he had the intention of committing treason.[4]

[3] This sentence supplements *FRLO* 143–44 F 2–6. Since the first law on "diminished majesty" (*maiestas minuta*) was introduced by L. Appuleius Saturninus in 100 (*LPPR* 329–30), there was a tendency, fostered by the rhetorical schools, to expand the concept; cf. Thomas 1991, 375–77.

[4] Literally, "of diminishing the grandeur" (sc. of the Roman people).

5–6 T 13 Quintilian, *The Orator's Education*

The Greeks call this part [of a speech] a *parekbasis*, the Latins an excursus or excursion. As I said, there are several of these that offer opportunity for various excursuses over the course of the whole case . . . Of this type is . . . that demagogic recital of the merits of Cn. Pompey in *On Behalf of C. Cornelius*, to which the superlative orator suddenly diverted after breaking off the speech he had begun, as if the course of his speech were held in check by the commander's very name.[1]

[1] Cf. 5 F 48.

5–6 T 14 Quint. *Inst.* 5.11.25

Sed ut hac corporis humani pro Cluentio, ita pro Cornelio equorum, pro Archia saxorum quoque usus est similitudine.

5–6 T 15 Quint. *Inst.* 5.13.18

Testes in Cornelium accusator lecti a tribuno codicis pollicetur; facit hoc Cicero supervacuum, quia ipse fateatur.

5–6 T 16 = 3 T 6

5–6 T 17 Quint. *Inst.* 8.3.3

An in causa C. Corneli Cicero consecutus esset docendo iudicem tantum et utiliter demum ac Latine perspicueque dicendo ut populus Romanus admirationem suam non adclamatione tantum sed etiam plausu confiteretur? Sublimitas profecto et magnificentia et nitor et auctoritas expressit illum fragorem. Nec tam insolita laus esset prosecuta dicentem si usitata et ceteris similis fuisset oratio.

5–6 T 14 Quintilian, *The Orator's Education*

But as he [Cicero] used this simile of the human body in *On Behalf of Cluentius*, so he used one of horses in *On Behalf of Cornelius* and one of stones as well in *On Behalf of Archias*.[1]

[1] *Clu.* 146, *Arch.* 19. J. T. Ramsey suggests (*per litt.*) that in our speech Cicero perhaps "introduced horses to illustrate the need for control to be exercised by a bit and bridal, much as by passing his two splendid laws Cornelius curbed praetors and powerful figures in the senate, the one law requiring praetors to abide by the terms of their edicts, the other requiring a quorum in the senate for a vote on *privilegia*."

5–6 T 15 [= T 18] Quintilian, *The Orator's Education*

The prosecutor holds in prospect witnesses who will testify against Cornelius that the tribune read the document; but Cicero makes this redundant, because the man confesses it himself.[1]

[1] Cf. 3 T 6 with note.

5–6 T 16 = 3 T 6

5–6 T 17 [= T 15] Quintilian, *The Orator's Education*

In the case of C. Cornelius, merely by instructing the jurors and by speaking to the advantage of his case and in good, clear Latin, did Cicero not cause the Roman people to confess their admiration not merely by shouts but even by applause? That roar was surely elicited by loftiness, splendor, polish, and authority. Nor would such unusual praise have attended the speaker had his speech been

Atque ego illos credo qui aderant nec sensisse quid face-
rent nec sponte iudicioque plausisse, sed velut mente cap-
tos et quo essent in loco ignaros erupisse in hunc volupta-
tis adfectum.

5–6 T 18 Quint. *Inst.* 10.5.12

Omnes enim [*sc.* causae] generalibus quaestionibus
constant. Nam quid interest Cornelius tribunus plebis
quod codicem legerit reus sit, an quaeramus "violeturne
maiestas si magistratus rogationem suam populo ipse reci-
tarit?"

5–6 T 19 Tac. *Dial.* 39.5

Satis constat C. Cornelium et M. Scaurum et T. Milonem
et L. Bestiam et P. Vatinium concursu totius civitatis et
accusatos et defensos, ut frigidissimos quoque oratores
ipsa certantis populi studia excitare et incendere potuerint.

5–6 T 20 Lactant. *Div. inst.* 6.2.15

Apud Ciceronem Catulus in Hortensio, philosophiam rebus omnibus praeferens, malle se dicit vel unum parvum
de officio libellum quam longam orationem pro seditioso
homine Cornelio.

ordinary and like others. Moreover, I believe that the attendees were neither aware of what they were doing nor applauded of their own accord and upon considered judgment but, as if deranged and not knowing where they were, burst into this ecstasy.

5–6 T 18 [= T 17] Quintilian, *The Orator's Education*

All cases consist of general questions. For what difference does it make whether Cornelius, a tribune of the plebs, is standing trial because he read the document or we ask, "Is treason committed[1] if a magistrate has read out his bill to the people himself?"

[1] Literally, "Is the grandeur [sc. of the Roman people] violated . . .?"

5–6 T 19 [= T 14] Tacitus, *Dialogue on Orators*

It is agreed that C. Cornelius, M. Scaurus, T. Milo, L. Bestia, and P. Vatinius were prosecuted and defended with the entire city gathered in attendance so that even the most lifeless orators could be roused and set aflame by the enthusiasm of a rooting populace.

5–6 T 20 [= T 9] Lactantius, *Divine Precepts*

In Cicero's *Hortensius* (fr. 21 G.), Catulus, who places philosophy before all else, says that he prefers even a single small book on duty to the long speech on behalf of the treasonous Cornelius.[1]

[1] Gigon 1962, 231–33, refers this remark to the defense of P. Cornelius Sulla. But Catulus' dislike is explicable from his role in our trial, and *Sull.* is not particularly long; cf. 6 F 9b.

5–6 T 21 Schol. Bob. ad *Vat.* 144.11St

. . . ⟨pro⟩bavit[1] nulli displicuisse illam defensionem quam Cornelio susceperit, cum sit non ita multo post consulari honore donatus.

  [1] probavit *Hildebrandt*

5–6 T 22 Grill. *Comm. in Cic. rhet.* 90.9 Jakobi

Rursum in Corneliana circuitione usus est, quia erat Cornelii persona vehementissime offensa.

5–6 T 23 = 3 T 9

5–6 T 24 (= 7 T 3) Fortun. 134.19 Calboli Montefusco (*RLM* 117.37)

In hypophoris quae cavenda sunt? Ne plene et copiose ponantur: quod tamen aliquando facimus duabus ex causis, aut inridendi adversarii gratia, si hoc augeat de quo nulla quaestio est, ut pro Cornelio maiestatis, aut si discrepans aliquid ostendamus, ut de rege Alexandrino.

5–6 T 25 Mart. Cap. 5.506 (*RLM* 472.8–10)

Et pro Cornelio primo refutata sunt crimina quae secuta sunt tribunatum, post ad ipsum tribunatum recursus est factus, quae dispositio artificialis, ut diximus, nominatur.

---

  [1] Namely, because it is nonchronological; see 1 T 8 with note. Thus in *Corn. I* the disruption of Cornelius' first trial (F 6–10) preceded the discussion of his tribunate (F 18–46); see the Appendix.

5–6 T 21 [= T 11] Bobbio Scholia on *Against Vatinius*

He offered as proof that the defense that he took on for Cornelius incurred no one's displeasure, since not so long afterward [sc. in 64] he was awarded the consulship.

5–6 T 22 Grillius, *Commentary on Cicero's* Rhetorica

Again, in the *Corneliana*, he used a roundabout approach, since Cornelius' person had given strong offense.

5–6 T 23 = 3 T 9

5–6 T 24 Fortunatianus, *Handbook of Rhetoric*

What points should be guarded against in citing an opponent's speech? That it not be cited in full and abundant form; but we sometimes do this, for two reasons, either to mock our opponent if he amplifies a point about which there is no dispute, as in *On Behalf of Cornelius* concerning treason,[1] or if we are highlighting some contradiction, as in *On the Alexandrian King*.

[1] Either a reference to Cornelius' reading out of his bill before the assembly, an act admitted by the defense (cf. T 15), or to the definition of treason (5 F 29).

5–6 T 25 [= T 4] Martianus Capella, *On the Marriage of Philology and Mercury*

In *On Behalf of Cornelius*, first the charges that followed his tribunate were refuted; afterward he returned to the tribunate itself. This is, as we have said, called an artificial arrangement.[1]

5 PRO CORNELIO I

*This was the second trial of C. Cornelius for treason (ma-
iestas),*[1] *based on his action as plebeian tribune of 67 in
reading out his law in defiance of the veto of his colleague
P. Servilius Globulus. The first trial, in 66, was marked by
irregularities: on the appointed day the praetor failed to
appear, and the prosecutors P. and C. Cominius fled before
a threatening mob; on the next day, with the praetor present but the prosecutors absent, the charge was dropped
(TLRR 203, 209; T 11.4).*[2] *In early 65, C. Manilius, whose*

---

[1] The term *maiestas* is difficult to render in English. As a
charge, we have generally used "treason" as the equivalent, but
more literally it is the "majesty" or "grandeur" sc. of the Roman
people, which could be "diminished" (*imminuta*: T 11.6, or
minuta: 5 F 29 and *30), "damaged" (*laesa*: 5 F 18), or violated
(*violari*: T 18), an offense that took shape in the late Republic
under a Lex Appuleia of 100 (cf. on T 12), a Varian Law (on 5
F 58), and a Cornelian Law (4 T 5 n.). The scope of *maiestas* was
much expanded under the empire as a kind of catchall for offenses against the emperor and the state. See the detailed studies
by Gundel 1963; Drexler 1988, 31–48; Thomas 1991, esp. 365–77
on developments during the Republic; Ferrary 2009; Williamson
2016, 335–42.

[2] On the dismissal of charges and on the Cominii, see on
T 11.4.

5 ON BEHALF OF CORNELIUS I

earlier trial for extortion (de repetundis) *had been disrupted, had been convicted of* maiestas *(TLRR 205, 210), so P. Cominius took up the case again in the hope that he could prevail now that the public mood had shifted.*[3] *The trial is likely to have occurred circa February or March, 65.*[4] *In this speech, Cicero works to separate his client from*

---

[3] On the question whether Gaius again participated as assistant prosecutor (*subscriptor*), see above, on T 11.5.   [4] This assumes that Manilius' second trial occurred in late January/early February and that Cominius acted quickly to indict Cornelius, so as to take advantage of the public mood; see further note on introduction to no. 7. It is also relevant, as Khrustalyov 2022, 101n15, points out, that M. Crassus is attested as a juror in this trial (Asc. 76.10C) and that he could not have served as such once he entered office as censor (*MRR* 2:157). The evidence for the election of censors in the post-Sullan period is limited (cf. Mommsen 1887–1888, 2.1:352, who places such elections circa April) and pertains to Appius Claudius (cos. 54): in the first half of April 50, Cicero, writing from Cilicia, knew of his candidacy but not yet of his election as censor (*Fam.* 3.10[73].3); by *ca.* June 26 (Shackleton Bailey's dating with a query) Cicero expresses the hope that Appius is by now installed in the censorship (ibid. 3.11[74].5); he is first attested as exercising the office *ca.* August 8 (Caelius, *Fam.* 8.14[97].4). Since Crassus was still censor as late as December 5,

Manilius, to palliate Manilius' legislative record, and to blame the disruption of Manilius' first trial on certain un-named "important men" (F 13–14, 16–17). He also mocks the prosecutor's unheroic exit that put an end to Cornelius' first trial, faults the prosecutor for failing to prosecute those who disrupted that trial (F 8–10, 12), and argues that Cominius could have dropped the case altogether without dishonor (F 11). Cicero frames Cornelius' own legislative record as good (F 33–42) and his conduct at the public assembly at which he read out his law as irre-proachable, claiming that he was merely reviewing the law[5] and that he terminated the assembly at the first sign of violence (T 3, 11.2; F 43–45). He may also have argued that his reading of the law was protected by his "right of conducting business with the people" (ius agendi cum po-pulo) and that he had reached the part of the proceedings

---

when Cato became quaestor (a clash between the two is recorded at Plut. *Vit. Cat. Min.* 16.3–6; cf. *MRR* 3:170–71), Crassus' censorship will be a terminus ante quem for the trial, not a terminus post quem, as argued by Khrustalyov 2022, 101–2, whose attempt to discredit Plutarch's evidence is unconvincing.

[5] See on T 3.

5 F 1 Grill. *Comm. in Cic. rhet.* 89.90 Jakobi

Ut insinuationis exempla etiam de Cicerone ponamus, ecce insinuatione usus est per circuitionem in Corneliana ("Si umquam ulla fuit causa, iudices"), in qua initio di-

that were protected from veto (F 28).[6] *Toward the end of the speech, Cicero invokes the potent name of Pompey, who had been Cornelius' commander during the latter's quaestorship (T 11.1, 6, 13; F 48), and digresses on the history of the plebeian tribunate and its role as a guarantor of Roman liberty (F 49–58).*[7] *The speech concludes with the usual appeal for pity for his client (F 59).*[8] *The loss of the two speeches for Cornelius is perhaps the most to be regretted of any of Cicero's orations, because they are a rare example of* popularis *rhetoric employed before a jury of well-to-do citizens.*

[6] So Rilinger 1989, 495. However, Ferrary 2009, 247, proposes that Cicero argued that Cornelius' action still allowed Globulus to interpose his veto while the voters were being transferred to their tribal units.   [7] Cf. the "editorial comments" at the end of *Rosc. Am.* (§§153–54). Kenty 2020, 186, remarks: "Cicero portrays himself as an authority on historical memory, able to explain the origins of current disputes and take a broader perspective." On the relation of our speech to M. Antonius' defense of Norbanus (*FRLO* 65 F 22–30: *TLRR* 86), cf. Lintott 2008, 116–19; Ferrary 2009, 245–49. Zetzel 2022, 56–58, suggests that Cicero used details from his own speech to lend color to his account of Antonius' in *On the Orator*.   [8] See the Appendix for further details on the plan of the speech.

5 F 1 Grillius, *Commentary on Cicero's* Rhetorica

To cite examples of *insinuatio*[1] from Cicero as well, behold, he used *insinuatio* in a roundabout way in the defense of Cornelius ("If there ever was a case, jurors"), in which

[1] "A method of beginning a speech in which the favour of the judges is obtained by indirect means": *OLD* s.v.

cendi finxit se a diis petere quod a iudicibus postulabat.
Et quomodo illud Vergilianum "neque me Argolica de
gente negabo" (*Aen.* 2.78), sic et hic: "Nam primum[1] omnium tempore infestissimo causam dicimus."

---

[1] primum *Halm in app.*: primo *codd.*

5 F 2 Prisc. *GL* 2.294.2

DE DATIVO ET ABLATIVO PLURALI PRIMAE DECLINATIO-
NIS . . . Inveniuntur tamen quaedam pauca feminini generis . . . quae differentiae causa ablativo singulari "bus"
assumentia faciunt dativum et ablativum pluralem . . . ut
. . . "deabus" . . . Cicero pro Cornelio I: "Ut ab Iove optumo
maximo ceterisque diis deabusque omnibus opem et auxilium petam."

at the beginning of the speech he pretended that he was begging the gods for what he was demanding from the jurors. Just as the well-known Virgilian passage says "nor will I deny my Argive origin," so he says, "In the first place, I am pleading the case at the most prejudicial time of all."[2]

[2] A discrete allusion to the conviction of Manilius; see T 11.5 and F 5. The timing of the trial is also a topic, e.g., at *Clu.* 80, where Cicero remarks on the "prejudicial time" (*iniquitas temporis*) for his client in the aftermath of the Junian tribunal of 74 (*TLRR* 149).

5 F 2 Priscian, *Textbook of Grammar*

ON THE DATIVE AND ABLATIVE PLURAL OF THE FIRST DECLENSION . . . However, a few nouns of the feminine gender are found . . . which, for differentiation, form the dative and ablative plural by adding *bus* to the ablative singular . . . as for instance . . . *deabus* (goddesses) . . . Cicero, *On Behalf of Cornelius I*: "So that I may seek help and aid from Jupiter Best and Greatest and all the other gods and goddesses (*deabus*)."[1]

[1] The Elder Cato is said to have begun all his speeches with a prayer: Servius on *Aen.* 7.259; Aeschin. 3.180 is also a possible model; cf. Weische 1972, 65. There are similar prayers at *Rab. perd.* 5 and *Mur.* 1, as well as an elaborate prayer at the end of the Verrine corpus, on which see von Albrecht 1980.

5 F 3 Grill. *Comm. in Cic. rhet.* 93.85 Jakobi

At[1] certe nec narratio esse debet, sed aut a lege aut ab aliquo firmissimo argumento inchoare debet orator, sicut in Corneliana: "Unde igitur ordiar? An ab ipsa lege?"

[1] aut: *corr. Martin*

5 F 4 Ar. Mess. *Elocut.* 36.1 Di Stefano (*GL* 7.471.3)

Expedio me hac re. Cicero pro Cornelio I: "Eius modi mihi duos laqueos in causa esse propositos, ut, si me altero expedissem, tenerer altero."

5 F 5 Asc. 62.15C (50.20St)

VER. A PRIMO CIRCI. CLX[1]

"Postulatur a⟨pud⟩ me praetore⟨m⟩[2] primum de pecuniis repetundis. Prospectat videlicet Cominius quid agatur: videt homines faeneos in medium ad temptandum periculum proiectos."[3]

[1] CLXI: CLX *Kiessling-Schoell*
[2] a me praetore: *corr. Manutius*
[3] proiectus: *corr. Manutius*

5 ON BEHALF OF CORNELIUS I

5 F 3 Grillius, *Commentary on Cicero's* Rhetorica

But in fact there need not even be a narrative, but the orator ought to begin with either a law or some strong argument, as in the defense of Cornelius: "What, then, shall I take as my starting point? The law itself?"[1]

[1] The orator's dilemma is a topos going back to C. Gracchus (*FRLO* 48 F 61; Bonnet 1906); cf., e.g., Cic. *Lig.* 1 ("So I do not know where to turn"); Narducci 2004, 215–26. Cf. Kenty 2020, 108, who speaks (apropos of *Mil.*) of the orator taking "an intentionally weak and self-deprecating approach, creeping indirectly into a hostile audience's good graces."

5 F 4 Arusianus Messius, *Examples of Expressions*

I free myself from this thing. Cicero, *On Behalf of Cornelius I*: "Two snares were set for me in the case of such a kind that if I freed myself from the one, I would be caught by the other."[1]

[1] The Scylla and Charybdis he faces are evidently: (1) countering the five senior optimates testifying against Cornelius too sharply and thus angering them and (2) countering them too weakly and thus losing the case; cf. T 11.6.

5 F 5 [= F 7] Asconius

ABOUT 160 LINES FROM THE BEGINNING

"He [sc. Manilius] is first indicted before me as praetor on a charge of extortion. Cominius clearly has his eye on the proceedings: he sees dummies stuffed with hay thrown into the arena to test the danger."[1]

[1] In this allegory, the dummies filled with hay stand for Manilius; the bull, whose ferocity is being tested, will be the jurors: so Ramsey forthcoming ad loc.

5 F 6 Ar. Mess. *Elocut.* 12.1 Di Stefano (*GL* 7.453.18)

Adsum illi. Cicero pro Cornelio I: "Das[1] enim mihi facultatem eos qui tum adfuerint Cornelio nominandi."

[1] da *codd.*: *corr. edd.*

5 F 7 Prisc. *GL* 2.544.26 (~ *GL* 2.530.19)

"Sinor situs" et "desinor desitus" paenultima correpta. Cicero pro Cornelio in I:[1] "Coeptum igitur per eos qui agi volebant, desitum est per hunc qui decessit."

[1] in I: *om. GL 2.530.19*

5 F 8 Ps.-Acro ad Hor. *Sat.* 1.2.67

Et notandum fore numero singulari: . . . Item Cicero pro Cornelio: "Aperui forem scalarum," sed ex verbis accustores[1] ridentur, ut in Flacciana "strangulavit" posuit.

[1] accusatoris: *corr. Dyck*

5 F 6 [= F 12] Arusianus Messius, *Examples of Expressions*

I am supporting him. Cicero, *On Behalf of Cornelius I*: "You give me an opportunity to name those who supported Cornelius on that occasion."[1]

[1] Sc. Cornelius' trial of 66: *TLRR* 203. These included the two serving consuls; cf. T 11.4.

5 F 7 [= F 61] Priscian, *Textbook of Grammar*

Sinor situs (allow) and *desinor desitus* (desist) with shortened penult. Cicero, *On Behalf of Cornelius* in I: "It was, then, begun by those who wanted there to be a trial, but was ended by this man, who departed."[1]

[1] Perhaps a reference respectively to the optimates, who wanted the trial, and to Cominius, whose departure aborted Cornelius' first trial; for a different view, cf. Crawford 1994, 136–37.

5 F 8 [= F 9] Pseudo-Acro, *Commentary on Horace*

fore (door) in the singular should be noted . . . Likewise Cicero, *On Behalf of Cornelius*: "I opened the door of the staircase." The prosecutors are being mocked on the basis of their words, as in the defense of Flaccus he used "strangled."[1]

[1] Cf. Schol. Bob. on *Flac.* 5 (p. 95.5St), quoting Cicero: "He [sc. the prosecutor] preferred to say that they [i.e., the captured Catilinarian conspirators] had been strangled [*strangulatos*]."

5 F 9 Schol. ad Iuv. 7.118

Scalae sunt armariola advocatorum . . . Cicero in Corneliana: "'Correpsimus'[1] inquit 'in scalas.'"

[1] correpsimus LZκ: correpsit π

5 F 10 Fortun. 146.7 Calboli Montefusco (*RLM* 123.18)

Haec magnificentia atque magnitudo omnibus locis ac-
commodata est? Non omnibus. Cur ita? Quoniam sunt
quaedam partes causae perpetuae quae verba humilia
desiderent, ut "Latet in scalis tenebrosis Cominius."

5 F 11 Asc. 62.21C (51.1St)

"Quid? Metellus summa nobilitate ac virtute, cum bis iu-
rasset, semel privatim, ‹iterum lege, nonne›[1] privatim
patris,[2] publice legis ‹religione›[3] deiectus est? Ratione an
vi? At utri‹mque omnem›[4] suspicionem animi tollit ‹et

[1] *suppl. Kiessling-Schoell*
[2] privatum patre: *corr. Kiessling-Schoell*
[3] *lac. suppl. Beck*
[4] *lac. suppl. Kiessling-Schoell*

5 F 9 [= F 10] Scholia on Juvenal, *Satires*

scalae are lawyers' cupboards . . . Cicero in the defense of Cornelius: "'We crept,' he said, 'into the stairwell.'"[1]

[1] With the explanation "lawyers' cupboards," the scholiast evidently (wrongly) infers a meaning from this passage without reference to the general usage of the word; see further Wessner 1931, 267–68. The first-person plural shows that Cicero is quoting the prosecutor verbatim; this passage supplements the fragments of the Cominii at *FRLO* 143 + 144.

5 F 10 [= *F 11] Fortunatianus, *Handbook of Rhetoric*

Is this grandeur and greatness adapted to all topics? No. Why? Because there are certain parts of the whole case that require humble words, such as, "Cominius is hiding in the dark stairwell."[1]

[1] For hiding in a dark stairwell, cf. *Mil.* 40 (of P. Clodius).

5 F 11 [= F 8] Asconius

"Tell me this: though he had twice sworn an oath, once privately, the second time under a law, was Metellus,[1] a man of high nobility and character, not dislodged from a conscientious regard for his father in private, and the law in public? Did this happen by plan or by force? Yet on both sides, the character of C. Curio and the standing and re-

[1] As tribune of the plebs, Q. Caecilius Metellus Nepos was embroiled in controversy with Cicero as a result of the latter's actions as consul (see no. 13). Nevertheless, and although he was a cousin of P. Clodius, as consul in 57 Metellus allowed Cicero's recall from exile: *MRR* 2:174 and 199–200.

C. Curionis⟩[5] virtus ac dignitas et Q. Metelli s⟨pectata⟩[6] adulescentia ad summam laudem omnibus rebus ornata."[7]

[5] *lac. suppl. Manutius*
[6] *lac. suppl. Kiessling-Schoell*
[7] ornatam: *corr. Manutius*

5 F 12 Ar. Mess. *Elocut.* 33.9 Di Stefano (*GL* 7.469.6)

Experior cum his. Cicero pro Cornelio I: "Quid quod ne cum his quidem expertus es, quos duces operarum fuisse dixisti?"

spected youth of Q. Metellus, equipped in all respects for supreme merit, eliminate any suspicion of his intent."[2]

[2] Nepos' homonymous father (cos. 98) was prosecuted by C. Scribonius Curio (cos. 76); see further *TLRR* 82. On his deathbed, Nepos senior made his son swear an oath to exact vengeance by prosecuting Curio (Asc. 63.16–21C). Such transgenerational feuds were not uncommon in the late Republic; cf. Hinard 1980. In addition to the private oath to his father, Nepos had to swear a public oath when he filed suit against Curio. However, he dropped his suit under pressure; cf. Asc. 63.21–64.6C; *TLRR* 181. Cicero cites this example to suggest that such an indictment could be dropped without dishonor (on the text of Asc. 63.7–8C, see Ramsey forthcoming). Cicero claims that in view of the character of both Curio and Nepos, there can be no doubt that the latter swore his oaths in good faith. Cf. the similar suggestion at *Mur.* 63 that Cato should have dropped his vow to prosecute.

5 F 12 [= F 13] Arusianus Messius, *Examples of Expressions*

Go to law with them. Cicero, *On Behalf of Cornelius I*: "What of the fact that you did not even go to law with the men you said were the gang leaders?"[1]

[1] For the role of gang leaders in thwarting Cornelius' first trial, cf. T 11.4. Several times elsewhere Cicero cites the failure to prosecute a related charge to suggest that the current prosecution is unserious; cf. *Cael.* 20, *Planc.* 55.

5 F 13 Asc. 64.11C (52.3St)

"'Legem,' inquit, 'de libertinorum suffragiis Cornelius C. Manilio[1] dedit.' Quid est hoc 'dedit'? 'Attulit.' An rogavit? An hortatus est? Attulisse[2] ridiculum est, quasi legem aliquam aut ad scribendum difficilem aut ad excogitandum reconditam:[3] quae lex paucis his annis non modo scripta sed etiam lata esset."

[1] cum Mallio: *corr. Manutius*
[2] an tulit . . . an tulisse: *corr. Madvig*
[3] recognitam: *corr. ed. Iunt.*

5 F 14 Asc. 65.1C (52.13 St)

"In quo cum multa reprehensa sunt,[1] tum imprimis celeritas actionis."

[1] sint: *corr. Sigonius*

---

[1] A reference to Manilius' law on freedmen's suffrage; see n. 1 on previous fragment. According to Asconius (65.3–5C), Manilius enacted his law a few days after entering office as plebeian tribune on December 10, 67, during the Compitalia (a movable feast usually falling at the end of December). Dio (36.42.3) says

5 F 13 [= F 14] Asconius

"'Cornelius,' he said, 'gave C. Manilius the law concerning the suffrage of ex-slaves.'[1] What is this 'gave'? 'He supplied it to him.' Did he ask for it? Did he urge him? It is ridiculous for him to have supplied it, as if it were a law that was difficult to draft or recherché to think up, since this law was not only drafted but even enacted within these past few years."[2]

[1] He quotes the prosecutor: *FRLO* 143 + 144 F 6. The reference is to the law providing that freedmen be distributed among all the tribes, enacted within a few days of Manilius' entry into the plebeian tribunate but soon annulled by the senate: *LPPR* 375; *MRR* 2:153. The prosecutor aims to create a tight bond between Cornelius and Manilius, *tribuni plebis*, respectively, of 67 and 66, so that the former will bear some taint from the latter's recent conviction. For the individual *populares* related to each other as part of an ideal continuum with tralaticious program points, cf. Strasburger, *RE* 18.1:794.14–19 (s.v. Optimates); for such a proposal as "having a kind of life of its own," cf. Morrell 2023, 53–54.   [2] That is, in 88 by the plebeian tribune P. Sulpicius Rufus; it was, however, soon abrogated by Sulla; cf. *LPPR* 346; *MRR* 2:41. Though here Cicero ridicules the idea of a plebeian tribune receiving a ready-made law from someone else, at *Mil.* 33 he alleges that the scribe Sextus Cloelius, an associate of P. Clodius', had a portfolio of laws he wanted to pass on to a cooperative tribune (cf. on 16 F 1).

5 F 14 [= F 15] Asconius

"In this matter not only were many points criticized, but in particular the haste of the action."[1]

that the law was enacted on December 29 and annulled the following day, when the new consuls took office on January 1. Cf. Courrier 2014, 523–24.

5 F 15 (= 4 T 3) Asc. 65.6C (52.18St)

"Petivit tamen a me praetore[1] maxima ⟨in⟩ contione[2] ut causam Manili defenderem."

[1] praetore *Manutius*: praetor *ed. Iunt.*: p̄r̄ *codd.*

[2] in contione *Clark in app.* (*cf. F 35, Prov. 18; v.ll. ad Serv. Aen. 12.844 a v.d. Murgia et Kaster laud.*): contione *Ramsey, Leg. agr. 3.2 coll.*: constitutione *codd.*

5 F 16 Asc. 65.9C (52.20St)

VER. A PRI. DCCCL

Dicit de eodem Manili tribunatu: "Nam cum is tr. pl. duas leges in eo magistratu tulisset, unam perniciosam, alteram egregiam, quod summae rei publicae nocuisset[1] ab illo ipso tr. abiectum est, bonum autem quo[d] ⟨continetur⟩[2] summa res publica manet et †in vestri ordina . . . dis fuit."[3]

[1] summae rei publicae nocuisset *Clark*: summa resp. non hesit sed *codd.*

[2] quod . . . *codd.*: quo continetur *Dyck*

[3] in vestri ordina . . . dis fuit: imperi vestri ordinarios hostes dispulit *Mommsen*: *fort.* imperi vestri odio hostibus fuit

5 F 15 [= F 16] Asconius

"Nevertheless, at a huge public meeting, when I was praetor, he begged me to plead Manilius' case."[1]

[1] Asconius (65.8C) identifies the subject as C. Attilius Celsus (given as pr. 65 at *MRR* 2:157–58 and by Brennan 2000, 753, but he would have to be assigned to 66, if praetor is the subject of the verb; see on the Latin text and Ward 1970, 549n15; *MRR* 3:28–29). However, Cass. Dio (36.44.2 = 4 T 6) speaks of the tribunes as organizing the public meeting at which Cicero was compelled to justify himself, and this was the typical situation; cf. Pina Polo 2018, 108–13. Moreover, the career profile of C. Attilius Celsus fits a tribunate more neatly than a praetorship; see further Ramsey forthcoming ad loc.

5 F 16 [= F 17] Asconius

850 VERSES FROM THE BEGINNING

He likewise says of Manilius' tribunate: "When that plebeian tribune had enacted two laws in that magistracy, one harmful,[1] the other outstanding, the one that would have damaged the state interest was rejected by that tribune himself, the good one, however, on which the state interest depends, abides and was . . ."[2]

[1] This is Cicero's earliest reference to a harmful (*perniciosa*) law; cf. 5 F 21; *Pis.* 10; *Phil.* 2.72; Classen 1979, 286 and n. 72.

[2] The two laws were, respectively, the Manilian Law on Freedmen's Suffrage (see on F 13 and 14), and the Manilian Law transferring the war against Mithridates to Pompey: *LPPR* 375–76; *MRR* 2:153. The end of the fragment is damaged; possibly it read "was hated by your enemies" or the like.

5 F 17 (= 4 T 4) Asc. 66.1C (53.5St)

Dicit de disturbato iudicio Maniliano: "Aliis ille in illum furorem magnis hominibus auctoribus impulsus est qui aliquod institui[1] exemplum disturbandorum iudiciorum ‹rei publicae›[2] perniciosissimum, temporibus suis accommodatissimum, meis[3] alienissimum rationibus cupierunt."

[1] instituit: *corr. Manutius*
[2] *add. Patricius*
[3] eis: *corr. Manutius*

5 F 18 Mar. Vict. *Def*. 29.8St

Sic Tullius multis in locis et ipsa pro Cornelio, ubi quaeritur quid sit maiestatem minuere, tractat: "Quod malam legem tulit, quod legendo codicem intercessionem sustulit, quod seditionem fecit." In quibus omnibus definitur laesa maiestas; sed ita singula sunt[1] ut in ipsis singulis totum, id est laesa maiestas, possit ostendi.

[1] *fort.* conexa sunt

---

[1] This passage supplements *FRLO* 143–44. Cicero is summarizing the prosecutor's claims. The "bad law" is presumably Cornelius' proposal that exemption from the laws be granted only by the people, not the senate; the reading of the document and instigation of sedition will refer to actions that occurred in the assem-

5 F 17 [= F 18] Asconius, *On the Speech On Behalf of Cornelius*

He says of Manilius' disrupted trial: "He was pushed into that madness by the authority of others, important men[1] who were eager for some precedent for the disruption of trials to be established, a matter harmful to the state that was perfectly suited to their circumstances but utterly at odds with my strategy."[2]

[1] Asconius comments: "He seems to indicate L. Catiline and Cn. Piso" (66.7C), but it is hard to see Cn. Piso as an "important man" (cf. Gruen 1969, 23). It is usually assumed that Crassus is meant; cf. Ward 1977, 138–41; Crawford 1994, 110 with literature.   [2] For the disruption of Manilius' trial, see also 4 T 6. With "utterly at odds with my strategy," Cicero dissociates himself from the disruption: as Manilius' advocate, he planned to defend his client with arguments, not violence.

5 F 18 [= *F 19] Victorinus, *On Definitions*

Tullius treats it this way in many passages and even in *On Behalf of Cornelius*, where the question arises what it is to reduce majesty: "because he enacted a bad law, because he flouted a veto by reading the document, because he instigated sedition."[1] Damaged majesty is defined in all these ways; but the individual points are such that the whole, that is, damaged majesty, can be shown in the individual points themselves.

bly that was convened to vote on the matter (T 11.1–2). Malaspina 1997a, 587, suggests that "because he instigated sedition" is too general a point to be assigned to a direct quotation, but this may be a paraphrase rather than a direct quotation, and in Ciceronian tricola the final member is often a summarizing formulation.

5 F 19, 20, 21 Asc. 66.16, 67.6, 67.15C (53.16, 54.1, 54.7St)

VER. CIR. ∞X[1]

"Possum dicere hominem summa prudentia spectatum,[2] C. Cottam, de suis legibus abrogandis ipsum ad senatum rettulisse."

SEQUITUR

"Possum etiam eius‹dem›[3] Cottae legem de iudiciis privatis anno post quam lata sit a fratre eius ‹abrogatam›."[4]

STATIM

"Legem Liciniam et Muciam de civibus re‹di›gendis[5] video constare inter omnis, quam‹quam›[6] duo consules omnium quos vidimus sapientissimi tulissent, non modo inutilem sed perniciosam rei publicae fuisse."

[1] s XI: *corr. Kiessling-Schoell*
[2] captum: *corr. Kiessling-Schoell*
[3] *add. Manutius*
[4] *add. Manutius*
[5] redigendis *Schol. Bob. ad Sest. 30, Pighius*: regundis *codd.*
[6] *add. Halm*

---

[1] It is not clear which of his own laws C. Cotta (cos. 75) moved to abrogate (Asc. 66.21–67.5C could find no record of it). The actual abrogation may have occurred not in 75 but in the following year; see next note.

5 F 19, 20, 21 [= F 20, 21, 22] Asconius

CA. VERSE 1010

"I can say that a man admired for the utmost good sense, C. Cotta, consulted the senate himself concerning the abrogation of his own laws."[1]

THERE FOLLOWS

"I can also say that a law of the same Cotta concerning private trials was abrogated by his brother the year after it was enacted."[2]

IMMEDIATELY AFTER

"I see that everyone agrees that the Licinian and Mucian Law on restoring citizens (to their proper jurisdictions) was not only not advantageous but harmful to the state, even though two consuls had enacted it who were the wisest of all we have seen."[3]

[2] In the consulship of his brother M. Cotta (cos. 74), two of C. Cotta's laws were abrogated, the one mentioned pertaining to private cases, the other regulating censorial leases; cf. *LPPR* 365; *MRR* 2:96.

[3] A law passed in the consulship of L. Licinius Crassus and Q. Mucius Scaevola (95), perhaps in response to fraudulent claims of citizenship uncovered during the census of 98/7, established a tribunal to try any unqualified persons; cf. *LPPR* 335; *MRR* 2:11; Monaco 2006; Coskun 2009, 149–55; Bispham 2016, 86. Contrast *Off.* 3.47, where Cicero expresses approval of the law. By describing the law as "harmful," Cicero may imply that he thinks it contributed to the outbreak of the Social War; cf. Tweedie 2012; Santangelo 2018, 235; Helfberend 2022, 178.

5 F 22 Prisc. *GL* 2.527.12

In "lo" finientia praesens per "lui" exeunt in praeterito . . .
Alia quoque eiusdem terminationis "o" in "i" convertunt
. . . Cicero vero in I epistularum ad filium (fr. epist. VIII.1
Watt): "quare effice et elabora ut excelleas," quod est ab
"excelleo, excelles" . . . Idem tamen Cicero in Verrinis
"praecellunt" protulit secundum tertiam coniugationem
et in I pro Cornelio: "qui eloquentia ceteris antecellit."

5 F 23 Asc. 68.7C (54.19St)

"Quattuor omnino genera sunt, iudices, in quibus per senatum more maiorum statuatur aliquid de legibus. Unum
est eius modi placere legem abrogari:[1] ut Q. Caecilio M.
Iunio coss.[2] quae leges rem militarem impedirent, ut abro-
garentur."

[1] abrogare: *corr. Beraldus*
[2] iunio coss. *Lodoicus*: emilio cos. *codd.*

5 F 24 Asc. 68.19C (55.5St)

"Alterum,[1] quae lex lata esse dicatur, ea non videri populum teneri: ut L. Marcio Sex. Iulio coss.[2] de legibus Li-
viis."[3]

[1] quartum: *corr. Manutius*   [2] cos.: *corr Clark*
[3] iuniis *P*: viniis *M*: vivis *S*: *corr. Manutius*

---

[1] Laws of M. Livius Drusus (tr. pl. 91) providing land and
grain for the urban plebs and enrollment of three hundred equites in the senate were annulled as illegal (carried contrary to
auspices); for sources, see *LPPR* 336–37; *MRR* 2:20–22.

5 F 22 [= F 23] Priscian, *Textbook of Grammar*

[Verbs] that terminate the present in *–lo* end in *–lui* in the perfect . . . Others with the same ending change *o* to *i* . . . But in Book 1 of his letters to his son, Cicero writes: "Therefore exert yourself and bring about that you excel [*excelleas*]," which is from *excelleo, excelles* . . . Cicero likewise, however, used *praecellunt* according to the third conjugation in the *Verrines*[1] and in the first speech *On Behalf of Cornelius*: "who excelled [*antecellit*] others in eloquence."[2]

[1] An erroneous reference.

[2] A reference to L. Crassus, often praised for his supreme eloquence in *On the Orator* and *Brutus*.

5 F 23 [= F 24] Asconius

"There are in all four categories, gentlemen of the jury, under which decrees are passed by the senate about laws according to ancestral custom. One is of such a kind that it is resolved that a law be abrogated, as in the consulship of Q. Caecilius and M. Iunius [sc. 109] that the laws be abrogated that were hindering military operations."[1]

[1] *LPPR* 324; *MRR* 1:545.

5 F 24 [= F 25] Asconius

"The second, that it does not seem proper for the people to be bound by a law that is said to have been enacted, such as concerning the Livian Laws in the consulship of L. Marcius and Sextus Iulius [sc. 91]."[1]

5 F 25 Asc. 69.8C (55.1St)

"Tertium est de legum derogationibus,[1] quo de genere persaepe S. C. fiunt, ut nuper de ipsa lege Calpurnia cui[2] derogaretur."

   [1] abrogationibus: *corr. Manutius*   [2] que: *corr. Lambinus*

5 F 26 Asc. 69.14 (55.12St)

"P. Africanus ille superior dicitur non solum a sapientissimis hominibus qui tum erant verum etiam a se ipso saepe accusatus esse[1] quod, cum consul esset cum Ti.[2] Longo, passus esset tum primum a[3] populari consessu[4] senatoria subsellia separari."

   [1] est: *corr. Baiter*   [2] T.: *corr. Manutius*   [3] primum a *Manutius*: plurima *codd.*   [4] consensu: *corr. Poggius*

5 F 27 Prisc. *GL* 2.292.16

Est autem quando hunc quoque per concisionem proferunt, et maxime in compositis et patronymicis, ut "Graiugenum" pro "Graiugenarum" . . . sic "caelicolum" pro "caelicolarum" et "trinum nundinum" pro "trinarum nundinarum." Cicero pro Cornelio I: "Ex promulgatione trinum nundinum dies ad ferendum potestasque venisset."

---

   [1] This is evidently the beginning of the narrative of the disorderly assembly at which Cornelius' bill on immunization from the laws was to be enacted; cf. T 11.1–2. *nundinae* (market-days) occurred every eighth day (every ninth day according to Roman inclusive reckoning); cf. *OLD* s.v. *nundinae* 1. According to the Caecilian Didian Law of 98, three market-days had to intervene between the promulgation and voting of a law; cf. Lintott 1968; 1999, 44 and n. 20–21.

5 F 25 [= F 26] Asconius

"The third concerns the partial abrogation of laws; senatorial decrees are often passed concerning this category, as in the recent case of the Calpurnian Law itself, which was partially abrogated."[1]

[1] The Calpurnian Law on Electoral Malfeasance was enacted in 67 and replaced Sulla's Cornelian Law. It stiffened the penalty by imposing a lifelong ban on holding public office, rather than a ten-year exclusion; cf. *LPPR* 361, 374. Cicero's treatment of the fourth type (*obrogatio*) is lost; it involved passing a law to invalidate or modify an earlier law; cf. Reduzzi Merola 2000.

5 F 26 [= F 27] Asconius

"The Elder P. Africanus is said often to have been reproached not only by wise men who were his contemporaries but even by himself because, when he was consul together with Ti. Longus [sc. 194], he allowed the senators' seats to be segregated for the first time from the people's seating area."[1]

[1] Cicero construes the matter differently, as an example of the way things should be done (violated by Clodius), at *Har. resp.* 22–24; cf. Asc. 70.10–25C; Ungern-Sternberg 1975.

5 F 27 [= F 28] Priscian, *Textbook of Grammar*

There are times when this too [sc. the genitive plural] is abbreviated, especially in compounds and patronymics, such as *Graiugenum* (Greek) instead of *Graiugenarum* ... So *caelicolum* (heaven dwellers) instead of *caelicolarum* and *trinum nundinum* (three market-days) instead of *trinarum nundinarum*. Cicero, *On Behalf of Cornelius I*: "From promulgation the terminal day of three market-days and an opportunity for enactment had arrived."[1]

5 F 28 Asc. 71.5C (56.15St)

CIRCA MEDIUM

Quo loco enumerat,[1] cum lex feratur, quot loca intercessionis sint.[2] "⟨. . .⟩[3] iubeat discedere.[4] Est utique ius ve-
tandi, cum ea feratur, quam diu ⟨quibus ius est suffragii⟩[5]
ferundi transferuntur; id est ⟨dum recitatur⟩[6] lex, dum
privati dicunt, dum ⟨summovetur populus⟩,[7] dum sitella
defertur, dum aequantur sortes, dum sortitio fit, et si qua
sunt alia huius generis."

[1] numerat: *corr. Kiessling-Schoell*   [2] sunt: *corr. Sigonius*
[3] *lac. detexit Sigonius, qui* antequam qui legem fert populum
supplere voluit   [4] dicere: *corr. Sigonius*
[5] *lac. suppl. Buecheler*
[6] *lac. suppl. Kiessling-Schoell*
[7] *lac. suppl. Mommsen*

5 F 29 Quint. *Inst.* 7.3.35

Est interim certa finitio, de qua inter utramque partem
convenit, ut Cicero dicit: "Maiestas est in imperi atque in
nominis populi Romani dignitate." Quaeritur tamen an
maiestas minuta sit, ut in causa Corneli quaesitum est.

---

[1] Cf. *Divisions of Oratory* 105: "Majesty resides in the dignity
of the power and name of the Roman people, which is diminished
by one who has issued a summons to sedition by mob violence . . . ," a paraphrase from Antonius' defense of Norbanus
(supplementing *FRLO* 65 F 22–30). One might wonder whether
Quintilian is merely citing from the *Divisions of Oratory* and

5 F 28 [= F 30] Asconius

AROUND THE MIDDLE

In this passage he enumerates how many opportunities there are for a veto when a law is being enacted.[1] ". . . he orders to disperse.[2] Assuredly there exists the right of veto when it [a law] is being enacted as long as those who have the right to vote are being shifted [sc. to their tribal voting units], that is, while the law is being read out, while non-magistrates are speaking, while the general public is being removed, while the voting urn is being brought, while the lots are being shaken for fairness, while lots are being drawn, and any other such matters."

[1] On the "opportunities for veto" (*loca intercessionis*), see Meier 1968; Rilinger 1989.　[2] Following the lacuna, "he orders to disperse" is likely to be part of Cicero's text, since Asconius explains the technical sense of "disperse" in the sequel (not quoted here); see further Ramsey forthcoming ad loc.

5 F 29 [= p. 78, n. 16] Quintilian, *The Orator's Education*

Sometimes there is a fixed definition that both sides agree upon, as Cicero says: "Majesty resides in the dignity of the power and name of the Roman people." The question arises, however, whether majesty has been reduced, as was at issue in Cornelius' case.[1]

pointing out that the issue came up at Cornelius' trial (in which case, this would be a nonverbatim fragment), or citing the definition from the speech. But in view of F 18 it is certain that the definition figured in the speech; cf. also T 12. It is thus likely that the definition was cited by both Antonius and Cicero; cf. Zetzel 2022, 57n13.

*5 F 30 Quint. *Inst.* 4.4.8

Est et nuda propositio, qualis fere in coniecturalibus: "caedis ago," "furtum obicio," et[1] ratione subiecta, ut: "Maiestatem minuit C. Cornelius; nam codicem tribunus plebis ipse pro contione legit."

[1] est: *corr. Meister*

5 F 31 Quint. *Inst.* 5.13.25

Quod autem posui, referre quo quidque accustor modo dixerit, huc pertinet ut, si est minus efficaciter elocutus, ipsa eius verba ponantur; si acri et vehementi fuerit usus oratione, eandem rem nostris verbis mitioribus proferamus, ut Cicero de Cornelio: "Codicem attigit."

---

[1] Cominius presumably said, "he snatched the document" (*codicem arripuit*), or the like.

*5 F 30 [= *F 6] Quintilian, *The Orator's Education*

A proposition can be put forward on its own, as is the general practice in conjectural cases: "I am prosecuting for murder," "I am claiming theft," and with a reason attached, such as: "C. Cornelius reduced the majesty [of the Roman people], since as a plebeian tribune he himself read the document before the assembly."[1]

[1] According to the *status* theory of Hermagoras of Temnos (fl. 150 BC), a "conjectural case" is one in which the facts are at issue; cf. *Rhet. Her.* 1.18; Lausberg 1998, §§79–138. The fragment is not explicitly attributed (hence, the asterisk). If it is from Cicero's speech (and not that of Cominius; cf. *FRLO* 143 + 144 F 4), he is quoting the prosecutor's position. On the basis of this fragment, Bauman 1967, 74, followed by Briscoe 2019, 118, claims that the charge was that Cornelius violated his own tribunician power by reading the bill out himself (and not having this done by a herald) and points to *ipse* (himself) in the text to show an implied contrast to the normal procedure. Bauman is right about the implicit contrast, but was this the violation or that the law was read out at all, in defiance of tribunician veto? Cf. Hinard 1976, 733–34. Moreover, Bauman's view seems to be at odds with Asconius' narrative (58.14–24C = T 11.2). In addition, opposed to the idea that the law was against a "violation of tribunician majesty," cf. on T 11.6.

5 F 31 [= *F 29] Quintilian, *The Orator's Education*

The point of my statement, that it makes a difference how the prosecutor has said each thing, is this: if he spoke ineffectually, his very words should be cited; but if he used sharp and forceful language, we should express the same thing in our own milder words, as for instance Cicero concerning Cornelius: "He touched the document."[1]

5 F 32 Asc. 71.17C (57.1St)

PAULO POST

"Unum tamen quod hoc ipso tr. pl. factum est prae-
termittendum non videtur. Neque enim maius est legere
codicem cum intercedatur quam sitellam ipsum[1] coram[2]
ipso intercessore deferre, nec gravius incipere ferre quam
perferre, nec vehementius ostendere se laturum invito
collega quam ipsi collegae magistratum abrogare, nec cri-
minosius tribus ad legem accipiendam quam ad collegam
reddendum privatum intro vocare: quae vir fortis, huius
collega, A.[3] Gabinius in re optima fecit omnia; neque cum
salutem populo Romano atque omnibus gentibus finem
diuturnae [cupiditatis][4] turpitudinis et servitutis afferret,
passus est plus unius collegae sui quam universae civitatis
vocem valere et voluntatem."

[1] ipsam: *corr. Kiessling-Schoell*
[2] cum: *corr. Rinkes*
[3] aut: *corr. Poggius*
[4] *del. Madvig*

5 F 32 [= F 31] Asconius

A LITTLE LATER

"Nonetheless, it seems that one deed that was done when
my client was a plebeian tribune ought not to be passed
over in silence. For it is not a greater offense to read a
document when a veto is interposed than personally to
present the urn for drawing lots in the very presence of
the intercessor; nor is it a more serious matter to begin to
enact a measure than to complete the enactment, or more
headstrong to show that one will enact a law against a colleague's wishes than to abrogate a colleague's magistracy;
nor is it a more culpable act to call the tribes in to accept
a law than to make a colleague a private citizen. All these
things were done by my client's colleague A. Gabinius, a
gallant man, in a very good cause; since he was bringing
salvation to the Roman people and an end of prolonged
disgrace and slavery to all peoples, he did not suffer the
voice and will of one of his colleagues to have greater force
than those of the entire community."[1]

[1] Cicero compares Cornelius' action in reading his law de-
spite Globulus' veto with the more aggressive way his colleague
A. Gabinius broke the veto that another plebeian tribune, L. Tre-
bellius, had interposed against his bill awarding Pompey a three-
year command over the coasts of the Mediterranean to clear the
sea of pirates: *LPPR* 371–72; *MRR* 2:144–45. Though here Cicero
defends Gabinius' tactics, at *Mil.* 72 and *Leg.* 3.24 he criticizes Ti.
Gracchus' similar abrogation of M. Octavius' mandate (see further Dyck 2004, 507).

5 F 33 Asc. 72.22C (57.23St)

"At enim de corrigenda lege rettulerunt."

5 F 34 Ar. Mess. *Elocut.* 29.4 Di Stefano (*GL* 7.466.10)

Detraho tibi. Cicero pro Cornelio I: "Nihil senatui detraxisse Cornelium."

5 F 35, 36 Asc. 73.1, 73.22C (57.27, 58.7St)

"Idem, ⟨nisi⟩[1] haec ipsa lex quam C. Cornelius tulit obstitisset, decrevissent id quod palam iam isti defensores iudiciorum pugnaverunt, senatui non placere id iudicium de Sullae bonis fieri. Quam ego causam longe aliter praetor in contione defendi, cum id dicerem quod idem iu-

[1] *add. ed. Ald.*

5 F 33 [= F 32] Asconius

"But they referred (to the senate) the question of amending the law."[1]

[1] "They" will be the consuls C. Piso and M'. Glabrio; the "law" is Cornelius' Law on Immunization from the Laws, which at first encountered opposition but then was enacted in amended form; see T 11.1–3.

5 F 34 [= F 33] Arusianus Messius, *Examples of Expressions*

I take away from you. Cicero, *On Behalf of Cornelius I*: "Cornelius took nothing away from the senate."[1]

[1] Sc. in his Law on Immunization from the Laws; see T 11.3.

5 F 35, 36 [= F 34, 35] Asconius

"Had this very law enacted by C. Cornelius not stood in the way, the same men would have decreed what these 'defenders of the courts' already openly fought for, namely, that the senate was opposed to that trial being held concerning Sulla's goods.[1] As praetor, I defended this cause far differently in a public assembly, when I said the same

[1] A reference to Cornelius' law as amended to require a quorum of at least two hundred senators in order to exempt anyone from the laws: *LPPR* 370–71; *MRR* 2:144. According to Cicero, this prevented the senate from legislating an exemption for Faustus Sulla, who was prosecuted in 66 by a plebeian tribune on grounds of self-enrichment with public monies (*de peculatu*), i.e., the money his deceased father, the dictator L. Sulla, realized from the sale of goods of the proscribed and other corrupt sources; see *TLRR* 196.

dices postea statuerunt, iudicium aequiore tempore fieri oportere."

STATIM

"Antea vero quam multorum reorum[2] iudicia sublata sint, et quia scitis praetereo[3] et ne quem in iudicium oratio mea revocare videatur."

[2] multarum rerum: *corr. Ramsey*
[3] praeterea: *corr. Manutius*

5 F 37 Asc. 74.9C (58.18St)

PAULO POST

"Non Cn. Dolabella C. Volcacium, honestissimum virum, communi et cotidiano iure privasset."

---

[1] An example of an injustice that would have been prevented if Cornelius' law requiring praetors to rule according to their edicts had been in existence earlier (see on T 11.3). Nothing more is known about the case cited (*TLRR* 127). There were two men named Cn. Cornelius Dolabella at this period, one consul in 81,

thing that the jurors later decided, namely, that the trial ought to be held at a less prejudicial time."[2]

IMMEDIATELY AFTER

"Indeed, I forbear to mention how many defendants' trials were previously thwarted, both because you are aware of them and so that my words may not be thought to be hailing anyone into court again."[3]

[2] As praetor, Cicero spoke at a public assembly, arguing that it was unfair for Faustus to be prosecuted by a tribune (*Clu.* 94); see further Crawford 1984, 61–63. In the event, the jurors declined to hear the case; for this (rare) move, cf. Mommsen 1899, 372 and n. 2; Santalucia 2009a, 98–102.   [3] Asconius seems to be mistaken in referring this to the suspension of most court business because of the Social War (73.25–74.7C). It is more likely that Cicero alludes to cases in the 70s, in which trials were thwarted by political influence; cf. Badian 1969, 453. There is a similar rhetorical move, turning away from an argument that might implicate others, at *Rosc. Am.* 94.

5 F 37 [= F 36] Asconius

A LITTLE LATER

"Cn. Dolabella would not have deprived C. Volcacius, a most honorable man, of a universal, everyday right."[1]

the other praetor in 81 (Münzer, *RE* s.v. Cornelius 134 and 135, respectively; *MRR* 2:74 and 76). Of these, the latter appears to be the more likely candidate since he is known to have been praetor urbanus and thus in charge of civil cases (he issued a ruling complained of by Cicero at *Quinct.* 9 and 30–31); cf. Brennan 2000, 750.

5 F 38 Asc. 74.13C (58.23St)

"Non denique homo illorum et vita et prudentia longe dissimilis, sed tamen nimis in gratificando iure liber,[1] L. Sisenna, bonorum Cn. Corneli possessionem ex edicto suo P. Scipioni, adulescenti summa nobilitate, eximia virtute praedito, non dedisset."

[1] liberalis *Halm*

5 F 39 Ar. Mess. *Elocut.* 23.16 Di Stefano (*GL* 7.462.1)

Concedo gratiae. Cicero pro Cornelio: "Cur nunc redeant, si tunc gratiae concesserint?"

5 F 38 [= F 37] Asconius

"Finally, a man far different from them in his manner of life and good sense but nonetheless too free in dispensing favors by means of the law, L. Sisenna, would not have failed, in line with his edict, to grant possession of the goods of Cn. Cornelius to P. Scipio, a young man of high nobility, endowed with outstanding character."[1]

[1] L. Cornelius Sisenna, pr. 78, the historian (see *FRH* 26). He had died in 67, but the criticism is nonetheless mitigated, perhaps because of his ties to Pompey; cf. *MRR* 2:86, 148. Cn. Cornelius is otherwise unknown. This was an inheritance case in which Sisenna diverted a legacy from young P. Scipio contrary to the principles set out in his edict (*TLRR* 134 wrongly has Sisenna finding for, rather than against, Scipio). The victim of this action may have been the man later adopted by a Metellus and thereafter known as Q. Caecilius Metellus Pius Scipio Nasica. He subsequently became the father-in-law of Pompey, who chose him to be his consular colleague for the final months of 52; he later commanded the Republican forces defeated by Caesar in North Africa in 46 and committed suicide in the aftermath (*MRR* 2:234–35, 297).

5 F 39 [= F 38] Arusianus Messius, *Examples of Expressions*

I yield to influence. Cicero, *On Behalf of Cornelius*: "Why would they now return, if at that time they yielded to influence?"[1]

[1] Perhaps still apropos of the praetors' edicts: once they had deviated from their original policy to please a petitioner, why would they go back to it later?

5 F 40 Mart. Cap. 5.492 (*RLM* 468.16)

A repugnantibus argumentum, cum ostenditur duo sibi
cohaerere non posse . . . Eius loci exemplum est in re magis ipsa quam forma verborum . . . et in Corneliana[1] prima
repugnare dicit ut divisores, quos honoris sui ministros
esse voluerat, lege ambitus vellet affligere.

¹ cornelia: *corr. Halm*

5 F 41, 42 Asc. 74.21, 75.4C (58.28, 59.5St)

"Quare cum haec[1] populus Romanus videret et cum a
tribunis plebis doceretur, nisi poena accessisset[2] in divisores, exstingui[3] ⟨ambitum⟩[4] nullo[5] modo posse, legem
hanc Corneli flagitabat, illam quae ex S. C. ferebatur repu-
diabat, idque iure, ut[6] docti sumus[7] duorum consulum
designatorum calamitate." Et eadem de re paulo post: "Ut
spectaculum illud [duorum designatorum consulum cala-
mitatis][8] re et tempore salubre ac necessarium, genere
⟨et⟩[9] exemplo miserum ac funestum videremus."

¹ hunc: *corr. Rau*   ² accessisse: *corr. Poggius*
³ exstinct(i): *corr. M²*, *Poggius*   ⁴ *lac. suppl. Halm*
⁵ ullo: *corr. M, Poggius*   ⁶ iure ut *Madvig*: urebus *PM*: &
rebus *S*: vir is *π in mg.*: e re p. ut *Clark in app.*
⁷ docti sumus *Madvig*: doctissimus *codd.*
⁸ *del. Madvig*   ⁹ *add Manutius*

---

¹ Namely, P. Autronius Paetus and P. Cornelius Sulla, both
convicted as consuls designate under the Calpurnian Law on
Electoral Malfeasance after the elections of 66: *TLRR* 200–201.
Cicero implies that the Calpurnian Law (*LPPR* 374), enacted in
place of Cornelius' bill, was insufficient to deter such wrongdoing;
see also on 9 F 9.   ² Asc. 75.7–9C identifies the occasion as
the conviction of the two consuls designate; see previous note.

5 F 40 [= F 39] Martianus Capella, *On the Marriage of Philology and Mercury*

An argument from contradictories is when it is shown that two things cannot cohere . . . An example of this topic lies in the matter rather than the form of words . . . and in the first speech for Cornelius he says[1] that it is contradictory that with a law on electoral misconduct he would want to crush the bribery agents, whom he had wanted as assistants in his own advancement to office.[2]

[1] Cicero is identified as the subject both by the name of the speech and by the fact that a quotation from *Deiot.* 15 immediately precedes.   [2] Cicero explains why it was illogical for Piso's bill on electoral misconduct to impose penalties on the bribery agents (*divisores*); see Lintott 1990, 7–8; Cosi 1998. The pluperfect tense of the verb "had wanted" (*voluerat*) refers to Piso's canvas for the consulship in 68, which nearly subjected him to a prosecution for *ambitus* (*TLRR* no. 190). It is not clear whether pressure from the tribunes forced Piso ultimately to target bribery agents in a revised bill. In any case, further senatorial decrees had to be issued to curb their excesses in 61; see further Ramsey on Asc. 74C.

5 F 41, 42 [= F 40, 41] Asconius

"Therefore, when the Roman people saw this and when they were apprised by the plebeian tribunes that, unless a punishment for the bribery agents were added, electoral misconduct could by no means be blotted out, they demanded this law of Cornelius' and repudiated the other one, which was being brought to a vote in keeping with a senatorial decree, and rightly so, as we have been taught by the disaster of two consuls designate."[1] And a little later about the same matter: "Hence we saw that spectacle, salutary and necessary as regards its substance and timing, but wretched and ruinous in kind and example."[2]

5 F 43 Prisc. *GL* 2.435.20

CIRCUMEOR. Cicero pro Cornelio: "Circumitis rostris ei-
cerentur lapidibus homines."

5 F 44 Mar. Vict. *Def*. 41.16, 26St

Nona species definitionis est καθ᾽ ὑποτύπωσιν, id est per
quandam imaginationem . . . Item pro Cornelio maiestatis:
"Replicate, ipsa sunt, legite, ut legebatis: hinc intellegetis
nulla tenuissima suspicione describi aut significari Cornelium."

5 F 45 Asc. 75.10C (59.11 St)

"Quid ego nunc tibi argumentis respondeam posse fieri
ut alius aliquis Cornelius sit qui habeat Philerotem ser-
⟨vum⟩,[1] volgare nomen esse Philerotis, Cornelios[2] vero ita
multos ut iam etiam collegium constitutum sit?"

[1] res: *corr. Madvig*
[2] Cornelius: *corr. ed. Ald.*

5 F 43 [= F 42] Priscian, *Textbook of Grammar*

circumeor (I am surrounded). Cicero, *On Behalf of Cornelius*: "When the rostra had been surrounded, people were driven off with thrown rocks."

5 F 44 [= *F 43] Victorinus, *On Definitions*

The ninth type of definition is by sketch,[1] that is, by a certain mental picture . . . Likewise *On Behalf of Cornelius on Treason*: "Unroll (the book): this is the very passage. Read it, as you did previously. From this you will understand that there is not the slightest suspicion that Cornelius is being described or indicated."[2]

[1] See on 8 F 5.   [2] As J. T. Ramsey suggests (*per litt.*), this request is perhaps addressed to the Cominii as the prosecutors (hence, the plural) and refers to a deposition submitted by C. Calpurnius Piso, who was currently governing the two Gauls (*MRR* 2:159) and, hence, could not testify in person; for such a request to the prosecutor(s), see *Sull.* 36. His deposition evidently contained no evidence connecting Cornelius with the rioting, apart from the fact that a slave named Phileros, owned by a Cornelius, was involved; see note on following fragment.

5 F 45 [= F 44] Asconius

"Why should I now reply to you by arguing that it can be the case that there is some other Cornelius who has a slave named Phileros; that Phileros is a common name; that there are so many Cornelii that by now they have even formed a club?"[1]

[1] Evidently, a slave named Phileros, belonging to a Cornelius, was thought to be a ringleader in the rioting. Cicero turns the claim aside with humor. For mistaken attribution of ownership of a slave, cf., e.g., *Verr.* 2.5.17.

5 F 46 Asc. 75.20C (59.19St)

"At enim extremi ac difficillimi temporis vocem illam, C. Corneli,[1] consulem mittere coegisti: 'Qui rem ⟨publicam⟩[2] salvam esse vellent, ut ad legem accipiendam adessent.'"

[1] Cornelio: *corr. Manutius*
[2] *add. ed. Ald.*

5 F 47 Asc. 76.5C (59.26St)

Plebem ex Maniliana offensione victam et domitam esse dicit: "Aiunt[1] vestros animos[2] propter illius tribuni plebis temeritatem posse adduci ut omnino ⟨a nomi⟩ne[3] illius potestatis abalienentur:[4] qui restituerunt eam potestatem,

[1] ante: *corr. Madvig*
[2] annos: *corr. Patricius*
[3] *lac. suppl. Stangl*
[4] potestate abalienemur: *corr. Madvig*

5 F 46 [= F 45] Asconius

"But you, C. Cornelius, compelled the consul to utter that cry of last resort in crises: 'Let those who want the state to be secure lend support to the enactment of the law.'"[1]

[1] A variant of the famous utterance of P. Cornelius Scipio Nasica Serapio (cos. 138) in taking up arms against Ti. Gracchus in 133: "Let those who want the state to be secure follow me" (*FRLO* 38 F 4); a similar exhortation is attributed to the young Scipio (later Africanus) in 215 after the disaster at Cannae: Livy 22.53.7; Scullard 1970, 29–30. Cf. also Lintott 1990, 8–9; Manuwald 2021, 175 and 176. The consul mentioned is C. Calpurnius Piso (cos. 67), who uttered these words before the vote on his own law against electoral bribery (see above, on F 41). Cicero may perhaps be quoting or paraphrasing the prosecutor's argument (cf., e.g., *Sull.* 81–82), accusing Cornelius of causing the disorder at the time when Piso's law was enacted; if this is right, this passage would supplement *FRLO* 143–44. See further Ramsey forthcoming ad loc. But cf. also Marshall 1985, 264, who thinks that these are Cicero's words as he "tries to turn the situation to his client's advantage."

5 F 47 Asconius

He says that as a result of the resentment at Manilius, the plebs were conquered and subdued: "They[1] say that because of the rashness of that plebeian tribune you can be induced to be altogether alienated from the very name of that [sc. tribunician] power; that of those who restored

[1] Presumably the Cominii brothers, not the witnesses, who had not yet testified; cf. on F 44. For a different view, cf. McDermott 1977, 52.

alterum nihil unum posse contra multos, alterum longe abesse."

5 F 48 Quint. *Inst.* 9.2.54

Ἀποσιώπησις, quam idem Cicero reticentiam, Celsus obticentiam, nonnulli interruptionem appellant, et ipsa ostendit adfectus, vel irae . . . vel sollicitudinis . . . vel alio transeundi gratia: "Cominius autem—tametsi ignoscite mihi, iudices." In quo est et illa, si tamen inter schemata numerari debet, cum aliis etiam pars causae videatur, digressio; abit enim causa in laudes Cn. Pompei, idque fieri etiam sine ἀποσιωπήσει potuit.

that power, one is powerless on his own against many, while the other is far away."[2]

[2] The reference is to Crassus and Pompey, the latter currently on campaign in Asia. As consuls in 70, they had restored the full powers of the plebeian tribunate (*LPPR* 369; *MRR* 2:126). Asconius (76.11–12C) reports that Crassus was among the jurors in this trial, information likely to have been drawn from the speeches of Cicero, who sometimes mentions individual jurors in his pleadings (cf., e.g., *Verr.* 29–30; *Vat.* 25; *Mil.* 44). This fragment leads to the encomium of Pompey; he is more likely to have been mentioned first in this general way in contrast to Crassus and then by name, rather than vice versa.

5 F 48 [= F 46] Quintilian, *The Orator's Education*[1]

Aposiopesis, which Cicero calls *reticentia*, Celsus *obticentia*, some *interruptio*,[2] is itself an indicator of emotions, either of anger . . . or of concern . . . or is used to change the subject: "Cominius, however—but pardon me, jurors." This example involves that digression,[3] if it ought to be counted among the figures, though others think it part of a cause, for the speech moves on to a panegyric of Cn. Pompey,[4] and this could have been done without an aposiopesis.

[1] For the placement of this fragment after, not before, the oblique mention of Pompey in F 47, see Kumaniecki 1970, 26–27.   [2] Cic. *De orat.* 3.205; Cels. fr. rhet. 16 Marx (on Celsus, an encyclopedist writing under Tiberius, see *OCD* s.v. Cornelius Celsus, A.); *interruptio* is not attested elsewhere in this sense.

[3] With "that digression" Quintilian refers back to *Inst.* 9.1.28, a citation of *De or.* 3.203, where "Crassus" includes digression among the figures.   [4] Cf. T 13. For another digression on Pompey, see *Balb.* 9–16.

5 F 49 Grill. *Comm. in Cic. rhet.* 35.28 Jakobi

Et Scipio, tantus vir, qui productus a tribuno plebis eos
dixit iure caesos videri, favore nobilitatis hoc fecit, quia et
ipse ex optimatibus erat, nam[1] sicut in Cornelianis Tullius:
"Hic mos iam apud illos antiquos et barbatos fuit, ut per-
sequerentur[2] populares homines."

[1] nam γ: non α
[2] persequantur: *corr. Halm*

5 F 50 Asc. 76.13C (60.1St)

"Tanta igitur in illis virtus fuit ut anno XVI post reges exac-
tos propter nimiam dominationem potentium secederent,
leges sacratas ipsi[1] sibi restituerent, duo tribunos crearent,
montem illum trans Anienem qui hodie Mons Sacer nominatur, in quo armati consederant, aeternae memoriae
causa consecrarent. Itaque auspicato postero anno [de-
cem][2] tr. pl. comitiis curiatis creati sunt."

[1] ipsis: *corr. Manutius*
[2] x *PM*: *om.* S

---

[1] For this criticism of the early Republic, cf. *Rep.* 2.56; *Leg.*
3.15–16.

[2] *leges sacratae* were laws the violation of which rendered
any perpetrators and their property forfeit to the offended deity:
OLD s.vv. *sacratus* 3a, *sacer* 2; see further Liou-Gille 1997; Pellam 2015.

5 F 49 [= 6 *F 4] Grillius, *Commentary on Cicero's* Rhetorica

Scipio, great man that he was, who, upon being led before an assembly by a plebeian tribune, said that they seemed to have been rightly slain,[1] did this with the support of the nobles, since he was himself one of the optimates, for as Tullius says in the speeches *On Behalf of Cornelius*: "This was already the custom among those ancient and bearded figures, to harass the *populares*."

[1] Namely, Ti. Gracchus and his followers. This incident is also cited by Cicero at *Mil.* 8; for further testimonia, cf. Rieger 1991, 176ff.

5 F 50 [= F 48] Asconius

"They had, then, such great courage that in the sixteenth year after the expulsion of the kings they seceded because of the excessive dominance of the powerful,[1] they restored the sacred laws for themselves,[2] elected two tribunes, sanctified for eternal memory the mountain across the Anio that today is called the Mons Sacer, where they had encamped under arms. Therefore, in the following year, upon the taking of auspices, plebeian tribunes were elected in curiate elections."[3]

[3] In curiate elections (*comitia curiata*) the assembly was organized by *curiae*, the original division of the citizen body established by Romulus: *OLD* s.vv. *curia* 1, *curiatus*. For historical sources, see *MRR* 1:15 (under the year 493); for recent interpretations of the conflict of the orders, cf. papers in Raaflaub 2005. After these words, Asconius appends the following fragment, indicating further content of this passage.

5 F 51   Asc. 77.9C (60.19St)

Reliqua pars huius loci, quae pertinet ad secundam consti-
tutionem tribunorum et decemvirorum finitum imperium, et breviter et aperte ab ipso dicitur. Nomina sola non
adicit, quis ille ex decemviris fuerit qui contra libertatem
vindicias[1] dederit, et quis ille pater contra cuius filiam id
decrevit.

[1] vindictae: *corr. Beraldus*

5 F 52   Asc. 77.19C (60.26St)

"Tum interposita fide per tris legatos amplissimos viros
Romam armati revertuntur. In Aventino consederunt;
inde armati in Capitolium[1] venerunt; decem tr. pl. ⟨per⟩[2]
pontificem, quod magistratus nullus erat, creaverunt."

[1] capitolio: *corr. Beraldus*
[2] *add. Manutius*

---

[1] The Second Secession (449). The three envoys were Sp.
Tarpeius, C. Iulius (or Iullus), and Serv. (or P.) Sulpicius, all of
consular rank: *MRR* 1:49. The priest is identified as the pontifex
maximus M. Papirius (Asc. 77.25–26C), but Rüpke 2008, 69 and

5 F 51 Asconius

The remainder of this passage pertaining to the second establishment of tribunes and the termination of the power of the Decemviri was briefly and clearly narrated by him [sc. Cicero]. It was only the names that he did not add—which of the Decemvirs granted interim possession (*vindiciae*) against liberty [sc. Appius Claudius] and who the father was against whose daughter he decreed it [sc. L. Verginius].[1]

[1] When the lovely Verginia caught Appius' eye, a plot was concocted by which Appius' client M. Claudius claimed her as his slave, an incident that precipitated the fall of the Decemvirate; cf. the detailed narrative by Livy (3.44–49). Litigation over servile status involved competing claims of the alleged owner and a third party acting on behalf of the person claiming to be free (cf. Franciosi 1961; Watson 1967, 218–25). For *vindiciae*, see Gaius 4.16: "The praetor declared *vindiciae* in favor of one of them, that is, he established someone as interim possessor."

5 F 52 [= F 49] Asconius

"Then when three envoys, who were important men, had pledged their word, they returned to Rome under arms. They encamped on the Aventine; from there they came under arms to the Capitoline. With a priest as their presiding officer, since there was no magistrate, they elected ten plebeian tribunes."[1]

826n4, is skeptical. There were no magistrates, since the Decemviri still held power. The ten tribunes replaced the original two (F 50) and remained canonical for the rest of the Republic.

CICERO

5 F 53 Asc. 78.1C (61.3St)

"Etiam haec recentiora praetereo:[1] Porciam, principium iustissimae libertatis; Cassiam, qua lege suffragiorum ius potestasque convaluit; alteram Cassiam, quae populi iudicia firmavit."

[1] praeterea: *corr. Manutius*

5 F 54 Aq. Rom. *Fig.* 23.10 Elice (*RLM* 26.31)

Μετάστασιν,[1] transmotionem,[2] quidam inter figuras nominavit, cum rem a nobis alio transmovemus, [non][3] ita ut ibi causam constituamus . . . Tale et[4] illud pro Cornelio videri potest de aerario: "Refertum" inquit "tribuniciis legibus, exhaustum a quibus sit, ipsi sciunt."

[1] μετάστασις *vel* μετάθεσις *vel* metastasis: *corr. Halm*
[2] transmutatio(nem): *corr. ed. Basil.*   [3] *secl. Dyck; coll. Alex. 26.30–31 Sp.*   [4] et *N^2*: est *rell.*

---

[1] The rhetorician Alexander (fl. AD 200) left a work on figures of thought and speech; our passage alludes to p. 26.23 Sp.

[2] Implicitly responding to an optimate claim that tribunician laws bankrupted the treasury; cf. *Tusc.* 3.48 and *Off.* 2.72, where Cicero blames C. Gracchus for draining the treasury (with his grain dole); cf. also T 3 apropos of Vatinius.

126

5 F 53 [= F 50] Asconius

"I also leave aside these more recent enactments: the Porcian Law, the beginning of true liberty; the Cassian Law, by which the right and power of voting were strengthened; and the second Cassian Law, which reinforced the popular tribunals."[1]

[1] Three Porcian Laws were enacted in the second century, but they are insufficiently distinguished in our sources; cf. *LPPR* 268–69; Elster 2003, 296–301. The one attributed to Cato the Elder and probably to be dated to 195 forbade Roman citizens from subjection to the lash; cf. Santalucia 1998, 71–74. Asconius remarks (78.6) that Cicero "said a little earlier that Cassius enacted a law so that the people might vote by ballot." This occurred in 137, under sponsorship of L. Cassius Longinus Favilla (cos. 127) and provided for use of the secret ballot in people's courts (except in cases of treason [*perduellio*]); cf. *LPPR* 297; *MRR* 1:485; Dyck 2004, 530. The second Cassian Law was enacted by L. Cassius Longinus as tr. pl. of 104 and provided that anyone whose office or command had been abrogated by the people also be expelled from the senate: *LPPR* 327; *MRR* 1:559.

5 F 54 [= *F 51] Aquila of Rome, *On Figures*

A certain authority [sc. Alexander] has named *metastasis*, diversion, among the figures, when we transfer a matter from ourselves to another in such a way as to place the cause there . . .[1] In *On Behalf of Cornelius* the following point about the treasury may also seem to be of this kind: "It [sc. the treasury]," he said, "was filled by tribunician laws; they themselves know by whom it was drained."[2]

5 F 55 Asc. 78.17C (61.15St)

Dicit de nobilibus:[1] "Qui non modo cum Sulla verum
etiam illo mortuo semper hoc per se summis opibus reti-
nendum putaverunt, inimicissimi C. Cottae fuerunt, quod
is consul paulum tribunis plebis non potestatis sed dignitatis addidit."

[1] dicit de nobilibus *P in mg.*: *om. M*

5 F 56 Prisc. *GL* 2.361.25

"Plurium," quod solum in "us" terminans talem habuit
genetivum pluralem, tam in "es" quam in "is" finit accusa-
tivum . . . Cicero pro Cornelio I: "Quae intermissa compluris annos."

5 F 55 [= F 52] Asconius

He says of the nobles: "Those men, who not only under Sulla but also after his death supposed that they always ought to maintain this particular principle with all their might, were bitterly hostile to C. Cotta, since as consul he enhanced a bit not the power of the plebeian tribunes, but their standing."[1]

[1] With his Cornelian Law on Tribunician Power of 81, Sulla had clipped the wings of the plebeian tribunes in various ways, including a prohibition of their candidacy for higher office: *LPPR* 350–51; *MRR* 2:74–75 (for date). As consul in 75, Cotta enacted the Aurelian Law, annulling that restriction (while leaving Sulla's other strictures in place): *LPPR* 365; *MRR* 2:96. In speaking of the hostility stirred by Cotta's move, Cicero may be alluding to Catulus and Hortensius, two of the principal witnesses against Cornelius, who were also opponents of Cotta's law (Ps-Asc., p. 255.16–17St). Cicero may, however, be exaggerating the hostility; cf. Ramsey forthcoming on Asconius 78C.

5 F 56 [= F 60] Priscian, *Textbook of Grammar*

Plurium. Since [*plus*] alone ending in *us* had such a genitive plural, it ends the accusative in *es* as well as in *is* . . . Cicero, *On Behalf of Cornelius I*: "which, interrupted for some [*compluris*] years."[1]

[1] Perhaps the antecedent of "which" is the "rights of tribunes" (*iura tribunicia*), in which case this fragment would form part of his survey of the history of the plebeian tribunate, and the "interruption" would be the period between 81 and 70; see on F 47 and F 55.

5 F 57 Asc. 78.26C (61.22St)

"Quam diu quidem hoc animo erga vos illa plebs erit quo
se ostendit esse cum legem Aureliam, cum Rosciam non
modo accepit sed etiam efflagitavit?"

5 F 58 Asc. 79.3C (61.28St)

"Memoria teneo cum primum senatores cum equitibus
Romanis lege Plotia iudicarent, hominem dis ac nobilitati
perinvisum Cn. Pomponium[1] causam lege Varia de maiestate dixisse."

[1] Pompeium: *corr. Pighius*

5 F 57 [= F 53] Asconius

"How long will the plebs maintain the attitude toward you that it showed it had when it not only accepted but even demanded the Aurelian Law and the Roscian Law?"[1]

[1] "You" (plural) will be the optimates. The Aurelian Law referred to here is the one that provided for the tripartite division of jury panels; see on T 11.6. One of the tribunes of 67, L. Roscius Otho, enacted a law providing preferential seats in the theater for the equites: *LPPR* 374–75; *MRR* 2:145. On the incident at the games involving Roscius during Cicero's consulship, see the introduction to no. 11 below.

5 F 58 [= F 54] Asconius

"I recall that as soon as the senators began serving as jurors together with the Roman equites under the Plotian Law, Cn. Pomponius, a man deeply loathed by the gods and the nobles, pleaded his case on a charge of treason under the Varian Law."[1]

[1] For the Plotian (or Plautian) Law enacted in 89 and of short duration, also mentioned at *Mil.* 35, cf. *LPPR* 342. It is perhaps cited as an example of a law that, though enacted by a tribune (M. Plautius Silvanus: *MRR* 2:34), benefited senators. Cn. Pomponius was one of the tribunes of 90 (the restoration of this name instead of that of Cn. Pompeius [sc. Strabo] is generally accepted); cf. Badian 1969, 465–75; *MRR* 2:26 and 31n9, and 3:166; *TLRR* 110. The Varian Law, enacted in 90 by the plebeian tribune Q. Varius Hybrida, created a special tribunal to try for treason those responsible for causing the Social War: *LPPR* 339–40; *MRR* 2:26–27. Cf. Gruen 1965; Badian 1969.

5 F 59 Ar. Mess. *Elocut*. 34.21 Di Stefano (*GL* 7.470.9)

Expellit hoc loco. Cicero pro Cornelio I: "Satius hominem
miserum atque innocentem eripi populo Romano,[1] expelli
patria, divelli a suis."

> [1] populo Romano: rei publicae *ci. Halm*

5 F 60 Ar. Mess. *Elocut*. 15.7 Di Stefano (*GL* 7.455.26)

Abest tot milia . . . Cicero pro Cornelio I: "Sed ab urbe[1]
dierum abfuerunt iter[2] complurium."

> [1] ad urbem: *corr. Ursinus*
> [2] abfuerunt iter *Keil*: tres fuerit *codd.*

5 F 61 Ar. Mess. *Elocut*. 19.18 Di Stefano (*GL* 7.459.9)

Certamen illi cum illo est. Cicero pro Cornelio I: "Quod[1]
enim mihi certamen est cum accusatore aut contentio?"

> [1] quid: *corr. Patricius*

5 F 59 [= F 55] Arusianus Messius, *Examples of Expressions*

He expels from this place. Cicero, *On Behalf of Cornelius I*: "It is better for a wretched and innocent man to be snatched from the Roman people, expelled from his homeland, parted from his family."[1]

[1] Evidently taken from the peroration, this probably either is sarcastic or forms part of a question. For Cicero's emphasis on his client's danger in this speech, see 3 T 9. Cicero was noted in general for his ability to elicit pity in the final part of the speech (*Brut.* 190, *Orat.* 130). The following fragments from lexicographical or grammatical sources are too brief to be securely placed, though a possibility is raised in the note on F 63.

5 F 60 [= F 56] Arusianus Messius, *Examples of Expressions*

He is so many miles away . . . Cicero, *On Behalf of Cornelius I*: "But they were several days' journey away from the city."

5 F 61 [= F 57] Arusianus Messius, *Examples of Expressions*

One man has a point of contestation with another. Cicero, *On Behalf of Cornelius I*: "What point of contestation or dispute do I have with the prosecutor?"[1]

[1] Perhaps a reference to the fact that Cornelius did not deny reading out the bill in the assembly; cf. 3 T 6, 5–6 T 11.6 and 7, T 15.

5 F 62 Ar. Mess. *Elocut*. 12.3 Di Stefano (*GL* 7.453.20)

Adsum ad hoc. Idem pro Cornelio: "Facite ut facitis, qui ad causam adestis."

5 F 63 Ar. Mess. *Elocut*. 32.16 Di Stefano (*GL* 7.468.25)

Demo de hoc. Cicero pro Cornelio I:[1] "Demi medius fidius de his ornamentis aliquantum malim."

[1] *fort.* II

5 F 64 Prisc. *GL* 2.435.25

"Gratificor, gratificaris," deponentia. Cicero pro Cornelio in I: "Num alicui gratificabatur aut homini aut ordini?"

5 F 62 [= *F 58] Arusianus Messius, *Examples of Expressions*

I support this. The same author *On Behalf of Cornelius*: "Those of you who are supporting the case, do as you are doing."[1]

[1] He probably means that they should continue to show restraint. On Cornelius' concern about disruption of the trial by his supporters, see on T 11.5. Rosillo-López 2017, 119, remarks that the "lack of mechanisms of control of audiences in the courts made them at the same time a powerful ally and a dreadful hazard."

5 F 63 [= F 59] Arusianus Messius, *Examples of Expressions*

I take away from this. Cicero, *On Behalf of Cornelius I*: "I would prefer, by God, for these ornaments to be somewhat reduced."[1]

[1] Possibly, this should be assigned to *Corn. II*, with its discussion of wealth, including reference to the "decorations of villas" (*ornamenta . . . villarum*: 6 F 8).

5 F 64 [= F 62] Priscian, *Textbook of Grammar*

"I do a favor, you do a favor," deponents. Cicero, *On Behalf of Cornelius in I*: "Surely he was not doing a favor for either a person or a group, was he?"[1]

[1] Evidently, a defense of one of Cornelius' laws, perhaps that on electioneering.

6 PRO CORNELIO II

Much less survives of the second speech for Cornelius. The main subject matter is the three witnesses (6 F 3 with note), who would have been called to testify after the set speeches of both sides.[1] As Quintilian remarks (Inst. 5.7.6), such material was sometimes incorporated into defense speeches. This could be done in cases argued in more than one session (typically extortion cases), whereby witnesses testified at the end of the first session so that reference could be made to their testimony in the second session (cf., e.g., Scaur. 38–45a). Cicero has chosen to publish this material, as he did later in Against the Witness Vatinius, memorializing a phase of the trial of P. Sestius in 56. In our speech he had to beware of giving offense by aggressive questioning, since his further career depended on, if not the goodwill, at least the nonopposition of leading optimates. Hence, to remove the invective edge, he decided to repackage this material as if it were a conventional forensic speech; cf. analysis by Crawford 1994, 137; Guérin 2015, 156–61. A fragment evidently from his plan of pro-

---

[1] There is no need to posit a change from the usual procedure, as has sometimes been thought; cf. Guérin 2015, 155–56.

6 ON BEHALF OF CORNELIUS II

cedure suggests that Cicero divided the chief witnesses into two groups, whereby he portrays the leading members of the second group as ideological opponents of tribunician power (F 3), thus continuing the line of attack pursued in Corn. I (5 F 49–58). Some fragments show how he very politely backs the witness Q. Catulus into a corner by comparing Cornelius' tribunate with the (from an optimate standpoint) more pernicious tribunate of Catulus' maternal uncle, Cn. Domitius Ahenobarbus (tr. pl. 104: F 4–7). The digression on the tribunate in the first speech has its counterpart here in a digression arguing that wealth is a relative value (F 8).[2] The speech concludes with a glance back at the four-day course of the trial (F 9) and a peroration combining an appeal for pity for Cornelius with advice on the importance of safeguarding liberty (F 10–16).

[2] This was a well-worn literary topos; cf. Mouritsen 2022, 89–90. On Cicero's general attitude toward wealth, cf. Raskolnikoff 1977, 369–71; Pina Polo 2016.

6 F 1 Aq. Rom. *Fig*. 17.12 Elice (*RLM* 25.15 ~ Mart. Cap. 5.523)

Διαπόρησις, addubitatio. Hac utimur cum propter aliqua volumus videri addubitare et quasi ab ipsis iudicibus consilium[1] capere, quo potissimum genere orationis utamur, quale est pro Cluentio . . . Item pro Cornelio: "Pugnem aperte contra nobilissimorum hominum voluntates?[2] Studia consilia cogitationesque[3] eorum aperiam?" et cetera: quae quasi dubitans an sibi facienda sint dicit.[4]

> [1] inchoamenti consilium *Capella*
> [2] voluntates *om. Capella*
> [3] rationesque *Capella*
> [4] quae . . . dicit *om. Capella*

6 F 2 Cic. *Orat*. 225 (Rufin. *Comp. orat.*, *RLM* 579.32–38; cf. Quint. *Inst*. 9.4.123, Diom. *GL* 1.466.7–13)

Incisim autem et membratim tractata oratio in veris causis plurimum valet, maximeque iis locis, cum aut arguas aut refellas, ut nos[1] in Corneliana secunda: "O callidos homines, o rem excogitatam, o ingenia metuenda!" Membratim adhuc; deinde caesim: "Diximus"; rursus membratim: "Testis dare volumus." Extrema sequitur comprehensio, sed ex duobus membris, qua non potest esse brevior: "Quem, quaeso,[2] nostrum fefellit ita vos esse facturos?"

> [1] nostra: *corr. Rufinus*
> [2] quas(i): *corr. unus cod. rec.*

6 F 1 Aquila of Rome, *On Figures*

Diaporēsis, doubt. This is what we use when for some reason we want to appear to be in doubt and, as it were, take advice from the jurors themselves as to what kind of discourse we employ. An example is in *On Behalf of Cluentius* [sc. §4] . . . Likewise in *On Behalf of Cornelius*: "Should I fight openly against the wishes of the nobles? Should I reveal their partisan spirit, plans, and thoughts?" etc.[1] He says this as if hesitating as to what he should do.

[1] Cf. 5 F 3 for a similar pretense of hesitancy or doubt in the exordium. This fragment could be assigned to *Corn. I* but is perhaps better located here, since the second speech dealt specifically with the nobles' opposition to his client.

6 F 2 Cicero, *Orator*

Speech that is managed in short phrases and short clauses is powerful in real-life cases, especially in passages in which you are either offering proof or refutation, as I did in my second speech *On Behalf of Cornelius*: "O clever men, o well thought-out project, o formidable intellects!" These are in short clauses, then in a short phrase: "I have spoken";[1] in a short clause again: "I want to offer witnesses." A final grouping follows, but comprising two members, than which nothing can be briefer: "I ask you, which of us failed to see that you would act in this way?"[2]

[1] That is, this signals the end of the defense case.
[2] The "you" is plural, referring either to the prosecutors (cf. on T 11.5) or to the optimates behind the prosecution.

6 F 3 Asc. 79.16C (62.2 St)

"Num in eo qui sint hi testes haesitatis? Ego vobis edam. Duo reliqui sunt de consularibus, inimici tribuniciae potestatis. Pauci praeterea adsentatores[2] eorum atque adseculae subsequuntur."

[1] *add. in mg. Poggius*
[2] senatores: *corr. Poggius*

6 F 4 Asc. 80.7C (62.16St)

"Sed si familiariter ex Q. Catulo sapientissimo viro atque humanissimo velim quaerere: utrius tandem tibi tribunatus minus probari potest, C. Corneli, an—non dicam P. Sulpici, non L. Saturnini, non Gai Gracchi, non Tiberi, neminem quem isti seditiosum existimant nominabo, sed avunculi tui, Q. Catule,[1] clarissimi patriaeque[2] amantissimi viri? Quid mihi tandem responsurum putatis?"

[1] Catuli: *corr. Patricius*
[2] atque: *corr. Manutius*

---

[1] Cicero's direct addresses to Servius Sulpicius Rufus at *Mur.* 15–16 show a similar tone and manner. Though Asconius usually quotes the fragments in the order in which they appear in Cicero's text, F 4 and 5 are an exception, as he explains at 80.4–6C; cf. Crawford 1994, 140.　　[2] These four names recur at *Har. resp.* 41; they seem to have formed a kind of canon of *popularis* tribunes; all of them died a violent death.　　[3] That is, the optimates.　　[4] Q. Lutatius Catulus (cos. 78) was the son of the homonymous consul of 102 and a Domitia who was the sister of Cn. Domitius Ahenobarbus (cos. 96). He was probably the

6 F 3 Asconius

ON BEHALF OF CORNELIUS II

"Surely you do not have any uncertainty, do you, who these witnesses are? I will disclose them to you. Two remaining are from among the ex-consuls, enemies of tribunician power. In addition, a few of their toadies and 'yes-men' come after them."[1]

[1] Cicero is evidently laying out his plan of procedure, dividing the witnesses into two groups. According to Asconius (79.20–24C), the three dealt with in this speech were Q. Catulus, Q. Hortensius, and Q. Metellus Pius; the remaining two mentioned here were M. Lucullus and M'. Lepidus; cf. n. 11 on T 11.6.

6 F 4 [= F 5] Asconius

"But if I should wish to pose a friendly question to Q. Catulus, a wise and cultured man:[1] of the two, which man's tribunate can you approve of less, that of C. Cornelius or—I shall not say that of P. Sulpicius, L. Saturninus, Gaius Gracchus, or Tiberius:[2] I shall not name any whom they[3] account seditious, but of your uncle, Q. Catulus, a most distinguished and patriotic man? What reply do you suppose he will give me?"[4]

stepson of Servilia, daughter of Q. Servilius Caepio (cos. 140); cf. Badian 1964, 232–33, against Münzer, *RE* 13.2:2073.40–61. On Domitius' plebeian tribunate, dated to 104 according to Asc. 80.18–19C, cf. *MRR* 1:559. Guérin 2015, 292–93, suggests that at the trial Cicero asked Catulus in turn whether he preferred the plebeian tribunate of Sulpicius, Saturninus, etc., to that of Cornelius, and concluded the series with the surprise item, Catulus' own uncle.

6 F 5 Asc. 79.25C (62.9St)

"Quid? Avunculus tuus clarissimus vir, clarissimo patre
avo maioribus, credo, silentio, favente nobilitate, nullo
intercessore comparato populo Romano dedit[1] et poten-
tissimorum hominum conlegiis eripuit cooptandorum
sacerdotum potestatem?"

[1] populo Romano dedit *Manutius*: proderit *codd.*

6 F 6 Asc. 80.16C (62.23St)

SEQUITUR

"Quid?[1] Idem Domitius M. Silanum, consularem hominem, quem ad modum tr. pl. vexavit?"

[1] quod: *corr. ed. Ald.*

---

[1] M. Iunius Silanus (cos. 109) was prosecuted by Domitius
before a popular tribunal on the ground of waging an illegal war
against the Cimbri but was acquitted (*TLRR* 63).

6 F 5 [= F 6] Asconius

"Tell me: did your uncle, a distinguished man, of a distinguished father, grandfather, and ancestors, without uproar, I suppose, with the nobility in favor[1] and no one recruited to interpose a veto, snatch away the power of co-opting priests from the boards of powerful men and give it to the Roman people?"[2]

[1] North 2011, 40, argues that "Domitius himself was trying to reach a consensus that would satisfy all the interests involved," with supporting arguments. However, Ramsey forthcoming on the Asconian passage suggests that Cicero, for his purposes, chooses to emphasize the controversy; he therefore interprets this remark as ironic, the irony perhaps signaled by *credo* (I suppose). [2] *LPPR* 329, dated to 103 by Vell. 2.12.3 (Marius' third consulate). On the unconvincing attempt of Sumner 1973, 97–100, to harmonize this date with that of Domitius' plebeian tribunate, cf. Marshall 1985, 277–78, and *MRR* 3:82. The procedure, by which candidates were elected by seventeen of the thirty-five Roman tribes, was borrowed from the one used since the third century to elect the Pontifex Maximus; see further Manuwald 2018, 228–29. The catalyst for the reform is said to have been the failure of a priestly board to co-opt Domitius himself: Asc. 21.3–5C; Suet. *Ner.* 2.1 (albeit Asc. speaks of augurs, Suet. of priests). If Catulus approved his uncle's action, which was not markedly different from Cornelius' policies, both having taken privileges away from the nobles, how could he denounce the latter? Cf. Guérin 2015, 299.

6 F 6 [= F 7] Asconius

THERE FOLLOWS

"Tell me: how savagely did the same Domitius as plebeian tribune harass M. Silanus, an ex-consul?"[1]

6 F 7 Asc. 81.1C (63.1St)

Haec est controversia eius modi ut mihi ⟨probetur⟩[1] tr. pl.
Cn. Domitius, Catulo M. Terpolius.[2]

[1] *lac. suppl. Madvig*
[2] Turpilius *Pighius*

6 F 8 Cic. *Orat.* 232

Quantum autem sit apte dicere experiri licet, si aut com-
positi oratoris bene structam collocationem dissolvas per-
mutatione verborum; corrumpatur enim tota res, ut et
haec nostra in Corneliana et deinceps omnia: "Neque me
divitiae movent, quibus omnis Africanos et Laelios multi
venalicii mercatoresque superarunt": immuta paululum,
ut sit "multi superarunt mercatores venaliciique": perierit
tota res. Et quae secuntur: "Neque vestis aut caelatum
aurum et argentum, quo nostros veteres Marcellos Maxi-

6 F 7 [= F 8] Asconius

"This is a controversy of such a kind that the plebeian tribune Cn. Domitius wins my approval, M. Terpolius that of Catulus."[1]

[1] M. Terpolius (tr. pl. 77) is known only from this passage, and Asconius' comment giving his date and stating that his was the "most insignificant name" among the post-Sullan tribunes (81.3–8C); indeed the tribunes from 80 to 75 were "unambitious nonentities" (Sumner 1973, 7) because they were barred by Sulla's legislation from holding higher office (cf. 5 F 55 with note). Cicero's step-by-step questioning forces Catulus, with his ideological objections to tribunician activity, to prefer a nonentity to a distinguished tribune related to himself; for a similar rhetorical ploy, cf. *Fin.* 4.66. As consul two years later, Cicero invoked Domitius as a worthy plebeian tribune in contrast with his current opponent, P. Servilius Rullus (*Leg. agr.* 2.18–19).

6 F 8 [= F 9] Cicero, *Orator*

You may test how great is the power of speaking aptly if you either dissolve the well-constructed combination of a polished orator by changing the words; the whole thing would be ruined, as are these words of mine in the defense of Cornelius, as well as all the next examples: "I am unmoved either by riches, in respect of which many slave dealers and merchants have surpassed [*multi venalicii mercatoresque superarunt*] all the Africani and Laelii."[1] Change it a little so as to read *multi superarunt mercatores venaliciique*. The whole thing will be ruined. And the sequel: "Or by clothing or embossed gold and silver, in re-

[1] The pairing with (C.) Laelius shows that Cicero has the younger Africanus in mind (cos. 147, 134).

mosque multi eunuchi e Syria Aegyptoque vicerunt":
verba permuta sic, ut sit "vicerunt eunuchi e Syria Aegyptoque." Adde tertium: "Neque vero ornamenta ista villarum, quibus L. Paullum et L. Mummium, qui rebus his
urbem Italiamque omnem referserunt, ab aliquo video
perfacile Deliaco aut Syro potuisse superari"; fac ita:
"potuisse superari ab aliquo Syro aut Deliaco." Videsne ut
ordine verborum paululum commutato, isdem tamen verbis stante sententia, ad nihilum omnia recidant, cum sint
ex aptis dissoluta?

6 F 9a Asc. 62.3C (50.11St)

Cicero, ⟨ut⟩[1] ipse significat, "quadriduo" Cornelium defendit.

[1] *add. Kiessling-Schoell*

spect of which many eunuchs from Syria and Egypt have vanquished [*eunuchi e Syria Aegyptoque vicerunt*] our ancient Marcelli and Maximi."[2] Change the words so as to read *vicerunt eunuchi e Syria Aegyptoque*. Add a third: "Or even those decorations of villas, in which I see that L. Paullus and L. Mummius, who stuffed the city and all Italy with these things[3] could easily be defeated by some Delian or Syrian [*ab aliquo . . . Deliaco aut Syro potuisse superari*]." Alter as follows: *potuisse superari ab aliquo Syro aut Deliaco.* Do you see that when the order of words is slightly changed, even though the thought remains with the same words, they are all reduced to nothing, since they have been dissolved from what is apt?[4]

[2] Maximus will be Q. Fabius Maximus Verrucosus (cos. I 233), the famous "Delayer" (Cunctator). Paired with him is another hero of the Hannibalic War, M. Claudius Marcellus (cos. I 222), famed for the capture of Syracuse.   [3] A reference to L. Aemilius Paullus (cos. II 168) and L. Mummius (cos. 146), the respective conquerors of Perseus of Macedonia and the Achaean League, who sent many plundered Greek artworks to Italy in the aftermath.   [4] For discussion of the differences in rhythm in the first two sets of examples, cf. Pinkster 2015–2021, 2:970.

6 F 9a [= T 21.83] Asconius

As he himself indicates, Cicero defended Cornelius "for four days."[1]

[1] This statement is assigned to the second speech, since it was evidently part of the summary at the end of his pleading, and it is assumed that the published speeches preserved verisimilitude in this respect; cf. T 7.

6 F 9b Plin. *Ep.* 1.20.8

Idem pro Cluentio ait se totam causam vetere instituto
solum perorasse, et pro C. Cornelio "quadriduo" egisse,
ne dubitare possimus quae per plures dies (ut necesse
erat) latius dixerit, postea recisa ac repurgata in unum librum grandem quidem unum tamen coartasse.

6 F 10 Ar. Mess. *Elocut.* 16.9 Di Stefano (*GL* 7.456.20)

Adiudico illud huic. Cicero pro Cornelio II: "Si vos huius
fortunas paucorum odio adiudicaveritis."

6 F 11 Ar. Mess. *Elocut.* 28.15 Di Stefano (*GL* 7.465.17)

Dedo ad hoc. Cicero pro Cornelio II: "Ad miserrimum
crudelissimumque dominatum dedi patiamini."

---

[1] This interpretation assumes that this is the apodosis of the
protasis in the previous fragment, so that "fortunes" continues as
the object, but the precise context is unclear. The "dominion" will
be that of the leading optimates arrayed against Cornelius. Mou-

6 F 9b [= 5–6 T 19] Pliny, *Letters*

He likewise says that he pleaded the entire case on behalf of Cluentius alone by ancient custom,[1] and he pleaded on behalf of C. Cornelius "for four days," so we cannot doubt that what he said at length in the course of several days (as was necessary) he later pruned and reduced to a single book, albeit a large one.[2]

[1] *Clu.* 199.   [2] It is hard to believe that Pliny was unaware of *Corn. II*, which must have comprised a book on its own. Perhaps his statement is based on a distinction between the (set) speech (*Corn. I*) and the proceedings of the trial (*Corn. II*), cf. Guérin 2015, 154. An alternative possibility, suggested by J. T. Ramsey (*per litt.*), is that this fragment should be assigned to *Corn. I* on the ground that Pliny otherwise shows no awareness of *Corn. II* and that he may have known a version of *Corn. I* as a "fully contained speech," i.e., subsuming the matter of *Corn. II*. Cf. also Lo Monaco 1990, 175n21.

6 F 10 Arusianus Messius, *Examples of Expressions*

I award this to him. Cicero, *On Behalf of Cornelius II*: "If you award my client's fortunes to the hatred of a few men."

6 F 11 Arusianus Messius, *Examples of Expressions*

I surrender to this. Cicero, *On Behalf of Cornelius II*: "You would allow (them) to be surrendered to a most wretched and cruel dominion."[1]

ritsen 2022, 211, suggests that Cicero may have won this case (cf. T 10) precisely because of his strategy of depicting Cornelius as the victim of the nobles.

6 F 12 Ar. Mess. *Elocut.* 32.11 Di Stefano (*GL* 7.468.21)

Diligens huius rei. Cicero pro Cornelio II: "Quam diligentes libertatis vos oporteat esse."

6 F 13 Serv. ad Verg. *Aen.* 11.708

VENTOSA FERAT CUI GLORIA FRAUDEM: haec est vera et antiqua lectio . . . nam "fraudem" veteres poenam vocabant . . . Cicero in Cornelianis: "Ne fraudi sit ei qui populum ad contentionem[1] vocarit."[2]

[1] *fort.* contionem
[2] vocari *F*: vocavit *Ambros.*: *corr. edd.*

6 F 14 Ar. Mess. *Elocut.* 32.13 Di Stefano (*GL* 7.468.23)

Dumtaxat, id est "tantum modo" vel "hoc solo." Cicero pro Cornelio II: "qui commodis populi Romani <non>[1] lingua dumtaxat ac voluntate consuluit."

[1] *add. Dyck*

6 F 15 Ar. Mess. *Elocut.* 5.7 Di Stefano (*GL* 7.449.6 = Prisc. *GL* 3.217.1)

Abundans illa re. Cicero pro Cornelio libro II: "Quis tam abundans copiis?"

6 F 12 Arusianus Messius, *Examples of Expressions*

Careful with this matter. Cicero, *On Behalf of Cornelius II*: "how careful you ought to be with your liberty."

6 F 13 Servius, *Commentary on Virgil*

TO WHOM VAIN GLORY BRINGS PUNISHMENT: This is the true and ancient reading . . . For the ancients called a penalty *fraus* . . . Cicero in the speeches for Cornelius: "that he who has summoned the people to a dispute not be liable to punishment."[1]

    [1] This fragment could be assigned to *Corn. I*.

6 F 14 Arusianus Messius, *Examples of Expressions*

Dumtaxat, that is, "merely" or "by this alone." Cicero, *On Behalf of Cornelius II*: "who took counsel for the interests of the Roman people not merely with his tongue and will."[1]

    [1] This seems to be an encomium of Cornelius for going beyond the usual parameters (and implying a contrast to deeds); hence, the insertion of the negative; cf. *Fin.* 2.21: *qui . . . non reprehenderentur eo nomine dumtaxat* (who would not be criticized only on that account . . .).

6 F 15 Arusianus Messius, *Examples of Expressions*

Abounding in such and such a thing. Cicero, *On Behalf of Cornelius* in Book II: "Who so abounding in resources . . . ?"

6 F 16 Ps.-Prob. *Nom.* 69.8 Passalacqua (*GL* 4.212.8)

Minister an ministrator? Minister cotidiani officii videtur esse, ministrator autem, ut administrator in re publica vel saepius quid faciens. Itaque Cicero oratione secunda pro Cornelio: "Quare hominem inpugnare non desinunt, nisi remotis ministratoribus."

6 F 17 Ar. Mess. *Elocut.* 74.9 Di Stefano (*GL* 7.497.11)

Offendi apud vos. Cicero pro Cornelio: "Quid[1] me apud equites Romanos offendisse dicebant?"

 [1] qui *Garatonius in Cic. Mil.* 99: aliquid *dubitanter Keil*

6 F 18 Ar. Mess. *Elocut.* 35.4 Di Stefano (*GL* 7.470.12)

Expellit a loco. Cicero pro Cornelio II: "Expelleret a dispensantibus."

6 F 16 Pseudo-Probus, *On the Noun*

Minister (assistant) or *ministrator* (attendant)? It seems that a *minister* is one who performs a daily function, whereas a *ministrator* is like an administrator in the state or one who often does something. Hence Cicero in the second speech *On Behalf of Cornelius*: "Therefore, they do not cease to attack the man, unless their attendants have been removed."[1]

1 Possibly referring to high magistrates and the lictors who protect them: the removal of the lictors would make it impossible to attack Cornelius in the face of public opinion in his favor.

6 F 17 Arusianus Messius, *Examples of Expressions*

I have given offense among you. Cicero, *On Behalf of Cornelius*: "What offense did they say that I had given among the Roman equites?"[1]

1 "They" are probably the prosecutors. Was the offense Cicero's mockery of Cominius, who was an eques, regarding his flight in 66 (cf. 5 F 8–10)?

6 F 18 Arusianus Messius, *Examples of Expressions*

He drives away from a place. Cicero, *On Behalf of Cornelius II*: "He would drive away from the administrators."[1]

1 Possibly, these "administrators" (*dispensantes*) are the people elsewhere called *divisores*, i.e., the bribery agents (see 5 F 40 with note), and the object would then be candidates for office; cf. *OLD* s.v. *dispenso* 2a.

7 DE REGE PTOLEMAEO[1]

Delivered in 65, this is Cicero's first attested speech before the senate.[2] *It is cited as both* On King Ptolemy *(F 7) and* On the Alexandrian King *(T 2–4), with the more generic title found in the later tradition. It was delivered during a senate debate in the year 65 on M. Crassus' proposal that Rome invade and take control of Egypt.*[3] *Crassus' arguments, insofar as we can reconstruct them, were that*

[1] Ptolemaeo F 7: Alexandrino *auctores inferioris aetatis (T 2, 3, 4)*.

[2] Cicero also spoke twice in the senate on January 1–2, 56, on a plan to restore Ptolemy XII Auletes to the Egyptian throne (*Fam.* 1.2[13].1). At that time, Cicero was not opposed to the expedition per se but was backing the claim of P. Cornelius Lentulus Spinther (cos. 57) to lead it, whereas in our speech he apparently opposes taking up the legacy of Ptolemy X Alexander I and thus any expedition; hence, these testimonia and fragments are attributed to the earlier debate, which is dated to 65 at Cic. *Leg. agr.* 2.44 (for a possible exception, see on *T 1); cf. Strasburger 1938, 112–13; Crawford 1984, 150–51, and 1994, 43–46. In the Bobbio Scholia, however, this speech is oddly placed between *Against Clodius and Curio* (no. 14 below) and *On Behalf of Flaccus*, which dates from the year 59 (cf. pp. 91–93St). On oratory before the senate, see Ramsey 2007.

[3] The sources: Cic. *Leg. agr.* 1.1 and 2.41–44; Plut. *Vit. Crass.*

7 ON KING PTOLEMY (65 BC)

*Egypt rightfully belonged to Rome since it had been be-
queathed under the will of Ptolemy X Alexander I (ca.
140–88) and that the current monarch, Ptolemy XII Auletes, bore responsibility for the murder of his predecessor,
Ptolemy XI Alexander II, in ca. 80 and had no right to
rule.[4] In reply, Cicero casts doubt on the claim that the
Romans had accepted the legacy of Ptolemy X (F 3 and 5)
and seeks to rehabilitate the character of Ptolemy XII by
absolving him of the murder of his predecessor, which is
explained as a mob action triggered by outrage at Ptolemy
XI's murder of his popular sister/consort Cleopatra Berenice (F 9–10). He also attacks the policy advocated by
Crassus as greedy and immoral (F 1–2, 8); he thus takes
up from* Leg. Man. *38–39 his critique of Roman greed in*

13.2; Suet. *Iul.* 11. For the political background, see Rawson
1978, 83–84. Suetonius' claim that Julius Caesar was angling to
get a special command for Egypt at this time (*Iul.* 11) should be
treated with reserve; cf. Strasburger 1938, 113–14; Gruen 1974,
75 and n. 117.

[4] His illegitimate birth, alluded to by Cicero at *Leg. agr.* 2.42,
no doubt figured in this debate as well; cf. Khrustalyov 2018, 255.

dealing with allies. Later, Cicero would, however, effectively cede to Cato the role of "conscience of the empire"; cf. Morrell 2017, ch. 3. Perhaps Cicero took a stand against Crassus' proposal in order to restore his standing with the optimates, which may have been damaged by his defense

*7 T 1 Strabo 17.1.13 (798C)

τῆς Αἰγύπτου δὲ τὰς προσόδους ἔν τινι λόγωι Κικέρων φράζει, φήσας κατ᾽ ἐνιαυτὸν τῶι τῆς Κλεοπάτρας πατρὶ τῶι Αὐλητῆι προσφέρεσθαι φόρον ταλάντων μυρίων δισχιλίων πεντακοσίων.

of Cornelius earlier in this same year.[5] *In the event, Catulus, Crassus' colleague in the censorship this year (*MRR *2:157), thwarted the initiative (*Plut. *Vit. Crass. 13.2). Cicero may, however, have thus stirred the weighty opposition of Crassus to his consular candidacy (cf. 9 T 2.2 = Asc. 83C.2–4).*

[5] When on December 29, 66, Cicero scheduled the first trial of Manilius, he yielded to pressure from the crowd to allow at least ten days to prepare the defense (4 T 5–6); that would put the trial circa mid-January. After the proceedings were disrupted by mob violence (5 F 17), the senate probably met and voted tightened security for Manilius' second trial (4 T 2 = 5–6 T 11.5), probably held in late January/early February. Cornelius' (second) trial will have been scheduled shortly thereafter (5 F 5), perhaps still in the first half of February. Since the senate ordinarily took up foreign affairs in February (cf. *LPPR* 373; Mommsen 1887–1888, 3:1155–56; Pina Polo 2011, 321), the senate's deliberations over Egypt could have followed Cornelius' acquittal.

*7 T 1 [= Test. inc. 3] Strabo

Cicero discusses the revenues of Egypt in a certain speech, asserting that tribute of 12,500 talents per year was paid to Cleopatra's father, [Ptolemy] Auletes.[1]

[1] It is not certain that this testimonium refers to the debate of 65 rather than 56 (hence, the asterisk). The amount of the revenues of Ptolemy XII would, however, be relevant to his claim that the proponents of the expedition in 65 were motivated by greed (F 1–2); hence, this testimonium would fit with the argument of our speech.

7 T 2 Fortun. 129.8 Calboli Montefusco (*RLM* 115.1)

Omnis partitio qualis est? Aut nostra, quae προηγουμένη[1] διαίρεσις dicitur, aut adversarii, quae ἀναγκαία διαίρεσις nominatur, aut communis, quae μικτή potest dici, ut Cicero de rege Alexandrino.

[1] prohegoumenos: *corr. Capperonnerius*

7 T 3 = 5–6 T 24

7 T 4 *Adnotationes super Lucanum* 8.518

PURGANDUM GLADIO: Pompeius prior egit hac causa, ut huic traderetur imperium post patris mortem, postea Cicero, quae oratio ‹in›scribitur[1] de rege Alexandrino.

[1] scribitur: *corr. Endt*

7 F 1 Schol. Bob. 91.31St

"Ut rapiat, ut latrocinetur."

7 T 2 [= T 1] Fortunatianus, *Handbook of Rhetoric*

What is the nature of every division? Either it is our own, which is called the "preferred division," or it is our opponent's, which is called the "compulsory division," or it is shared, which can be called "mixed," as Cicero (used) in *On the Alexandrian King*.

7 T 3 [= T 2] = 5–6 T 24

7 T 4 [= Test. inc. 2] *Annotations on Lucan*

TO BE CLEANSED BY THE SWORD: Pompey previously acted with the motive of transferring power to this man [sc. Ptolemy XIII, in 51 BC] after his father's death, and Cicero did later in a speech that is entitled *On the Alexandrian King*.[1]

[1] In view of the explicit citation, this must be listed among the testimonia, but the scholiast is confused: his information is not relevant to our speech since it concerns the possible role played by Pompey in 51, after the death of Ptolemy Auletes, to ensure that Ptolemy XIII was installed as ruler; see further Crawford 1994, 47–48.

7 F 1 Bobbio Scholia

"So that he may snatch and steal."[1]

[1] Cicero uses highly prejudicial language to describe the plan. Cf. Unplaced F 19, which might come from this context.

7 F 2 Schol. Bob. 92.3St

"Si hercle in nostris rebus tam acres ad pecuniam, tam attenti, tam avari soleremus esse."

7 F 3 Schol. Bob. 92.17St

"Sed tamen quae sunt nostra iudicia?"

7 F 4 Schol. Bob. 92.23St

"Debent esse modestissima, quoniam quidem est hoc summi imperii nosmet ipsos de nostris rebus iudicare."

---

[1] The scholiast comments: "The orator wants it to be understood that it is almost shameless for the senate to have wanted to be judge of its own case, though it is natural that no one can preserve fairness when thinking above all of his own profit, which people generally try to claim even against propriety." On "judging one's own case," cf. also *Rosc. Am.* 102.

7 F 2 Bobbio Scholia

"If, by God, in our own affairs we were wont to be so keen on money, so attentive, so greedy."[1]

[1] The scholiast connects this with Cicero's general disapproval of Crassus' character. Cicero also heaps opprobrium on a thinly disguised Crassus at *Parad.* 46 and criticizes him by name at *Off.* 1.25 and 109, and 3.73 and 75.

7 F 3 Bobbio Scholia

"But what are our judgments?"[1]

[1] The scholiast comments (92.18–21St): "Crassus had tried to assert that there were prior judgments about this legacy of Egypt not just once, but on many occasions: first, at the time when recovery of money seemed to be sought from the Tyrians and brought to Rome, money that was recently withdrawn by King Alexa. Therefore, he had to meet (these arguments) in order for them to be refuted." Here, "King Alexa" refers to Ptolemy X Alexander I (ca. 140–88). Roman equites lent him money (deposited at Tyre) to build a fleet to try to recover his kingdom; and so he bequeathed his kingdom to Rome. On his death, the senate sent an embassy to Tyre to recover the money (*Leg. agr.* 2.41). The issue was whether the Romans had committed to accept the legacy, with Crassus maintaining, on the basis of a proposal in the senate that was vetoed by a tribune, that they had. Cf. Badian 1967; Manuwald 2018, 284–87; Khrustalyov 2018, 253–54.

7 F 4 Bobbio Scholia

"(The claims) ought to be very modest, since it is characteristic of supreme power for us to pass judgment on our own interests."[1]

7 F 5 Schol. Bob. 92.29St

"Qui ex hereditate tanta unum solum nomen agnoverimus."

7 F 6 Schol. Bob. 92.33St

"Si[1] est iusta causa belli, sicuti Crassus commemoravit cum Iugurtha fuisse."

[1] sic: *corr. Niebuhr*

7 F 7 Aq. Rom. *Fig.* 23.3 Elice (*RLM* 26.16 ~ Mart. Cap. 5.524)

Ἀντεισαγωγή,[1] compensatio. Est autem huius modi, ubi aliquid difficile et contrarium confitendum est, sed contra

[1] ἀνταναγωγή EO, *alii alia: corr. Stephanus in mg.*

7 F 5 Bobbio Scholia

"Since out of so great a legacy we have recognized one item alone."[1]

[1] Cf. on F 3. Schoell 1918 ad loc. thought that F 3–5 are all (in this order) from the same sentence, but the scholiast's comment (92.21–22St) makes it clear that F 3 is part of the refutation, whereas F 4 is the beginning of Cicero's own argument (*propositio*), so only F 4–5 are continuous.

7 F 6 Bobbio Scholia

"If there is a just cause of war, as Crassus recalled that there had been with Jugurtha."[1]

[1] This item supplements Crassus' fragments collected at *FRLO* 102. The scholiast goes on to explain the background (92.35–93.3St): "It is well known that upon the death of Micipsa, king of Numidia, there was a tripartite division of the kingdom among Atherbal, Hiempsal, and Jugurtha. This Jugurtha, however, killed the other two partly by force, partly by treachery. This was the particular cause for his waging war against the Roman people. After crushing many commanders, he was, however, finally defeated when C. Marius was the supreme commander." This is Cicero's first allusion to a "just war," a concept he famously elaborated at *Rep.* 3.25(35) and *Off.* 1.35–41; see Atkins 2022. The proponents of the bill were evidently trying to make a moral case for war; on this and on the analogy to the Jugurthine War, cf. Khrustalyov 2018, 254–55.

7 F 7 Aquila of Rome, *On Figures*

COMPENSATORY ANTITHESIS, compensation. It is of this kind: when something difficult and at odds with the case has to be admitted, but an equally strong point is intro-

inicitur non minus firmum. Qualia sunt haec de rege Ptolemaeo apud Ciceronem: "Difficilis ratio belli gerendi, at
plena fidei, plena pietatis."

7 F 8 Schol. Bob. 93.4St

"Non patiar hanc exaudiri vocem huius imperii: 'Ego te,
nisi das aliquid, hostem, si quid dederis, socium et amicum
iudicabo.'"

7 F 9 Schol. Bob. 93.9St

"Cum ille rex sit interfectus, hunc puerum in Syria fuisse."

7 F 10 Schol. Bob. 93.16St

"Atque illud etiam constare video: regem illum, cum regi-
nam sororem suam, caram acceptamque populo, manibus
suis trucidasset, interfectum esse impetu multitudinis."

duced in opposition. Such are these remarks in Cicero *On King Ptolemy*: "The policy of waging war is difficult, but abounding in faithfulness and loyalty."[1]

[1] Cicero is evidently quoting an argument from Crassus' speech; see F 6 with note. Alternatively, these words could be taken as establishing a standard for legitimate warfare that the current proposal fails to meet; so Khrustalyov 2018, 258 and n. 63.

7 F 8 Bobbio Scholia

"I shall not allow our empire to utter these words: 'I shall judge you an enemy unless you give something, but a friend and ally if you do.'"[1]

[1] The argument from the moral soundness (*honestas*) of a position was in general the line to take in the senate according to *Part. or.* 90–92; cf. Leonhardt 1998–1999, 281.

7 F 9 Bobbio Scholia

"When the former king was slain, the current one was a child in Syria."[1]

[1] As the scholiast remarks (93.11–15St), Cicero thus argues that Ptolemy Auletes lacked both the will and the capacity to kill his predecessor.

7 F 10 Bobbio Scholia

"Moreover, I see that this point also is agreed: since the king had slain the queen, his sister,[1] who was held in affection and favor by the people, with his own hands, he was killed by an attacking mob."

[1] Reference to Ptolemy XI Alexander II and Cleopatra Berenice.

*7 F 11 Quint. *Inst.* 1.5.13

Sed in prorsa quoque est quaedam iam recepta inmutatio
(nam Cicero "Canopitarum exercitum" dicit, ipsi Canobon
vocant) . . .

*7 F 11 Quintilian, *The Orator's Education*

But some substitutions are now accepted even in prose, for Cicero said "the army of the Canopitans," whereas they themselves say "Canobos."[1]

---

[1] Since the Canopitae were inhabitants of Canopus, a town and island on the western mouth of the Nile (cf. *OLD* s.v. Canopus), this fragment may be assigned to either our speech or one of the speeches of January 56 (see the introduction to this speech); hence, the asterisk.

8 PRO C. FUNDANIO

Cicero represented C. Fundanius (TLRR 207), whose case had the strong backing of members of his sodalitas *(club).*[1] *As a result, Cicero received a commitment from the members* (sodales) *to support his consular candidacy. Fundanius was one of four clients he agreed to represent in exchange for such group support (T 1). In the speech Cicero also refers to one of his competitors in the elections as a backer of the prosecution (F 5), which fixes the date of the trial to roughly the second half of 65 or first half of 64, the time when Cicero is known to have been canvassing for consul (Att. 1.1[10].1). The evidence for the speech is sparse. There are some indications that the charge, or one of the charges, was misconduct in canvassing for office* (ambitus; *cf. F 4 and on T 4). However, at least one of the witnesses against Fundanius appears to have been Greek (T 2), a fact suggestive of extortion charges arising from*

[1] For the sense of the word here, see on 5–6 T 1.

8 T 1 = 5–6 T 1 = 10 T 1

8 ON BEHALF OF C. FUNDANIUS (2ND HALF 65/1ST HALF 64 BC)

governorship of a Greek-speaking province, possibly, Macedonia. A Greek also plays a role in F 2; but the reference to Arcadians (T 4 and 5) may have a different explanation; see on T 4. It is not clear whether our defendant can be identified with any of the known office holders bearing the same name.[2] The outcome is not expressly attested, but a certain Fundanius appears as a creditor in 59 (QFr. 1.2[2].10); if it is the same man, it would follow that he was acquitted.

[2] He has been identified with the plebeian tribune of 68 (*MRR* 2:138 and 568 [in the latter, the year is given with a query]) and with the brother-in-law of the polymath M. Terentius Varro (cf. *R* 1.2.1 for a C. Fundanius as his father-in-law); see further Syme 1963, 58 and n. 40 = *RP* 2:563 and n. 2; Tatum 2018, 232. If the tribunate can be dated to 72, rather than 68 (cf. Crawford 1994, 58–59), he could conceivably have served as praetor, governed a province, and returned to face extortion charges in 65.

8 T 1 = 5–6 T 1 = 10 T 1

8 T 2 Quint. *Inst.* 1.4.14

Nam contra Graeci aspirare ei [*sc.* f] solent, ut pro Fundanio Cicero testem qui primam eius litteram dicere non possit inridet.

*8 T 3** Quint. *Inst.* 6.3.86

Dissimulavit Cicero cum Sex. Annalis testis reum laesisset et instaret identidem accusator: "Dic, M. Tulli, si quid potes de Sexto Annali"; versus enim dicere coepit de libro Enni annali sexto: "Quis potis ingentis causas[1] evolvere belli?"

[1] oras *Ennius*

8 T 2 [= T 4] Quintilian, *The Orator's Education*

On the other hand, the Greeks are in the habit of aspirating it [sc. *f*], as for instance Cicero in *On Behalf of Fundanius* mocks a witness who is unable to pronounce the first letter of his client's name.[1]

---

[1] Since Ancient Greek lacked the voiceless fricative /f/ (cf. Allen 1987, 18), this witness sounded the letter as an aspirate, i.e., said *Hundanius*; cf. Adams 2003, 108 and 432.

*8 T 3 [= T 5] Quintilian, *The Orator's Education*

When Sextus Annalis had damaged the defendant with his testimony and the prosecutor repeatedly pressed, "Speak, Marcus Tullius, if you can say anything about Sextus Annalis," Cicero pretended not to understand: he began to recite the verses from Ennius, *Annals* Six: "Who can unroll the vast causes of the war?"[1]

---

[1] Cicero pretends that with *dic . . . de Sexto Annali* (speak . . . about Sextus Annalis) the prosecutor meant "recite . . . from the sixth *Annal*," a possible meaning of the Latin words. Cf. Quint. *Inst.* 6.3.49 for another instance where Cicero deflects insistent questioning by a prosecutor with humor. An asterisk is placed before this item, since it is not expressly attributed to this speech; the assignment assumes that the Sextus Annalis mentioned is the same as the Villius Annalis of F 1, which is not quite certain. If this passage is connected with our case, it is evidently an anecdote that arose from the questioning of witnesses following the set speeches of each side.

8 T 4 Lact. Plac. ad Stat. *Theb.* 4.275 (p. 270.694 Sweeney)

ARCADES HUIC: Cicero pro Fundanio opinionis huius
meminit, cum de nobilitate tractaret.

8 T 5 Serv. ad Verg. *G.* 2.342

INMISSAEQUE FERAE SILVIS ET SIDERA CAELO: Hunc
ordinem propter Arcadas tenuit, qui se proselenos esse
adserunt, id est ante lunam natos, quod et Cicero in Fundaniana commemorat et Statius, qui ait "Arcades . . . astris
lunaque priores" (*Theb.* 4.275).

8 F 1 Prisc.*GL* 2.335.18

. . . si inveniantur propria appellativis similia in "i" finien-
tibus ablativum, illa per "e" proferunt eum . . . Cicero pro

8 T 4 [= T 3] Lactantius Placidus, *Commentary on Statius*

TO HIM THE ARCADIANS:[1] Cicero mentioned this belief in *On Behalf of Fundanius* when he treated the topic of the nobility.[2]

[1] The full statement reads: "To him [sc. Parasias] you old Arcadians, prior to the stars and the moon, give loyal troops" (*Arcades huic veteres, astris lunaque priores, / agmina fida datis*).

[2] Cf. T 5. Although the Arcadians claimed great antiquity, by the first century the area was a backwater. This may be part of an argument, such as Cicero makes in his defenses of Murena and Plancius, that a noble family does not count for much with voters these days (*Mur.* 15–17; *Planc.* 17–18, 31–32).

8 T 5 [= T 2] Servius, *Commentary on Virgil*

AND WILD BEASTS INTRODUCED TO THE FORESTS AND STARS TO THE SKY: He kept this order because of the Arcadians, who assert that they are prelunar, that is, born before the moon.[1] Cicero mentions this in the speech *On Behalf of Fundanius*[2] as does Statius, who says, "the Arcadians . . . predating the stars and the moon."

[1] This claim is attested as early as Aristotle (fr. 591 Rose).
[2] Cf. T 4 with note.

8 F 1 Priscian, *Textbook of Grammar*

. . . if proper nouns are found similar to common nouns that have ablatives ending in *i*, those nouns express that case with *e* . . . Cicero, *On Behalf of Fundanius*: "Not only

Fundanio: "Non modo hoc a Villio[1] Annale, sed vix mehercule a Quinto Muttone[2] factum probari potest."

[1] a villio *Patricius*: ab iulio *codd.*
[2] matone: *corr. Keil*

8 F 2 Prisc. *GL* 2.221.4

In "on" . . . haec tamen antiqui solent ablata "n" proferre et secundum Latinorum regulam in "o" terminantium . . . declinare . . . unde Cicero . . . idem pro Fundanio: "Essetne id quod Meno[1] nuntiasset?," pro "Menon."

[1] Parmeno *Ruhnken, fort. recte (cf. inc. sed. F 17)*

8 F 3 Serv. ad *Aen.* 9.675

DUCIS IMPERIO COMMISSA: . . . "commissura" enim dicitur tabularum coniunctio, sicut Cicero in Fundaniana meminit.

8 F 4 Ps.-Acro ad Hor. *A.P.* 343

"Puncta" dicuntur populi suffragia. Usus est hoc verbo etiam Cicero in Fundaniana.

can this deed not be approved by Villius Annalis [*Annale*], but scarcely, by God, by Quintus Mutto."[1]

---

[1] The Villius Annalis of this fragment has been assumed to be the same man as the Sextus Annalis of *T 3: so Gundel, *RE* s.v. Villius 8. The Quintus (Titius) Mutto referred to here may be the son of the homonymous man mentioned contemptuously at *Scaur.* 23, as Münzer, *RE* s.v. Titius 33, suggests. This looks like the kind of argument met with, e.g., at *Scaur.* F 9 Olechowska, in which a certain behavior is claimed to be impossible for x because it would not even be plausible for y, who is much worse.

8 F 2 Priscian, *Textbook of Grammar*

(Greek proper names ending) in *on* . . . The ancients are, however, in the habit of expressing these with the *n* removed and to inflect them according to the rule of Latin nouns ending in *o* . . . Hence Cicero [several speeches are cited] . . . Likewise in *On Behalf of Fundanius*: "Would that be what Meno announced?," instead of *Menon.*[1]

---

[1] See on Unplaced F 17.

8 F 3 Servius, *Commentary on Virgil*

ENTRUSTED BY THE LEADER'S COMMAND: . . . the place where tablets are joined is called the "juncture," as Cicero mentions in his speech for Fundanius.

8 F 4 Pseudo-Acro, *Commentary on Horace*

The votes of the people are called "dots."[1] Cicero also used this word in his speech for Fundanius.

---

[1] That is, because they are indicated with marks pressed in tablets coated with wax: *OLD* s.v. *punctum* 2.

8 F 5 Mar. Vict. *Def.* 41.23St

Nona species definitionis est καθ' ὑποτύπωσιν, id est per quandam imaginationem . . . Item subvenit in eo genere dictionis ubi aliquem pudor aut metus est nominare . . . pro Fundanio ita: "Descripsistine eius necessarium, nostrum competitorem, istum ipsum cuius nunc studio et gratia tota accusatio ista munita est?" In metu fuerat nominare, ideo descriptus est.

8 F 5 Marius Victorinus, *On Definitions*

The ninth type of definition is by sketch,[1] that is, by a certain mental picture . . . It is likewise helpful in the type of expression where one is embarrassed or fearful of naming someone . . . thus *On Behalf of Fundanius*: "Have you described his friend, my competitor, the very man by whose zeal and influence your entire prosecution has been fortified?"[2] Since he was afraid to name him, he was described.

---

[1] ὑποτύπωσις (*hypotyposis*) in rhetoric is a figure "by which a matter was vividly sketched in words": LSJ s.v. 3, referring to Quint. *Inst.* 9.2.40. Cf. also 5 F 44.   [2] It is uncertain which of Cicero's competitors (for the consulate of 63; cf. 9 T 2.1) is meant: perhaps Catiline, who was also facing prosecution for extortion around this time (cf. on 9 F 4), but it is unclear how Fundanius' conviction could have helped him.

9 IN TOGA CANDIDA

This speech was delivered by Cicero dressed in the tradi-
tional whitened garb of a candidate for office (cf. T 5).
Though formal speeches did not ordinarily play a part in
Roman electoral politics, this example is an exception (cf.
Tatum 2013, 134–35). In the run-up to the elections of 64,
bribery was so rife that the senate attempted to pass a
decree sharpening the penalties for improper canvassing.
This was vetoed, however, by the plebeian tribune Q. Mu-
cius Orestinus, who may have been a relation of Catiline's
wife Aurelia Orestilla (so RE s.v. Mucius 12). The previous
day, whether in a public assembly or in the senate, by way
of explaining his veto, Orestinus had declared Cicero un-
worthy of the consulship (F 27; cf. Tatum 2013, 149). Cat-
iline spoke in a similar vein, whether on that or another
occasion, emphasizing his own high standing (as a born
patrician) and expressing his contempt for Cicero (as a
"new man"): F 6, 20; cf. T 3. When the matter was brought
up for discussion in the senate the next day, Cicero was
called on to speak and delivered this oration, a passionate
denunciation of his two leading rivals, Catiline and Anto-
nius, not without aspersions cast on the tribune Orestinus
(F 27). The speech was not extemporaneous (Cicero doubt-

9 IN A WHITE TOGA
(64 BC, SHORTLY BEFORE
THE ELECTIONS)

less knew the matter would be raised in the senate and had a day to prepare) but was fueled by real indignation and passion (he speaks of being annoyed [F 27] and of what he could not bear with equanimity [F 6]).[1]

The two standard topics of speeches about Roman elections are (1) whether bribery took place and (2) which candidate had a motive for bribery, i.e., was likely to lose without recourse to bribery. F 1 seeks to establish the former point, alleging a nighttime (i.e., clandestine) meeting among his rival candidates (Catiline and C. Antonius), a financial supporter, and their bribery agents. Most of the rest of the speech argues that Catiline and Antonius were the ones who had a motive to resort to bribery, since their support was otherwise weak. Cicero systematically surveys and rules out the possible bases of support for their candidacies, beginning with friends and clients (F 2) and going on to Catiline's alienation of leading citizens, senators, equites, and the common people (F 11–16). He alerts

---

[1] Cf. *Att.* 4.2[74].2 on the outrage (*dolor*) that fueled Cicero's successful defense of his right to the Palatine property on which his house had stood.

*the senators to the dangers posed by both Antonius and
Catiline, warnings that would excite particular anxiety
in the aftermath of Spartacus' revolt (F 7–8). This threat
is reinforced at the end of the speech with a suggestive
picture of his rivals as "two daggers [being unsheathed]
against the republic" (F 28). On his side, Cicero, too, can
deploy a threat, namely, that of future prosecution, and,
pointing to the recent convictions of several of Sulla's
henchmen, he suggests that Catiline's case would be even
weaker than theirs (F 17–19). He addresses the question
of the relative public standing (*dignitas*) of himself and
Catiline by contrasting inherited status with the status
acquired by one's own actions (F 20). There is also a general attack on Catiline's character in private and public life, much of it in the form of a direct address to
his opponent (F 11–13, 15, 18–21, 23–24), anticipating a*

9 T 1 Asc. 82.1C (64.4St)

Haec oratio dicta est L. Caesare C. Figulo coss. post annum quam pro Cornelio dixerat.

tactic used in Cat. 1. *He does not shrink from lurid details (F 16, 21).*[2]

Antonius receives less extensive treatment in the preserved fragments (F 1, 2, 7, 10, 25–26). It is unclear whether this is an accident of transmission or reflects the balance of the original speech. These criticisms, partly again taking the form of a dialogue, mostly center on Antonius' ingratitude for Cicero's enabling him to be returned third in the polling for praetor in 67 (F 25–26). The emphasis on Catiline, if such it was, was perhaps not so much because Cicero had a premonition that he would have to work with Antonius as his colleague (so Kumaniecki 1961, 165) but rather because he saw Catiline as the more dangerous and difficult to control as a colleague in the consulship, and so made him the prime target.

The results of the election (T 3) suggest that the speech, though not the sole cause of Cicero's success (cf. Tatum 2018, 104–5), helped to frighten the senators away from Catiline and shore up his own position as an alternative.

[2] This similarity may help explain why *In a White Toga* failed to survive, as is suggested by Ramsey forthcoming in his introduction to the speech. Other factors may have been its allusiveness (cf. Stone 1998, 488n7), which made it difficult for readers to interpret, and the fact that it lacked the protection of membership of a corpus.

9 T 1 Asconius

This speech was delivered in the consulship of L. Caesar and C. Figulus [sc. 64], the year after he had spoken on behalf of Cornelius.

9 T 2 Asc. 82.4C (64.7St)

1. Sex competitores in consulatus petitione Cicero habuit, duos patricios, P. Sulpicium Galbam, L. Sergium Catilinam; quattuor plebeios, ex quibus duos[1] nobiles, C. Antonium, M. Antoni oratoris filium, L. Cassium Longinum, duos qui tantum[2] non primi ex familiis suis magistratum adepti erant, Q. Cornificium et C. Licinium Sacerdotem. Solus Cicero ex competitoribus equestri erat loco natus; atque in petitione patrem amisit.

2. Ceteri eius competitores modeste se gessere, visique sunt Q. Cornificius et Galba sobrii ‹ac›[3] sancti viri, Sacerdos nulla improbitate not‹at›us;[4] Cassius quamvis[5] stolidus tum magis quam improbus videretur, post[6] paucos menses in coniuratione Catilinae esse eum apparuit ac cruentissimarum sententiarum fuisse auctorem. Itaque hi quattuor probe[7] iacebant. Catilina autem et Antonius, quamquam omnium maxime infamis eorum vita esset, tamen multum poterant. Coierant enim ambo ut Ciceronem

1 duo: *corr. Sigonius*

2 tamen: *corr. Manutius*

3 *add. Beraldus*

4 corr. Lucarini

5 quamvis *Buecheler*: qui ineius *SP*: qui iners *Poggius, M*: qui iners ac *ed. Iunt.*

6 post *Manutius*: sed *codd.*

7 probe *Dyck*: pro re *codd.*

9 T 2 Asconius

1. Cicero had six competitors in canvassing for the consulship: two patricians, P. Sulpicius Galba and L. Sergius Catiline; four plebeians, of whom two were nobles, C. Antonius, the son of the orator M. Antonius, and L. Cassius Longinus; two who merely had not been the first of their families to obtain a magistracy, Q. Cornificius and C. Licinius Sacerdos.[1] Cicero alone of the competitors had been born of equestrian rank; and during the campaign he lost his father.[2]

2. His other competitors behaved moderately: Q. Cornificius and Galba showed themselves to be temperate and upright men; Sacerdos bore no mark of disloyalty; although at that time Cassius seemed more stupid than seditious, a few months later it became evident that he was involved in Catiline's conspiracy and had, in fact, been the proponent of very cruel schemes.[3] And so these four were completely out of the running. On the other hand, Catiline and Antonius, although their lives were the most infamous of all, were nonetheless potent rivals. Both had in fact

[1] P. Sulpicius Galba, pr. by 66; Catiline, pr. 68; C. Antonius, pr. 66 (on the name "Hybrida" sometimes attached to him, see Buongiorno 2006, who argues that it was an informal designation, perhaps indicating that his mother was not a Roman citizen); L. Cassius Longinus, pr. 66; Q. Cornificius, pr. by 66; C. Licinius Sacerdos, pr. 75.

[2] A mistake: Cicero's father died in 68, as we know from *Att.* 1.6[2].2; see further Dyck forthcoming, Appendix 5.

[3] It was he who took charge of the planned acts of arson in the city; cf. *Cat.* 3.14 and 4.13; cf. also *Cat.* 3.9 (instructions to the Allobroges to provide cavalry).

consulatu deicerent, adiutoribus usi firmissimis M. Crasso
et C. Caesare. Itaque haec oratio contra solos Catilinam
et Antonium est. Causa orationis huius modi in senatu
habendae Ciceroni fuit quod, cum in dies licentia ambitus
augeretur propter[8] praecipuam Catilinae et Antoni auda-
ciam, censuerat senatus ut lex ambitus aucta etiam cum
poena ferretur; eique[9] rei Q. Mucius Orestinus tr. pl. in-
tercesserat. Tum Cicero graviter senatu intercessionem
ferente surrexit atque in coitionem[10] Catilinae et Antoni
invectus est ante dies comitiorum paucos.

[8] praeter: *corr. Poggius, M*
[9] et quoque: *corr. Manutius*
[10] contionem: *corr. Manutius*

9 T 3 Asc. 93.24C (72.17St)

Huic orationi Ciceronis et Catilina et Antonius contume-
liose responderunt,[1] quod solum poterant, invecti in novi-
tatem eius. Feruntur quoque orationes nomine illorum
editae, non ab ipsis scriptae sed ab Ciceronis obtrectato-
ribus: quas nescio an satius sit ignorare. Ceterum Cicero
consul omnium consensu factus est; Antonius pauculis

[1] responderant: *corr. Manutius*

formed an alliance to keep Cicero out of the consulship[4] and enjoyed the very strong support of M. Crassus and C. Caesar. Accordingly, this speech is directed solely at Catiline and Antonius. Cicero's reason for delivering such a speech in the senate was this: since electoral bribery was unchecked and increasing on a daily basis because of the particular brazenness of Catiline and Antonius, the senate had decreed that a law against electoral bribery be enacted with a stiffened penalty, but the plebeian tribune Q. Mucius Orestinus had vetoed it. Then, with the senate being displeased at the intercession, Cicero got to his feet and attacked the electoral alliance of Catiline and Antonius a few days before the elections.

[4] Such an alliance, called a *coitio* in Latin, was legal, though it could be associated with improper campaign practices. Hypotheses about the origin of the combination are offered by Stone 1993, and Tatum 2018, 101 and n. 569.

9 T 3 Asconius

Catiline and Antonius offered an insulting reply to this speech of Cicero's, doing the only thing they could do, attacking his family background.[1] Speeches are also in circulation that were published under their names, albeit not written by the candidates themselves but by Cicero's detractors; I think it is better to ignore them. Cicero, moreover, was elected consul by general consensus, whereas

[1] Literally, his "newness" (*novitas*), i.e., the fact that he came from a family with no previous record in politics. Appian (*B Civ.* 2.2.5) describes a similar reaction on the part of Cicero's targets (after the election).

centuriis Catilinam superavit, cum ei propter patris nomen paulo copiosior[2] manus suffragata esset quam Catilinae.

[2] speciosior: *corr. Lucarini*

9 T 4 (= 14 T 4) Quint. *Inst.* 3.7.2

Sed mos Romanus etiam negotiis hoc munus inseruit [*sc.*
laudis ac vituperationis] . . . et editi in competitores, in L.
Pisonem, in Clodium et Curionem libri vituperationem
continent et tamen in senatu loco sunt habiti sententiae.

9 T 5 Isid. *Orig.* 19.24.6

Toga candida eademque cretata in qua candidati, id est
magistratum petentes, ambiebant, addita creta quo candi-
dior insigniorque esset. Cicero orationem quam habuit
contra conpetitores "In toga candida" ‹in›scripsit.[1]

[1] orationem . . . inscripsit *Dyck*: in oratione . . . scripsit *codd.*

9 F 1 Asc. 83.14C (65.1St)

"Dico, patres conscripti, superiore nocte cuiusdam hominis nobilis et valde in hoc largitionis quaestu noti et cogniti
domum Catilinam et Antonium cum sequestribus suis
convenisse."

---

[1] The "financial agents" (*sequestres*) were persons who re-
ceived sums earmarked for bribery; cf. *OLD* s.v. *sequester* 1b.
Asconius (83.18C) identifies the "nobleman" as either Caesar or
M. Crassus. But Stone 1998 argues cogently that the reference is

Antonius outpolled Catiline by very few centuries,[2] since, in view of his father's fame,[3] a somewhat more ample faction supported him rather than Catiline.

[2] A reference to the divisions of the Roman electorate for the purposes of the consular elections.
[3] Cf. T 2. M. Antonius was cos. 99; his oratory was much admired by Cicero, as is shown by *On the Orator* and *Brutus.*

9 T 4 Quintilian, *The Orator's Education*

But Roman custom has introduced this task [sc. of praising or blaming individuals] even into matters of business . . . and the books published against his competitors, against L. Piso, and against Clodius and Curio contain invective but were delivered as opinions in the senate.

9 T 5 Isidore, *Origins*

A white toga, i.e., one whitened with chalk, in which the candidates, i.e., those canvassing for a magistracy, went about, with the chalk applied so that it would be whiter and more distinct. Cicero gave the title *In a White Toga* to the speech that he delivered against his competitors.

9 F 1 Asconius

"Gentlemen of the senate, I assert that on the night before last Catiline and Antonius gathered with their financial agents at the house of a certain nobleman who is known and recognized in this business of offering largesse."[1]

to P. Sulla. There is a similar reference to a nocturnal meeting, including verbal echoes of our passage, at *Cat.* 1.8; cf. Pieper 2020, 216–17.

9 F 2 Asc. 83.26C (65.11St)

"Quem enim aut amicum habere potest is qui tot civis trucidavit,[1] aut ‹clientem›[2] qui in sua civitate cum peregrino negavit se iudicio aequo certare posse?"

[1] trucidari: *corr. Poggius*
[2] *add. Manutius*

9 F 3 Asc. 85.1C (66.4St)

"Nec[1] senatum[2] respexit,[3] cum gravissimis vestris decretis absens notatus est."

[1] ne: *corr. Patricius*
[2] si (se *PM*) iam tum: *corr. Halm*
[3] despexit: *corr. Poggius*

9 F 2 Asconius

"What friend can a man have who has butchered so many
fellow citizens, or what client can a man have who said that
in his own community he could not compete with a for-
eigner in a fair trial?"[1]

[1] The two subjects are, respectively, Catiline and Antonius.
He alludes to Catiline's role in the Sullan proscriptions (Asc.
84.4–11C; cf. F 13–14). Apropos of Antonius, Asconius explains
that he plundered the province of Achaea with a squadron of
Sullan cavalry (84.12–25C). When the Achaeans pressed charges
before M. Lucullus (pr. peregr. 76: *MRR* 2:93), Antonius called
on the tribunes to intervene and declared that he could not receive a fair trial (*TLRR* 141). Antonius' claim is likewise quoted
at Q. Cic. (?), *Comment. pet.* 8. See Balzarini 1968, 379–81, arguing that the charge was either extortion or theft; Damon and
MacKay 1995 suggest that Lucullus allowed the prosecution in
the peregrine court on the fiction that the Achaeans were Roman
citizens, whereupon Antonius protested to the tribunes that the
procedure was unfair (and they quashed the trial).

9 F 3 Asconius

"Nor did he have regard for the senate when he was
branded *in absentia* with your severe decrees."[1]

[1] This refers to Catiline's governorship of Africa in 67–66. As
Asconius remarks, the provincials sent ambassadors to complain
before the senate and "many severe opinions" (*multae . . . graves
sententiae*) were pronounced about him on that occasion: 85.3–
6C; cf. *MRR* 2:147 and 155, as well as F 12 below.

9 F 4 Asc. 85.7C (66.9St)

"In iudiciis quanta vis esset didicit cum est absolutus: si
aut illud iudicium aut illa absolutio nominanda est."

9 F 5 Asc. 87.16C (68.5St)

"Populum vero cum inspectante populo collum secuit
hominis maxime popularis quanti faceret ostendit."

9 F 4 Asconius

"He learned how much power resides in the courts when he was acquitted—if that should be called a tribunal or that an acquittal."[1]

[1] A reference to Catiline's trial for extortion as governor of Africa, held in the second half of 65 (*TLRR* 212). It is not clear whether Cicero insinuates that the prosecutor, P. Clodius, colluded with the defense (the claim he raises at *Har. resp.* 42 and *Pis.* 23) or attributes the result to massive bribery (so Q. Cic. [?], *Comment. pet.* 10). Urso 2019, 142, explains the difference by the fact that after Catiline's death, Cicero changed his target.

9 F 5 Asconius

"He showed how highly he valued the people when, in full view of the people, he cut the throat of an outstandingly popular man."[1]

[1] The subject is again Catiline; the victim, M. Marius Gratidianus, pr. 85–84: *MRR* 2:57 and 60 with a query. The supposition that he was praetor in 82, based on Val. Max. 9.2.1 and promoted by some scholars (Urso 2019, 88 and n. 11), is not credible; cf. *MRR* 3:140. This is the second use (after *Clu.* 77) of *popularis* in a political context (there is a similar exploitation of the derivation of *popularis* from *populus* at *Har. resp.* 42; cf. Seager 1972, 333). The first attested use of *optimates* also occurs in this speech (F 24); the two are first contrasted, however, at Q. Cic. (?), *Comment. pet.* 5. Gratidianus won his popularity by means of a ruse; cf. Cic. *Off.* 3.80; Plin. *HN* 33.132. See further F 15–16 and on the latter; Asc. 84.7–9, 87.19–20, and 90.1C. On Gratidianus, see Nicolet 1974, 945–46. On the popular cult of Gratidianus as a step toward the cult of the emperors, cf. Marco Simón and Pina Polo 2000.

9 F 6 Asc. 87.21C (68.8St)

"Me qua amentia inductus sit[1] ut contemneret constituere
non possum. Utrum aequo animo[2] laturum putavit? At in
suo familiarissimo viderat me ne aliorum ‹quidem›[3] iniu-
rias mediocriter posse ferre."

[1] est: *corr. Madvig*
[2] an in: *corr. Madvig*
[3] *add. ed. Ald.*

9 F 7 Asc. 87.26C (68.13St)

"Alter pecore omni vendito et saltibus prope addictis[1] pas-
tores retinet, ex quibus ait se cum velit subito fugitivorum
bellum excitaturum."

[1] additis: *corr. Beraldus*

9 F 6 Asconius

"I cannot ascertain what madness has led him to despise me.[1] Did he think I would take this calmly? And yet he had seen, in the case of his close friend, that I could even be strongly moved by the wrongs suffered by other people."[2]

[1] Catiline's attitude was apparent when, charged with extortion (*TLRR* 212), he refused Cicero's advocacy (cf. *Att.* 1.2[11].1); acceptance would no doubt have entailed an electoral alliance between the two consular candidates. Catiline was represented instead by his fellow patrician L. Manlius Torquatus (cos. 65); cf. *Sull.* 81.

[2] Catiline's alleged friend is C. Verres, with allusion to the latter's treatment of the Sicilians as governor of the island from 73 to 71, prosecuted by Cicero in 70: Asc. 87.25C; *MRR* 2:112, 119, 124; *TLRR* 177.

9 F 7 Asconius

"One of the two, though he has sold all his flocks, and his pastures have been largely assigned [sc. to creditors], retains his shepherds and says he will use them, whenever he wishes, to stir up a rebellion of runaway slaves on the spur of the moment."[1]

[1] A reference to Antonius (Asc. 84.23–35 and 87.29C), whose impecuniousness was one of the causes of his expulsion from the senate in 70: *MRR* 2:126–27. Ryan 1995, 47, suggests that the liquidation was for electoral bribery. The slave revolt of Spartacus (73–70) was a recent memory. It began as a breakout from a gladiatorial school in Capua but expanded by recruitment of pastoralists on large *latifundia* in Southern Italy; cf. *OCD* s.v. Spartacus.

9 F 8 Asc. 88.1C (68.17St)

"Alter induxit eum quem potuit ut repente gladiatores
populo non debitos polliceretur; eos[1] ipse consularis candidatus perspexit et legit et emit; ‹id›[2] praesente populo
Romano factum est."

[1] quos *Poggius*
[2] *add. Orelli*

9 F 9 Asc. 88.10C (68.23St)

"Quam ob rem augete etiam mercedem,[1] si voltis, Q. Muci
ut perseveret[2] legem impedire, ut coepit senatus con-

[1] mercede(s): *corr. Madvig*
[2] Q. mutium perreverti *codd.*: *corr. Madvig*

9 F 8 Asconius

"The other talked a man amenable to his persuasion into suddenly promising gladiators to the people even though they were not owed. He, though a candidate for consul, personally inspected and chose and bought them. This occurred in full view of the Roman people."[1]

[1] That "the other" is Catiline is shown by the date of the consular candidacy (66), which could not apply to Antonius, who was praetor that year (*MRR* 2:151–52); cf. Ryan 1995, 48. Asconius (88.5C = 10 T 3) identifies the man "amenable to his persuasion" as Q. Gallius; he is followed by Ryan 1995, who supposes (47–48n8) that Cicero refrains from naming Gallius to avoid offending a supporter of his consular campaign (5–6 T 1). However, Ramsey 1982 argues convincingly that Catiline was a candidate for consul not in the regular elections of 66, when Gallius was a candidate for praetor, but (briefly) in the new elections that were called when the winners of the regular consular elections were convicted of bribery; only this hypothesis will explain how Catiline's candidature could have been disallowed for having been filed too late (Sall. *Cat.* 18.3), i.e., because he had not filed for the regular elections. Ramsey identifies "the man amenable to persuasion" as P. Sulla. On gladiators as a potential threat to public safety, see the note on the previous fragment. Cicero's own Tullian Law on Electoral Malfeasance would later ban candidates from offering gladiatorial shows within two years of the elections in which they wished to compete (unless they were required by the terms of a will): *LPPR* 379; Ville 1981, 82–84; Nadig 1997, 48–55, 215–16.

9 F 9 Asconius

"Therefore, even increase Q. Mucius' wages, if you wish, so that he may go on blocking the law, as he began (to do

sultum;[3] sed ego ea lege contentus sum qua duos consules designatos uno tempore damnari vidimus."

[3] senter cos: *corr. Madvig*

9 F 10 Asc. 88.20C (68.31St)

"Atque ut istum omittam in exercitu Sullano praedonem, in introitu gladiatorem, in victoria quadrigarium."

9 F 11 Asc. 89.1C (69.4St)

"Te vero, Catilina, consulatum sperare aut cogitare non prodigium atque portentum est? A[1] quibus enim petis? A principibus civitatis, qui tibi, cum L. Volcacio cos. in consilio fuissent,[2] ne petendi quidem potestatem esse voluerunt?"

[1] ex: *corr. Manutius*
[2] fuisset: *corr. Madvig*

---

[1] L. Volcacius Tullus was cos. 66 (*MRR* 2:161). Asconius (89.9–12C) reports that Volcacius' council recommended that Catiline's candidature be disallowed because of his pending trial for extortion (the case came to trial in the second half of 65; see on F 4), whereas Sallust says that the reason was that he had not filed within the deadline (*Cat.* 18.3). Either way, this was not the kind of judgment of inherent unfitness that Cicero implies. Puccioni 1972, 76–77, joins this fragment with F 12, 13, and 15 as one continuous text: if so, F 14 may come from another part of the

with) the senate's decree. But I am content with the law by which we saw two consuls designate simultaneously convicted."[1]

[1] That is, P. Autronius Paetus and P. Cornelius Sulla; the law was the Calpurnian Law on Electoral Malfeasance; Cicero also sees it as a sufficient tool for convicting a guilty candidate at *Mur.* 46. But at 5 F 41, 42 (where see note) Cicero implies a different attitude toward the law.

9 F 10 [= F 22] Asconius

"To pass this man over in silence, a brigand in Sulla's army, a cutthroat in his hostile entry, a charioteer in his victory."[1]

[1] In *praeteritio* (i.e., professing to omit points that are none-theless mentioned), Cicero alludes to Antonius. For his activity in Sulla's army, see on F 2. The reference to his being a cutthroat (literally, a gladiator) during Sulla's "hostile entry" refers to his role in the proscriptions. Finally, he was a charioteer at the circus games celebrating Sulla's victory (held in November 81 and annually thereafter): Asc. 88.23–29C; cf. F 25 with note.

9 F 11 Asconius

"Is it not a monstrous portent for you, Catiline, to hope for or contemplate the consulship? From whom are you seeking it? From the leading citizens of the community, who, when they were consulted by the consul L. Volcacius, did not even want you to have the opportunity to be a candidate?"[1]

speech. But it is also possible that Cicero added to F 13 content corresponding to F 14, which is not quoted verbatim; and of the fragments of the speech F 13 is the only one that relates to F 14; hence, its placement here.

9 F 12 Asc. 89.13C (69.14St)

"A[1] senatoribus, qui te auctoritate sua spoliatum ornamentis omnibus vinctum paene Africanis oratoribus tradiderunt?"

[1] an: *corr. ed. Iunt.*

9 F 13 Asc. 89.20C (69.19St)

"Ab equestri ordine, quem trucidasti?"

9 F 14 Asc. 84.4 C (65.14St)

⟨Dicitur⟩ [1] Catilina, cum in Sullanis partibus fuisset, crudeliter fecisse. Nominatim etiam postea Cicero dicit quos occiderit, Q. Caecilium,[2] M. Volumnium, L. Tanusium.[3]

[1] *suppl. Clark*
[2] Caucilium *Comment. pet. 9*
[3] *Manutius ex Comment. pet. 9*: Tantasium *codd.*

9 F 12 Asconius

"From the senators, who, by their authority, practically handed you over stripped of all distinctions and bound to the ambassadors from Africa?"[1]

[1] See on F 3. Cicero's language plays on the *deditio* (surrender) of a Roman commander who made a treaty not authorized by the senate: he was stripped and surrendered to the enemy, as was done to C. Hostilius Mancinus in 136; cf. *Rep.* 3.28 and *Off.* 3.109, with Dyck 1996, 633. Cicero uses such language of himself at *Dom.* 30 ("not so much deserted as practically surrendered [*deditum*]").

9 F 13 Asconius

"From the equites, whom you have butchered?"[1]

[1] Appian (*B Civ.* 1.11.95) gives 1,600 as the total number of equites put to death in the Sullan proscriptions of 82–81 BC.

9 F 14 Asconius

Catiline is said to have acted cruelly when he was on the Sullan side. Afterward Cicero names the men he killed: Q. Caecilius, M. Volumnius, and L. Tanusius.[1]

[1] Caecilius and Tanusius are named as examples of equites slain by Catiline at Q. Cic. (?), *Comment. pet.* 9, where the former is spelled "Caucilius" and is said to have been the husband of Catiline's sister, possibly the sister allegedly debauched by Catiline (ibid.). See further Münzer, *RE* s.vv. Caecilius 21 and Tanusius 1; Nicolet 1974, 806–7 and 1030–31; Tatum 2018, 202. Urso 2019, 91–92, argues convincingly that this man (and not M. Marius Gratidianus, as claimed in the Bern schol. ad Luc. 2.173) is the brother-in-law slain by Catiline. It is unclear whether M. Volumnius was also an eques; cf. H. Gundel, *RE* s.v. Volumnius 5; Nicolet 1974, 1081–82; Hinard 1985, 410–11. On Catiline's impending trial for murder, see on F 18.

9 F 15 Asc. 89.25C (69.23St)

"A plebe, cui spectaculum eius modi tua crudelitas prae-
buit, ut ‹te› nemo sine gemitu ac recordatione luctus aspi-
cere possit?"[1]

[1] ut te . . . possit *Madvig*: ut . . . posset *codd.*

9 F 16 Asc. 90.3C (69.27St)

"Quod caput etiam tum plenum animae et spiritus ad Sul-
lam usque ab Ianiculo ad aedem Apollinis manibus ipse
suis detulit."

9 F 15 [= F 14] Asconius

"From the common people, to whom your cruelty presented such a spectacle that none of them can look upon you without groaning and recollecting their grief?"[1]

[1] Another reference to M. Marius Gratidianus; see on F 5 and 16.

9 F 16 [= F 15] Asconius

"With his own hands he carried to Sulla that still living and breathing head all the way from the Janiculum to the temple of Apollo."[1]

[1] Presentation of the decapitated head was regular practice during the proscriptions and required in order to claim the reward; cf. *Tabula Heracleensis* 122; Suet. *Iul.* 11.2; Hinard 1985, 40–41; Urso 2019, 101. A similar account of the fate of M. Marius Gratidianus is given by Plutarch (*Vit. Sull.* 32.2), who adds that Catiline then washed his hands in the lustral water of Apollo. On Sulla's special relationship with Apollo, cf. Noble 2014, 51, 109n100, 158, 167; Urso 2019, 102. The act of purification when approaching a holy place after contact with death was routine, not a sacrilege or a parody of the procedure of returning soldiers, as some have thought; cf. Urso 2019, 102–3. Sallust has the victim murdered on the grave of Q. Catulus (cos. 102): Q. Cic. (?), *Comment. pet.* 10, and Sall. *Hist.* 1.36–38 R, including gruesome details of the murder; see further Dyck 1996, 599–600; Urso 2019, 98–99, 102. The order was given by Sulla, probably at the request of Catulus Jr. (cos. 78). Catiline's involvement has been doubted by Marshall 1985, 291–92, and Berry 2020, 13, but it is so firmly rooted in the tradition that even so determined a defender of Catiline as Urso (2019, 103–4) accepts it.

9 F 17 Asc. 91.1C (70.14St)

Circa eosdem dies L. quoque Bellienus damnatus est
quem Cicero ait avunculum esse Catilinae.

9 F 18 Asc. 90.16C (70.5St)

"Quid tu potes in defensione tua dicere quod illi non
‹dixerint? At illi multa›[1] dixerunt quae tibi dicere non
licebit."

[1] dixerint . . . multa: *suppl. Madvig*

9 F 19 Asc. 90.20C (70.8St)

ET PAULO POST:

"Denique illi negare potuerunt et negaverunt; tu tibi ne
infitiandi quidem impudentiae locum reliquisti. Qua re

9 F 17 Asconius

Around the same time L. Bellienus was also convicted, who Cicero said was an uncle of Catiline's.[1]

[1] L. Bellienus (pr. 107: *MRR* 1:551; Sall. *Iug.* 104.1) was recently convicted of the murder (on Sulla's orders) of Q. Lucretius Afella; for the identification of Bellienus as the murderer, see Khrustalyov 2022, 102–4, and for the trial, *TLRR* 215. Catiline's mother was thus a Belliena, but the Bellieni were not a noble family; cf. Schietinger 2017, 158, and for the family tree, Drumann and Groebe 1899–1929, 5:411.

9 F 18 [= F 16] Asconius

"What can you say in your defense that they have not said? And yet they said many things that you will not have license to say."[1]

[1] Cicero looks ahead to Catiline's impending trial for murder (at F 14 he shows he is already familiar with the prosecutor's case): *TLRR* 217. The plural subjects are L. Luscius (named in the next fragment) and Catiline's maternal uncle L. Bellienus, both recently convicted for murders committed in Sulla's service: *TLRR* 215 and 216. The former was richly rewarded, achieving a net worth of ten million sesterces; see further Santangelo 2007, 98–99 and n. 37. Besides that detail, Asconius (90.25–91.9C) discusses their victims and says that they could claim to have acted on the dictator's orders or deny the charge altogether (as they did, according to the next fragment). There is a similar argument that his target will have a more difficult defense compared to someone else at *Vat.* 5 (= 5–6 T 3).

9 F 19 [= F 17] Asconius

AND A LITTLE LATER:

"Finally, they could and did offer denials, but you have not even left yourself room for the brazenness of denial. And

praeclara dicentur[1] iudicia tulisse si, qui infitiantem Lus-
cium condemnarunt,[2] Catilinam absolverint confitentem."

[1] dicuntur: *corr. Manutius*
[2] condemnarint: *corr. Manutius*

9 F 20 Asc. 91.14C (70.24St)

"Hanc tu habes dignitatem qua fretus me contemnis et
despicis, an eam quam[1] reliqua in[2] vita es[3] consecutus,
cum ita vixisti ut non esset locus tam sanctus quo[4] non
adventus tuus, etiam cum culpa nulla subesset, crimen
afferret?"

[1] qua: *corr. Manutius*
[2] reliqua in *Clark*: reliquam *codd.*
[3] vite: *corr. Manutius*
[4] quod: *corr. Beraldus*

so the courts will be said to have produced brilliant results, if those who convicted Luscius in spite of his denial acquit Catiline in spite of his confession."[1]

[1] See on the previous fragment.

9 F 20 [= F 18] Asconius

"Is this the standing you have, based on which you condemn and despise me,[1] or the standing you have achieved during the rest of your life, when you have lived in such a way that there is no place so hallowed that your arrival there fails to bring an accusation, even in the absence of guilt?"[2]

[1] Presumably, a reply to claims raised by Catiline about his "standing" (*dignitas*), sc. as a patrician as opposed to Cicero's as a "new man." Cf. T 3 as well as Catiline's letter at Sall. *Cat.* 35.3 ("I failed to hold the position of my standing [*statum dignitatis*] . . . I saw unworthy men advanced in office"); Stone 1993, 3–4. Cicero treats the topic of claims to inherited status also at *Mur.* 15–17 and *Planc.* 16–18. Cf. the mockery of the claims of ancient lineage at 8 T 4 and 5, as well as at *Fam.* 3.7[71].5: "Do you suppose that any Appiety or Lentulity counts with me more than the ornaments of merit?" (trans. Shackleton Bailey).

[2] The same point is made at Q. Cic. (?), *Comment. pet.* 10. Cicero alludes to the trials in 73 in which several Vestal Virgins had to answer a charge of unchastity. One of them, Fabia, the cousin or stepsister of Cicero's wife Terentia (cf. Treggiari 2007, 30), was accused of relations with Catiline (*TLRR* 167) but acquitted, as was Catiline, in a separate trial, as Cadoux 2005 convincingly argues; cf. also Urso 2019, 121–22. Cicero must of course deny guilt but wants to use the matter anyway to cast aspersions on Catiline's character. For the theme of a miscreant's polluting presence, cf. *Clu.* 192–93.

9 F 21 Asc. 91.24C (71.1St)

"Cum deprehendebare in adulteriis, cum deprehendebas adulteros ipse, cum ex eodem stupro tibi et uxorem et filiam invenisti."

9 F 22 Asc. 86.23C (67.14St)

"Stupris se omnibus ac flagitiis contaminavit, caede nefaria cruentavit; diripuit socios; leges quaestiones iudicia violavit."

9 F 21 [= F 19] Asconius

"When you would be caught in adultery, when you would catch other adulterers, when from the same illicit affair you got yourself both a wife and a daughter."[1]

[1] L. Lucceius (pr. 67) repeated these charges when prosecuting Catiline for murder later this year (*TLRR* 217; *FRLO* 123 F 4). Asconius reports that he was unable to discover the names of the women in question (92.1–3C). Sallust gives Catiline's wife's name as Aurelia Orestilla (*Cat.* 15.2, 35.3, 6), but there is no other evidence that she was the daughter of a former mistress. On this marriage and its possible implications, cf. Syme 2016, 155–57; Schietinger 2017, 163.

9 F 22 [= F 10] Asconius

"He has sullied himself with all manner of sexual crimes and scandals and covered himself with the blood of unholy slaughter; he has plundered the allies; he has violated the laws, the criminal courts, the tribunals . . ."[1]

[1] This summary of Catiline's crimes is one of four fragments Asconius quotes out of sequence in order to refute Fenestella's contention (*FRH* 70 F 21 *apud* Asc. 85.13C) that Cicero defended Catiline on charges of extortion (the others are, in order of citation by Asconius, F 26, 27, and 23). This fragment has been variously placed by editors, but perhaps functions most effectively as a summary of points previously established: sexual crimes/scandals, F 21–22; slaughter, F 2, 5, 13–16; plundering of the allies (sc. in Africa), F 3, 12; crimes unpunished by courts, F 4.

9 F 23 Asc. 86.26, 92.4C (67.15, 71.7St quid . . . absolutus est)

ET POSTEA:

"Quid ego ut violaveris provinciam praedicem, cuncto populo Romano ‹re›clamante[1] ac resistente?[2] Nam ut te illic gesseris non audeo dicere, quoniam absolutus es.[3] Mentitos[4] esse equites Romanos, falsas fuisse tabellas honestissimae civitatis existimo, mentitum Q. Metellum Pium, mentitam Africam: vidisse puto[5] nescio quid illos[6] iudices qui te innocentem iudicarunt. O miser, qui non sentias illo iudicio te non absolutum verum ad aliquod severius iudicium ac maius supplicium reservatum!"

[1] *suppl. Halm*
[2] cuncto . . . resistente *Asc. 92.5C: om. Asc. 86.26C*
[3] *hactenus Asc. 92.4C*
[4] mentitum: *corr. ed. Iunt.*
[5] apud: *corr. Manutius*
[6] illo: *corr. Manutius*

9 F 23 [= F 20a–b] Asconius

AND AFTERWARD:

"Why should I declare publicly how, in the face of the protest and opposition of the entire Roman people, you harmed your province? I dare not mention how you behaved there, since you were acquitted. I suppose that the Roman equites lied, the depositions of a most honorable community were falsified, Q. Metellus Pius and the province of Africa told falsehoods. I imagine that those jurors who found you innocent saw something or other.[1] O you wretch, not to realize that you were not acquitted by that court but reserved for a more severe tribunal and an aggravated punishment!"[2]

[1] The sarcasm is palpable. The equites will be the *publicani*, who had bid for and obtained the right to collect taxes in the province. It is not known which African city sent representatives to testify against Catiline (Lewis 2008, 294, suspects that it was Utica). The other witness mentioned is Q. Caecilius Metellus Pius (cos. 80, pont. max. from 81; omitted at *TLRR* 212); he was presumably involved because he inherited patronage of the province from his father, Q. Caecilius Metellus Numidicus (cos. 109); cf. Münzer, *RE* 3.1:1224.21–26. For this trial, see on F 4.

[2] A hint of his looming prosecution; see on F 18. The theme of escaping one punishment only to be subject to another (implicitly according to divine providence) already occurs at *Verr.* 2.1.71: "Can you doubt that fortune did not so much want to rescue him [sc. Verres] from that danger [sc. the angry mob at Lampsacus] as reserve him for your tribunal?" The more specific claim that acquittal is a prelude to worse punishment is invoked apropos of Clodius at *14 F 33 and *Mil.* 86. For theodicy in Cicero generally, cf. Gildenhard 2011, ch. 11.

9 F 24 Asc. 92.11C (71.12St)

"Praetereo nefarium illum conatum tuum et paene acerbum et luctuosum rei publicae diem, cum Cn. Pisone so-
cio,[1] ne quem alium nominem,[2] caedem optimatum facere
voluisti."

[1] socium: *corr. Poggius*
[2] neque alio nemine: *corr. Gronovius*

9 F 25 Asc. 92.26C (71.23St)

"An oblitus es te ex me, cum praeturam peteremus, petisse
ut tibi primum locum concederem? Quod cum saepius
ageres et impudentius a me contenderes, meministi me
tibi respondere impudenter te facere qui id a me peteres
quod a te Boculus[1] numquam impetrasset?"[2]

[1] quod a te Boculus *A. Augustinus*: quod avunculus *codd.*
[2] impetrasses: *corr. Poggius, M*

9 F 24 [= F 21] Asconius

"I pass by in silence that nefarious plot of yours and a day almost bitter and calamitous for the republic, when, with Cn. Piso as your confederate (to name no one else[1]), you intended to perpetrate a massacre of the optimates."[2]

[1] Possibly a discrete allusion to M. Crassus; cf. on F 28.

[2] Asconius 92.17C paraphrases as "a slaughter of the senate" (*caedem senatus*); similarly *Mur.* 81: a "plot to slay the senate." This is the first use of *optimates* (see on F 5). This claim is the seed from which sprouted the myth of the "first Catilinarian conspiracy"; cf. Frisch 1948; Syme 1964, 86–94; Seager 1964; Levick 2015, 35–38; Berry 2020, 16; but cf. also Woodman 2021, defending the historicity of the affair. Ramsey 1982, 131, thinks the story of the conspiracy may have arisen from P. Sulla's use of a gang to further Catiline's candidacy for the consulship of 65 in opposition to his fellow patrician Torquatus. For Cn. Piso, see on F 28.

9 F 25 [= F 23] Asconius

"Have you forgotten that when we were canvassing for the praetorship you asked me to yield first place to you? Do you recall that, when you did this repeatedly and pressed me for it shamelessly, I replied that you were behaving brazenly since you were asking me for something that Boculus would never have been granted by you?"[1]

[1] Cicero now returns to Antonius. Boculus was famous as a charioteer in the circus: Asc. 93.8–9C; see on F 10.

9 F 26 Asc. 85.21C (66.19St)

"Nescis me praetorem primum esse factum, te concessione competitorum et collatione[1] centuriarum et meo maxime beneficio ex[2] postremo in tertium locum esse subiectum?"

[1] conlatine: *corr. Poggius*
[2] et: *corr. Kiessling-Schoell*

9 F 27 Asc. 86.3C (66.27St)

"Te tamen, Q. Muci, tam male de populo Romano[1] existimare moleste fero qui hesterno[2] die me esse dignum consulatu negabas. Quid? Populus Romanus minus diligenter sibi constitueret[3] defensorem quam tu tibi? cum te‹cum›[4] furti L. Calenus ageret, me potissimum fortunarum tuarum patronum esse voluisti. Cuius tute[5] consilium in tua turpissima causa delegisti, hunc honestissimarum rerum defensorem populus Romanus auctore te repudiare potest? Nisi forte hoc dicturus es te,[6] quo tempore cum L.

[1] male de p. R. *Gronovius*: malecie tr. *codd.*
[2] hesterna: *corr. ed. Ald.*
[3] constituere: *corr. Baiter*
[4] *suppl. Gronovius*
[5] tu et: *corr. Orelli*
[6] es (*Manutius*) te (*Stangl*): est *codd.*

9 F 26 [= F 24] Asconius

"Are you unaware that I was returned first as praetor and that by leave of your competitors and by a combination of centuries and above all by my kindness you were lifted from last to third place?"[1]

[1] Such maneuvers were evidently legal; see further Hall 1964, 287–90; Staveley 1972, 184; Ryan 2001, 408–13.

9 F 27 [= F 25] Asconius

"As for you, however, Q. Mucius, who yesterday declared me unworthy of the consulship, I am annoyed that you have such a poor opinion of the Roman people.[1] Tell me: would the Roman people be less careful in appointing a defender for itself than you for yourself? When L. Calenus was a plaintiff accusing you of theft, you wanted me in particular to be the protector of your fortunes.[2] Can the Roman people reject on your authority this man as defender of their most honorable affairs, the man whose counsel you yourself selected in your most disreputable case? Unless perchance you are going to claim that when you reached a settlement over the matter of theft with L.

[1] There is an implied contrast: Cicero's annoyance is not with Mucius' poor opinion of himself but with his poor opinion of the Roman people, since Mucius' opposition to his election implies that they are unworthy of the kind of protection Cicero had afforded Mucius in a lawsuit.   [2] The plaintiff L. Fufius Calenus may be the man who testified against Verres according to *Verr.* 2.2.23 and the brother of Q. Fufius Calenus (cos. 47); cf. Münzer, *RE* s.v. Fufius 8. Similarly, at *Red. pop.* 11 Cicero points out that he had defended another opponent, A. Gabinius.

Caleno furti depectus sis,[7] eo tempore in me tibi parum
esse auxili vidisse."[8]

[7] detectus sit: *corr. Kiessling-Schoell*
[8] vidisset: *corr. ed. Ald.*

9 F 28 Asc. 93.11C (72.7St)

"Qui postea quam illo ⟨quo⟩[1] conati erant Hispaniensi
pugiunculo nervos incidere civium Romanorum non
potuerunt, duas uno tempore conantur in rem publicam
sicas destringere."

[1] *add. Mommsen*

Calenus, at that time you saw me providing you too little assistance."[3]

[3] Nothing more is known about the case than is stated here; cf. Crawford 1984, 75; *TLRR* 213. A conviction for theft entailed *infamia*, a legal status that excluded one from certain privileges of citizenship, such as the holding of public office (cf. Mommsen 1899, 754); hence, Cicero's reference to "your most disreputable case." Kaser 1956, 251–52n139, collects similar expressions.

9 F 28 [= F 26] Asconius

"After they were unable to sever the sinews of Roman citizens by means of that Spanish stiletto with which they had tried, they are attempting simultaneously to unsheathe two daggers against the republic."[1]

[1] Asconius (93.10, 15–17) identifies "they" simply as "wicked citizens," the "Spanish stiletto" as Cn. Piso, and the "two daggers" as Catiline and Antonius; this description is also applied to his opponents at Q. Cic. (?), *Comment. pet.* 12 (Ramsey forthcoming on Asc. 93C argues that Cicero used the phrase "wicked citizens" [*mali cives*] in his speech). Cn. Piso governed Nearer Spain as propraetor in 65–64 and was murdered there by Spanish cavalrymen; cf. *MRR* 2:159 and 163. The appointment is said to have been supported by Crassus in the expectation that he would counter Pompey's interests, and some attributed his assassination to Pompey's machinations (Sall. *Cat.* 19); cf. also Suet. *Iul.* 9.3. However, Seager 1964, 346, argues that Piso's activity in Spain had no sinister purpose. The metaphorical use of "dagger" involving Catiline continues at *Mil.* 37, where Cicero speaks of "the dagger he (Clodius) had received from Catiline."

CICERO

9 F 29 Asc. 93.18C (72.12St)

Hunc vos scitote Licinium[1] gladiatorem iam immisisse
†lapillum†[2] Catilinae †iudic quā Q. ue† Curium[3] hominem quaestorium.[4]

[1] hunc . . . Licinium: *cf. Verr. 2.5.111: hunc scitote fuisse Hera-cleum*

[2] lapillum *S¹*: capillum *PM*

[3] iudic quā Q. ueturiū *S*: iudic quā Q. ue curiū *P*: iudic quāque
uecurium *M*: iudicemque Curium *Ramsey*

[4] quaestorium: quaestuarium *Schoell*

9 F 29 [= F 27] Asconius

"Be aware that this Licinius, a cutthroat, has already released Catiline's sling bolt (?) . . . Curius, a man of quaestorian rank."[1]

[1] The reference "this Licinius" requires that he was previously mentioned. This man is otherwise unknown (not in the *RE*). He is unlikely to be a literal gladiator, since gladiators generally had foreign names; the metaphorical sense "cutthroat" is more likely. Thus, Catiline was said to be "living with actors and cutthroats": Q. Cic. (?), *Comment. pet.* 10. The following text is corrupt. If *lapillum* (sling bolt) is right, it might possibly be a bold metaphor; cf. F 28, where Cn. Piso is alluded to as "that Spanish stiletto." After the corruption there seems to be a reference to one Curius, whom Asconius (93.21–23) identifies as a notorious gambler (it is possible, however, that Asconius has confused this man with the gambler Manius Curius, referred to in *Phil.* 5.13 and Quint. *Inst.* 6.3.72). Possibly, this Curius should be identified with Q. Curius, the later Catilinarian conspirator, named as a member of the senate by Sall. *Cat.* 17.3 (cf. Q. Cic. [?], *Comment. pet.* 10, declaring him to be "in the senate" [*in curia*]). If this Curius is the same man who was expelled from the senate in 70 (*MRR* 2:126), possibly he was reelected quaestor in the meantime. The addition of *quaestorium* (of quaestorian rank) is odd, however, since in no other speech before the senate does Cicero mention the rank of a fellow senator, except in connection with official duties as serving consul, praetor, etc.; hence, Schoell conjectured *quaestuarium* "acting for financial gain." Cf. detailed discussion by Bur 2013.

10 PRO Q. GALLIO

After serving as aedile in 67 and praetor in 65 (when he presided at C. Cornelius' trial: MRR 2:144 and 158; TLRR 209; 5–6 T 11.7), Q. Gallius was charged with corrupt electioneering the following year by M. Calidius, a skilled advocate (FRLO 140; Brut. 274–78; David 1992, 821–22), perhaps to avenge his father's conviction when he was prosecuted by Gallius (T 4). Calidius included in the charge an attempt on his own life (TLRR 214). Gallius was one of four clients who are identified as men influential in elections and members of clubs whom Cicero had agreed to represent in the run-up to the consular elections of 64 (5–6 T 1). The matter seems to have come to trial after the election (Asc. 88.5C).[1] The point that emerges most clearly from the fragments is that Cicero made light of the charge of attempted murder by calling attention to Calidius' matter-of-fact delivery (T 2, F 6). There were also remarks on the social and cultural milieu of the prosecutor, including a description of the scene in the aftermath of a luxurious banquet (F 1), criticism of an ignorant poet (F 2) and of someone (the prosecutor?) obtruding a Greek word (F 3). It is clear that Cicero is seeking to exploit cultural prejudices but difficult to say how he packaged the mate-

10 ON BEHALF OF Q. GALLIUS
(64 BC, AFTER NO. 9)

rial in a coherent case. After the trial, Gallius disappears from the historical record. This, together with the fact that Calidius was prosecuted by two Gallii[2] in 51 for corruption in canvassing for the consulate that year (Caelius at Fam. 8.4.[81].1; TLRR 330), suggests that Q. Gallius was convicted, and his sons sought to avenge their father's fate, thus continuing the vendetta between the families (cf. T 4; for parallels, see on 5 F 11; TLRR 71).

---

[1] When Asconius writes *quem postea reum ambitus defendit* (whom he afterward defended on a charge of electoral malpractice: T 3), *postea* would most straightforwardly mean "after this speech," i.e., the speech *In a White Toga* (for this usage cf. Asc. 93.21C). However, Sidoti and Cheminade 2016, 373n17, and Tatum 2018, 233, take it to mean "after the incident with the gladiators" Asconius has just cited; Tatum therefore dates the trial to "late 66." But if, as Asconius surmised, the incident of the gladiators occurred in 66, when Gallius was standing for the praetorship (see below), the trial could hardly have occurred before the incident, so *postea* would be redundant; cf. also Briscoe 2019, 172 with further references.

[2] Namely, M. (pr. by 44) and Q. (pr. 43) Gallius (the younger): Vonder Mühll, *RE* s.v. Gallius 5 and 7.

10 T 1 = 5–6 T 1 = 8 T 1

10 T 2 Cic. *Brut.* 277

Quin etiam memini, cum in accusatione sua Q. Gallio crimini dedisset [*sc.* M. Calidius] sibi eum venenum para-
visse idque a se esse deprensum seseque chirographa tes-
tificationes indicia quaestiones manifestam rem deferre
diceret deque eo crimine accurate et exquisite disputavis-
set, me in respondendo, cum essem argumentatus quantum res ferebat, hoc ipsum etiam posuisse pro argumento,
quod ille, cum pestem capitis sui, cum indicia mortis se
comperisse manifesto et manu tenere diceret, tam solute
egisset, tam leniter, tam oscitanter.

10 T 3 Asc. 88.5C (68.20 St)

Q. Gallium, quem postea reum ambitus defendit, signifi-

10 T 1 = 5–6 T 1 = 8 T 1

10 T 2 [= T 3] Cicero, *Brutus*

Moreover, I remember that, in the course of his prosecution speech, he [M. Calidius] charged Q. Gallius with having prepared poison for him and said that he had detected this and that he was presenting handwritten documents, attestations, proofs, and the results of interrogations under torture, an open-and-shut case, and argued carefully and meticulously about that charge.[1] In my reply, when I had argued how great a burden the charge required, I even used this very point as an argument, that although he claimed a threat to his own life and that he had obtained clear evidence of assassination and had it in hand, he had argued so languidly, so gently, and with such boredom.[2]

[1] For M. Calidius' speech, see *FRLO* 140 F 3–6 (our passage = F 3).

[2] Val. Max. 8.10.3 depends on this passage plus the following F 6; cf. Bloomer 1992, 200–201; Briscoe 2019, 172. For Cicero's critique of Calidius' style, cf. Aubert 2010, 105–6, as well as Douglas 1955, who cautions against classifying Calidius an Atticist on grounds of delivery; van den Berg 2021, 179, labels him a "proto-Atticist."

10 T 3 [= T 2] Asconius

He seems to be referring to Q. Gallius, whom he afterward defended on a charge of corrupt electioneering.[1] For

[1] For the reference of "afterward" (*postea*), see on the introduction to this speech.

care videtur. Hic enim cum esset praeturae candidatus,
quod in aedilitate quam ante annum gesserat bestias[1] non
habuerat, dedit gladiatorium ⟨munus⟩[2] sub titulo patri[3] se
id dare.

[1] vertias: *corr. Manutius*
[2] *suppl. Clark; cf. Asc. 31.7C*
[3] patris: *corr. Manutius*

10 T 4 Ps.-Asc. ad *Verr.* 1.38 (219.3St)

Q. Calidius damnatus dixerit, minoris sestertium tricies:
Q. Calidius, M. Calidi oratoris pater, ex praetura Hispaniensi accusatus a Gallio, pro quo postea Cicero dixit . . .

when he was a candidate for the praetorship, since he had not presented a show of wild beasts during the aedileship he held the previous year, he offered a gladiatorial show under the pretext that he was giving it in honor of his father.[2]

[2] A comment on 9 F 8. Asconius' identification of Gallius as the man mentioned there appears to be mistaken, however; see ad loc. In any case, Gallius was aedile in 67 (*MRR* 2:144), so the games will have occurred in 66. Gallius' father is otherwise unattested (not in the *RE*).

10 T 4 Pseudo-Asconius on Cicero, *Verrine Orations*

Upon being convicted, Q. Calidius said that for less than three million sesterces: Q. Calidius, the father of the orator M. Calidius, was indicted on the basis of his praetorship in Spain by Gallius, on whose behalf Cicero later pleaded . . .[1]

[1] Q. Calidius was plebeian tribune in 98, praetor in 79, propraetor in Nearer Spain 78: *MRR* 2:5, 83 (where "C." should be corrected to "Q."), 86; cf. Münzer, *RE* s.v. Calidius 5. For his trial in 77, cf. *TLRR* 139. According to Cicero, after his conviction Q. Calidius launched this sardonic quip about the cheap bribes paid to the jurors.

10 T 5 Iul. Sev. *Praec. rhet*. 11, p. 91.8 Castelli Montanari (*RLM* 360.29)

Propositis quibus responsuri sumus, quaerendum nobis erit an inter se comparata repugnantia sint, ut suis armis conruant, ut Cicero . . . Similiter pro Gallio, ubi accustor reo[1] pecunias obiecit; ibi enim dum singula inter se conparat, alterum altero Tullius diluit.

[1] reo *Halm*: tres *AV*: in se *EFP*

10 F 1a Quint. *Inst.* 8.3.66

Interim ex pluribus efficitur illa quam conamur exprimere facies, ut est apud eundem (namque ad omnium ornandi virtutum exemplum vel unus sufficit) in descriptione convivii luxuriosi: "Videbar videre alios intrantis, alios autem exeuntis, quosdam ex vino vacillantis, quosdam hesterna ex potatione oscitantis. Humus erat inmunda, lutulenta vino, coronis languidulis et spinis cooperta piscium."

10 T 5 Iulius Severianus, *Precepts on the Art of Rhetoric*

Once the points have been set out that we are going to answer, we have to ask whether, when they are compared against each other, they are at odds so that they collapse by their own weaponry, as for instance Cicero . . . Similarly, in *On Behalf of Gallius*, where the prosecutor made financial accusations against the defendant: there, in comparing point against point, Tullius refuted one by means of the other.[1]

[1] The financial charges evidently pertained to the alleged corrupt electioneering. Cicero used a similar tactic of offsetting one charge against another in the defense of Oppius (3 T 3).

10 F 1a [= *F 1c] Quintilian, *The Orator's Education*

Sometimes the picture that we are trying to sketch is made up of several elements, as for instance in the same author (for he alone suffices to exemplify all excellences of ornament) in the description of a luxurious dinner party: "I thought I saw some people entering, others exiting; some staggering from wine, others nodding off from yesterday's drinking party. The ground was fouled, pooled with wine and covered with languid little garlands and fishbones."[1]

[1] Iulius Victor, *Ars rhetorica* 90.14 Giomini-Celentano (= *RLM* 436.22), depends on this passage. All three relevant witnesses for this fragment are, exceptionally, printed separately so as to make clear the stages of transmission and the reason for deletion of matter in F 1c.

10 F 1b Quint. *Inst.* 11.3.165

Mollior nonnumquam cum reprensione diversae partis imitatio: "Videbar videre alios intrantis, alios autem exeuntis, quosdam ex vino vacillantis" . . .

10 F 1c Aq. Rom. *Fig.* 9.12 Elice (*RLM* 23.12)

⟨Λεπτολογία⟩[1] . . . tale pro Gallio de convivio luxurioso: "Fit clamor, fit convicium mulierum, fit[2] symphoniae cantus. Videbar mihi videre alios intrantes, alios autem exeuntes, partim ex vino vacillantes, partim ⟨ex⟩[3] hesterna potatione[4] oscitantes. [Versabatur inter hos Gallius unguentis oblitus, redimitus coronis.][5] Humus erat lutulenta vino, coronis languidulis et spinis cooperta piscium."

[1] *in mg. Stephanus*
[2] fit . . . fit . . . fit *Ruhnken*: ut . . . ut . . . ut *codd.*
[3] *supplevimus, monente Halm*
[4] potione *codd.*: *corr. Halm*
[5] *seclusimus, monente Russell, vel fort.* Calidius *pro* Gallius *legendum*

10 F 2 Hieron. *Ep.* 52.8

Marcus Tullius . . . in oratione pro Quinto Gallio quid de favore vulgi et de imperitis contionatoribus loquatur attende: "His autem ludis—loquor enim quae sum ipse nuper expertus—unus quidam poeta dominatur, homo

10 F 1b [= *F 1d] Quintilian, *The Orator's Education*

Sometimes there is a depiction of effeminacy combined with criticism of the other side: "I thought I saw some people entering, others exiting; some staggering from wine" . . .

10 F 1c [= F 1a] Aquila of Rome, *On Figures*

Subtlety . . . For instance, in *On Behalf of Gallius* apropos of a luxurious dinner party: "There is a shout, the voices of women quarreling, the strains of a band. I thought I saw some people entering, others exiting; some staggering from wine, others nodding off from yesterday's drinking party.[1] The ground was pooled with wine and covered with languid little garlands and fishbones."

[1] At this point the following sentence appears: "Among them Gallius was going about, smeared with perfumes, his hair bound with garlands." Russell 2001, 3:376–77n86, is skeptical, however, since this sentence is missing in the other citations, and, according to Quintilian's remarks at F 1b, the scene sought to portray the opposing counsel negatively. Hence, the sentence is deleted here, but alternatively *Gallius* might be an error for *Calidius*, given the similarity of the names and the preceding mention of Gallius. Similarly, Cicero depicts Piso's luxurious lifestyle in order to discredit his claim to philosophical austerity (*Pis.* 67–71).

10 F 2 Jerome, *Letters*

Hear what Marcus Tullius . . . says about the favor of the masses and about ignorant assembly speakers in his speech *On Behalf of Quintus Gallius*: "At the recent games—I am speaking of what I myself have just experienced—one particular poet holds sway, a highly literate fellow. He creates

perlitteratus, cuius sunt illa convivia poetarum ac philoso-
phorum, cum facit Euripiden et Menandrum inter se et
alio loco Socraten atque Epicurum disserentes, quorum
aetates non annis sed saeculis scimus fuisse disiunctas.
Atque his quantos plausus et clamores movet! Multos
enim condiscipulos habet in theatro qui simul litteras non
didicerunt."

10 F 3 Non. *Comp. doct.* 88L

LOGI, a Graeco sermone, dicta ridicula et contemnenda.
Cicero pro Gallio: "Ego te certo scio omnes logos, qui
ludis dicti sunt, animadvertisse."

10 F 4 Eugraph. *Comm. in Ter.* Eun. 235 (102.25
Wessner)

HOMINEM HAUD INPURUM: non malum; inpuros enim
crudeles et saevos appellant, unde et spurcos dicebant
saevissimos, ut Tullius in Galliana: "qui[1] spurce dictum
commemorarent in libera civitate."

[1] in Galliana qui *Wessner*: in gallia aqua *codd.*

banquets of poets and philosophers in which he depicts
Euripides and Menander and in another passage Socrates
and Epicurus holding converse, men whose lifetimes we
know were separated not by years but ages. And with these
scenes, what great applause and shouts he stirs! For he has
many fellow students in the theater who have all together
failed to learn their A, B, Cs."[1]

[1] Cf. Hilberg 1905, suggesting that the author of these anach-
ronistic banquets was an Epicurean.

10 F 3 Nonius Marcellus, *Compendium of Learning*

LOGI, from the Greek, things said that are ridiculous and
contemptible. Cicero, *On Behalf of Gallius*: "I know for a
fact that you paid attention to all the *mots* [*logos*] that were
uttered at the games."[1]

[1] Cicero seems to belittle the prosecutor's report of gossip,
possibly in preparation for F 4.

10 F 4 [= F 5] Eugraphius, *Commentary on Terence*

HARDLY A VILE MAN: not a bad one. For they call cruel
and savage men vile; hence they called utterly savage men
foul, as Tullius does in the defense of Gallius: "who mentioned that it was a foul thing to say in a free community."[1]

[1] The subject will be the prosecutors (in which case this fragment supplements *FRLO* 140). It has been conjectured that during his games Gallius made some seditious remarks that the prosecution used to stir prejudice against him: Vonder Mühll, *RE*
7.1:672.35–42. For the situation cf. *Planc.* 33, where Cicero must
likewise address the prosecutor's complaints about offensive remarks made by his client.

10 F 5 Charis. 179.12 Barw. (*GL* 1.141.29)

Poematorum et in II et in III idem Varro adsidue dicit et
his poematis, tam quam nominativo hoc poematum sit et
non hoc poema . . . Itaque Cicero pro Gallio "poematorum" et in Oratore "poematis" dixit.

10 F 6 Cic. *Brut.* 278 (~ Quint. *Inst.* 11.3.155)

"Tu istuc, M. Calidi, nisi fingeres, sic ageres? Praesertim
cum ista eloquentia alienorum hominum pericula defendere acerrume soleas, tuum neglegeres? Ubi dolor, ubi

---

[1] There is a similar contrast of attitudes toward the treatment
of others and of himself at 9 F 6. An anecdote is told of Demosthenes' skepticism that a would-be client had suffered injuries
because he failed to show the expected outrage (Plut. *Vit. Dem.*

10 F 5 [= F 4] Charisius, *Handbook of Grammar*

Both in the second and in the third book Varro continually uses the forms *poematorum* [of poems] and *his poematis* [these poems], as if it were *hoc poematum* [this poem] in the nominative and not *hoc poema* . . . Accordingly, Cicero uses the forms *poematorum* in *On Behalf of Gallius* and *poematis* in the *Orator* (§§70, 201, 227).[1]

[1] A reference to Varro's three-book treatise *On poems* (*De poematis*); cf. Varro, *GRF* pp. 192–93 (with Dahlmann 1953, 96–97, confirming the reference to *On Poems* and explaining the oddity that Charisius fails to cite Book 1) and *On the Latin Language* (*De lingua Latina*) 7.2. There was often difficulty in determining declensional forms of words borrowed from Greek. In this case, the older Latin practice was *in poematis* ("in poems": Plaut. *Asin.* 174), possibly to match the metrical shape of ἐν ποιήμασιν (so Leumann 1977, 456–57), as if from nom. *poematum*; Accius, Varro, and Cicero followed suit; only in the imperial period was *poema* firmly established as the nominative singular; cf. *OLD* and *TLL* s.v. *poema*.

10 F 6 Cicero, *Brutus* (immediately after T 2)

"Unless you were making this up, M. Calidius, would you plead this way? Especially since you are in the habit of warding off the dangers of others fiercely with that eloquence of yours, would you take your own lightly?[1] Where

11.2). For Calidius' confounding of the normally valid system for reading body language, cf. Guérin 2015, 319–21. For the expectation that an ancient orator would perform his anger, cf. Schneider 2000, 501–2.

ardor animi, qui etiam ex infantium ingeniis elicere voces et querelas solet? Nulla perturbatio animi, nulla corporis, frons non[1] percussa, non femur; pedis, quod minimum est, nulla supplosio. Itaque tantum afuit ut inflammares nostros animos, somnum isto loco vix tenebamus." Sic nos summi oratoris vel sanitate vel vitio pro argumento ad diluendum crimen usi sumus.

[1] frons non: non frons *Quint. codd.*

is the outrage, the fiery temper that is wont to elicit words of complaint even from the feelings of infants? No physical or mental agitation, no striking of the forehead or thigh; not even the slightest gesture, the stamping of a foot.[2] And so you were so far from setting our minds on fire that in that portion of your speech we scarcely kept from nodding off." In this way, we exploited the sobriety or fault of an outstanding orator as an argument for refuting the charge.

[2] Cf. the similar criticism of P. Rutilius' self-defense at *De orat.* 1.230, with Aubert 2010, 107–9.

11 DE OTHONE

An impromptu speech delivered before a public assembly called by Cicero as consul on the spur of the moment to meet a crisis. The cause was rival demonstrations at the games of Apollo that threatened to turn into a riot (T 3). The catalyst was the appearance at the games of the praetor L. Roscius Otho (MRR 2:167). Though as plebeian tribune in 67 he had sponsored a law reserving seats in the theater for equites (see on 5 F 57), that is unlikely to have sparked a spontaneous outburst four years later (in spite of T 2 and 3). Rather, he may have been praetor urbanus in charge of organizing the games and thus took a prominent role. In addition, this was a year of low liquidity and rising debt (cf. Off. 2.84 on the demand for debt relief during his consulate). The urban praetor is likely to have made himself unpopular with the plebs by strict decisions enforcing the terms of contracts (cf. Cat. 1.32 on men sur-

11 T 1 (= 12 T 1) Cic. *Att.* 2.1[21].3

Oratiunculas autem et quas postulas et pluris etiam mittam, quoniam quidem ea quae nos scribimus adulescen-

11 ON OTHO[1]
(JULY 63 BC)

rounding the praetor's tribunal, presumably in a threaten-
ing manner; Sall. Cat. 33.1, 5). That would explain the
opposing reactions of the plebs and the equites, a group
that included the moneylenders.[2] Cicero's speech must
have been a model of reproof and conciliation. This may
be the speech Cicero compared to a flutist's change of mode
in order to quiet the passions of inebriated young men
threatening the door of a chaste woman (On His Policies
F 3 Garbarino = FRH 30 F 6).

[1] This is the title used by Cicero (T 1); the author citing the
one preserved fragment identifies the quotation as "when he
called a public meeting from the games," but this was surely not
the title of the speech (for the tendency in the later tradition to
use more generic labels, see the introduction to no. 7); for a different view, cf. Ryan 2016.

[2] This is the interpretation of Ramsey 2021, 19–26.

11 T 1 Cicero, *Letters to Atticus*

I will send you the little speeches, both the ones you request and even more, since you take pleasure in the things

tulorum studiis excitati te etiam delectant. Fuit enim mihi
commodum . . . curare ut meae quoque essent orationes
quae consulares nominarentur. Quarum una est in senatu
Kalendis Ianuariis, altera ad populum de lege agraria, tertia de Othone . . . quinta de proscriptorum filiis . . . hoc
totum σῶμα curabo ut habeas.

11 T 2 (= 12 T 3) Plin. *HN* 7.116–17

Sed quo te, M. Tulli, piaculo taceam, quove maxime excel-
lentem insigni praedicem? . . . te suadente Roscio theatra-
lis auctori legis ignoverunt notatasque[1] discrimine sedis
aequo animo tulerunt; te orante proscriptorum liberos
honores petere puduit; . . .

[1] *post* notatasque *hab. R se: vel possis* notatosque se

11 T 3 Plut. *Vit. Cic.* 13.2–4

Δεῖγμα δ᾽ αὐτοῦ τῆς περὶ τὸν λόγον χάριτος καὶ τὸ
παρὰ τὰς θέας ἐν τῆι ὑπατείαι γενόμενον. Τῶν γὰρ
ἱππικῶν πρότερον ἐν τοῖς θεάτροις ἀναμεμειγμένων
τοῖς πολλοῖς καὶ μετὰ τοῦ δήμου θεωμένων ὡς ἔτυχε,
πρῶτος διέκρινεν ἐπὶ τιμῆι τοὺς ἱππέας ἀπὸ τῶν ἄλ-

I write down to satisfy the enthusiasm of young persons.[1]
It was in my interest . . . to see that I would also have
speeches that could be called "consular." Of these, one
was delivered in the senate on January 1, a second to the
people on the agrarian law, the third *On Otho* . . . the fifth
was about the sons of the proscribed . . . I will see that you
have this entire corpus.

[1] Elsewhere, too, Cicero claims that his speeches are popular
with young people and written up in response to readers' de-
mands; see above, xi n. 2.

11 T 2 Pliny, *Natural History*

But, Marcus Tullius, what appeasement could I offer for
passing over you in silence or by what distinctive mark
should I proclaim your excellence? . . . At your persuasion,
they [sc. the Roman people] pardoned Roscius, the sponsor of a law about the theater, and calmly accepted dif-
ferential seating; on your plea, the sons of the proscribed
were ashamed to canvass for office . . .

11 T 3 Plutarch, *Life of Cicero*

An incident that occurred at the games in his consulship
is a sample of his rhetorical charm.[1] Though the equites
previously mixed with the common people in the theater
and watched together with them in no particular order, as
praetor Marcus Otho was the first to distinguish the eq-

[1] The games are likely to have been the theatrical games (*ludi
scaenici*) dedicated to Apollo that were held July 9–13, and the
incident probably occurred on the first day of the event; cf. F 1;
Ryan 2006, 99–100; Lintott 2013, 151; Ramsey 2019, 235–42.

λων πολιτῶν Μᾶρκος Ὄθων στρατηγῶν, καὶ κατένει-
μεν ἰδίαν ἐκείνοις θέαν, ἣν ἔτι καὶ νῦν ἐξαίρετον
ἔχουσι. Τοῦτο πρὸς ἀτιμίαν ὁ δῆμος ἔλαβε, καὶ φα-
νέντος ἐν τῶι θεάτρωι τοῦ Ὄθωνος ἐφυβρίζων ἐσύριτ-
τεν, οἱ δ' ἱππεῖς ὑπέλαβον κρότωι τὸν ἄνδρα λαμπρῶς·
αὖθις δ' ὁ δῆμος ἐπέτεινε τὸν συριγμόν, εἶτ' ἐκεῖνοι
τὸν κρότον. Ἐκ δὲ τούτου τραπόμενοι πρὸς ἀλλήλους
ἐχρῶντο λοιδορίαις, καὶ τὸ θέατρον ἀκοσμία κατεῖ-
χεν. Ἐπεὶ δ' ὁ Κικέρων ἧκε πυθόμενος, καὶ τὸν δῆμον
ἐκκαλέσας πρὸς τὸ τῆς Ἐννοῦς ἱερὸν ἐπετίμησε καὶ
παρήινεσεν, ἀπελθόντες εἰς τὸ θέατρον αὖθις ἐκρό-
τουν τὸν Ὄθωνα λαμπρῶς, καὶ πρὸς τοὺς ἱππέας
ἅμιλλαν ἐποιῦντο περὶ τιμῶν καὶ δόξης τοῦ ἀνδρός.

11 T 4 Macrob. *Sat.* 3.14.12

Nam illam orationem quis est qui non legerit, in qua populum Romanum obiurgat quod Roscio gestum agente tu-
multuarit?

uites from the other citizens on the basis of rank, and he apportioned a special seating area for them, which they hold reserved to this day.[2] The common people took this as an affront and hissed insultingly when Otho appeared in the theater, whereas the equites received him with applause. The common people, for their part, continued their catcalls, the equites their applause. Then they turned to the other group, shouting insults, and the disorder spread over the whole theater. When Cicero learned of this and came on the scene, he summoned the common people to the temple of Bellona[3] and chided and exhorted them. When they returned to the theater, they applauded Otho, competing with the equites in honoring and glorifying the man.

[2] There are several problems: (1) the praenomen is wrong: this must be a reference to L. Roscius Otho; and (2) his law was a plebiscite that he enacted as plebeian tribune in 67, not as praetor in 63; cf. *LPPR* 374–75 and *MRR* 2:145 and 167. Cicero represents the law as uncontroversial (cf. 5 F 57 above; *Mur.* 40). The mistake made by Pliny and Plutarch is attributable to the fact that this law was what Roscius Otho was chiefly remembered for under the empire.   [3] This venue was chosen for its proximity to the scene of the games, held in the Circus Flaminius, both being in the Campus Martius; cf. A. Viscogliosi, *LTUR* s.v. Bellona, Aedes in Circo; Richardson 1992 s.v. Bellona, Aedes.

11 T 4 Macrobius, *Saturnalia*

Who has not read the famous speech in which he upbraids the Roman people for having made an uproar at a gesture used by Roscius?[1]

[1] Macrobius himself seems not to have read the speech, since he confuses the praetor with the actor Q. Roscius Otho!

11 F 1 Ar. Mess. *Elocut.* 64.4 Di Stefano (*GL* 7.490.23)

Ludi deorum sunt. Cicero cum a ludis contionem avoca-
vit: "Cerealia, Floralia ludosque Apollinares deorum im-
mortalium esse, non nostros."

11 F 1 Arusianus Messius, *Examples of Expressions*

The games belong to the gods. Cicero when he called a public meeting from the games: "The Cerealia, Floralia, and games of Apollo belong to the immortal gods, not us."[1]

---

[1] The Cerealia (April 12–19) and the Floralia (April 28–May 3) were two of the three sets of games for which Cicero had been responsible as plebeian aedile in 69 (*Verr.* 2.5.36); cf. Taylor 1939, reaffirmed with new arguments by Becker 2017, 237–45, against Daguet-Gagey 2013. For the games of Apollo, cf. on T 3 above.

12 DE PROSCRIPTORUM LIBERIS

Under the Roman Republic, the main issue was who would be admitted to the political class, with its associated advantages (cf. Pina Polo 1996, 65). The hardest fate was to have had full rights but for them to be stripped away. This is what happened to the children of the victims of Sulla's proscriptions, and it was perceived as a great injustice.[1] Cicero had sought to tap into this feeling for his client's

[1] Cf. Cic. *Nat. D.* 3.90 (speaking generically) and Plut. *Vit. Sull.* 31.4; Vedaldi Iasbez 1981.

12 T 1 = 11 T 1

12 T 2 Cic. *Pis.* 4

Ego adulescentis bonos et fortis, sed usos ea condicione fortunae ut si essent magistratus adepti, rei publicae statum convolsuri viderentur, meis inimicitiis, nulla senatus mala gratia comitiorum ratione privavi.

12 T 3 = 11 T 2

12 ON THE SONS OF THE PROSCRIBED

(BEFORE THE ELECTIONS, 63 BC)

benefit at Rosc. Am. *153. In his consulship, probably around the time when the elections were to be held, i.e., in July but after no. 11 (see 11 T 1 and on 11 T 3), the issue of the restoration of their rights came to a head and had to be addressed by Cicero, probably in a public meeting (see T 2). Though his rhetoric managed to calm the agitation for the time being, the problem continued to fester until in 49 Mark Antony, acting as Caesar's agent, enacted a law restoring their rights (LPPR 416; MRR 2:258).*

12 T 1 = 11 T 1

12 T 2 Cicero, *Against Piso*

I excluded from the electoral process young men who, while good and gallant, were in such a position that they evidently would have uprooted the constitution had they obtained magistracies; I did so at the expense of personal enmity but without the senate's incurring ill will.

12 T 3 = 11 T 2

12 F 1 Quint. *Inst.* 11.1.85

Mollienda est in plerisque aliquo colore asperitas orationis, ut Cicero de proscriptorum liberis fecit: "Quid enim
crudelius quam homines honestis parentibus ac maioribus
natos a re publica summoveri?" Itaque durum id esse sum-
mus ille tractandorum animorum artifex confitetur, sed ita
legibus Sullae cohaerere statum civitatis adfirmat ut iis
solutis stare ipsa non possit. Consecutus itaque est ut aliquid eorum quoque causa videretur facere contra quos
diceret.

12 F 1 Quintilian, *The Orator's Education*

The harshness of one's speech should in many cases be softened by some palliative, as Cicero did in *On the Sons of the Proscribed*: "What is more cruel than for people born of honorable parents and ancestors to be removed from the state?"[1] And so that supreme artist in the handling of feelings confesses that it is hard, but he affirms that the constitution is bound so tightly by Sulla's laws that it cannot stand if they are repealed. In this way he created the impression that he was doing something even for the sake of those against whom he was speaking.

[1] Whether these words should be taken as a direct quotation of Cicero's speech (Crawford 1994, 205–7) or merely a paraphrase (Russell 2001) is unclear.

13 CONTRA CONTIONEM
Q. METELLI

*When the new tribunes entered office on December 10, 63,
one of them, Q. Caecilius Metellus Nepos, took a strong
line against Cicero and the execution, under his supervision, of the captured Catilinarian conspirators on December 5. He interposed his veto to prevent Cicero from giving
a consul's customary valedictory speech upon leaving office on December 29 (Fam. 5.2[2].7). Metellus explained
that one who had violated the Sempronian law, which
guaranteed citizens the right to appeal to the people
against a capital conviction (LPPR 309–10), had forfeited
his own right to speak before the people (MRR 2:174;
FRLO 120 F 2). When Cicero's private overtures to him
were rebuffed, a vigorous debate between Cicero and Metellus ensued in the senate on January 1.[1] This was followed by a speech given by Metellus at a public meeting
on January 3, in which he variously denounced and threat-*

---

[1] *Fam.* 5.2[2].8. A no-holds-barred attack by Cicero, as can be
seen from the report that he included doubts about his opponent's
paternity; cf. Plut. *Vit. Cic.* 26.9–10; *RP* 3:1238.

13 AGAINST Q. METELLUS'
SPEECH IN A PUBLIC MEETING
(JANUARY 62)

ened the ex-consul.[2] *Cicero replied to Metellus' bluster
with this speech, probably delivered in the senate (*F 10
and 11).*[3]

[2] *Fam.* 5.2[2].8; cf. *FRLO* 120 F 3, assigning Metellus' speech
to a meeting of the senate, but if our speech was a reply to it,
it must have been given in a public meeting. The threat may
have been of prosecution under the Sempronian Law. Cass. Dio
(37.42.3) claims, however, that the senate passed a decree im-
munizing those who acted against the Catilinarian conspiracy and
declared a public enemy anyone who attempted to bring such a
person to book. Possibly this was a response to the current imbro-
glio. Moreau 2012, 40–42, argues that the Clodian Law on the
Life of a Roman Citizen (cf. on 15 F 8) specifically repealed that
measure.

[3] Shackleton Bailey 1977, 1:274, followed by Hall 2009,
239n45, dates this speech to January 7 or 8. At that point, what
was relevant and most on Cicero's mind was Metellus' recent
speech, i.e., his *contio* of January 3. Similarly, Cicero's speech *In
a White Toga* was a response in the senate to an attack made upon
him the day before by a plebeian tribune, Q. Mucius Orestinus;
cf. 9 F 27. For a possible additional fragment, cf. on Unplaced
F 5.

13 T 1 Cic. *Att.* 1.13[13].5

In illam orationem Metellinam addidi quaedam. Liber tibi mittetur, quoniam te amor nostri φιλορήτορα reddidit.

13 T 2 Gell. *NA* 18.7.9

Id autem quod potissimum expetebat [*sc.* Favorinus], "contionem" esse dictam pro verbis et oratione, docui titulo Tulliani libri qui a M. Cicerone inscriptus est Contra contionem Q. Metelli, quo nihil profecto significatur aliud quam ipsa quae a Metello dicta est oratio.

13 T 3 Schol. Gron. ad *Cat.* 4.10 (289.10St)

Lege Sempronia iniussu populi non licebat quaeri de capite civis Romani. Quintus Metellus, in quem postea dixit

13 T 1 Cicero, *Letters to Atticus*

I have made a few additions to the speech against Metellus. I will send you the book, since your fondness for me has made you a fancier of oratory.[1]

[1] This is from a letter dated January 25, 61; in this passage Cicero discusses several speeches he has sent Atticus to read and responds to his comments. He says he has changed an erroneous date (December 3), which might have been in our speech, describing events involving the Catilinarian conspirators (cf. F 9). He also speaks of adding, at Atticus' request, a topographical description of Misenum and Puteoli, but it is not clear how that could have enhanced this speech. Lintott 2008, 20n26, suspects a reference to a different speech, possibly *Leg. agr.* 1 or 3, but in that case the speeches on the agrarian law would not have been new to Atticus in June 60, as is implied by *Att.* 2.1[21].3.

13 T 2 [= T 3] Aulus Gellius, *Attic Nights*

Moreover, I apprised him[1] of what he most particularly sought, that *contio* was used of words and a speech, on the basis of the designation of Tullius' book, which was entitled by M. Cicero *Against Q. Metellus' Speech in a Public Meeting*, which surely signifies nothing else than the very speech that was pronounced by Metellus.

[1] Namely, Favorinus, a Greek sophist (ca. AD 85–155).

13 T 3 [= T 2] Gronovian Scholia

By the Sempronian law it was forbidden for a capital case involving a Roman citizen to be tried without an order from the people. Quintus Metellus, against whom he later

(et est Metelliana oratio), superiore die, cum deprehensi essent coniurati et adducti, omnia decrevit de coniuratis.

13 F 1 August. *Rhet.* 19 (71.1–12 Giomini)

Quia ante actionem et omnino curta et sine capite oratio est quae sine principio ab ipsis rebus orditur, utemur etiam principiis in bonae opinionis controversiis, sed brevioribus et erectioribus paulo et confidentibus et plenis dignitatis, sine iactantia dumtaxat, ne res pariat invidiam, ut est illud apud M. Tullium contra contionem Metelli, in qua exultare videtur contra tribunum pl.: "Ubi vis vel in ipsa consistere?[1] Sic enim ⟨agam⟩,[2] ut opinor: insequar fugientem, quoniam congredi non licet cum resistente." Quod numquam profecto tam magnifice dicere in exordio statim orsus fuisset, nisi et ipsius actoris esset honesta persona et res de qua locuturus erat non improba.

[1] ubi . . . consistere *ed. princ.*: *om. ceteri testes*
[2] agam *inseru. Madvig*

---

[1] The attribution to Augustine is very doubtful; see above, xx and n. 22.   [2] On Cicero's assumption of the persona of an attacker right away in the exordium, cf. Kenty 2020, 31: "this is where Cicero establishes a posture of strength and also where he is particularly careful to establish a balance for himself between aggression, moral rectitude, and wit, if only to build suspense for what is to come." In our passage Cicero also seems to be "enjoying himself, flexing his muscles as a rhetorician" (ibid., 50).

spoke (and there is an oration *Against Metellus*), two days earlier, when the conspirators had been seized and brought in, voted for all matters concerning the conspirators.[1]

[1] The reference will be to December 3, 63, when the conspirators first appeared before the senate to respond to charges; for *superiore die* = "two days earlier" (sc. than *Cat.* 4, delivered on December 5), cf. Dyck 2008a, 243–44. According to the scholiast, then, on December 3 Metellus Nepos agreed with the majority of the senate in condemning the actions of the captured conspirators, though he may have absented himself from the meeting of December 5 that determined their punishment (cf. *Cat.* 4.10). This item supplements the speeches of Metellus at *FRLO* 120.

13 F 1 Augustine, *On Rhetoric*[1]

Since a speech before a suit that begins without an exordium from the facts themselves is incomplete and headless, we will even use exordia in disputes over good reputation, but ones that are briefer, a bit more straightforward, confident, and dignified, but free of boasting, so as not to stir envy, as the passage in M. Tullius against Metellus' speech in a public meeting in which he seems to let himself go against the plebeian tribune: "Where do you wish to take your stand on this very matter? I shall, I think, proceed as follows: I shall pursue him as he flees, since I cannot join battle with him as he puts up resistance." He would surely not have begun to say this so boastfully right away in the exordium unless the person of the speaker himself were honorable and the subject about which he was going to speak were not disreputable.[2]

**13 F 2 *Accessus ad auctores* 43.11 Huygens

Materiam habet [*sc.* Lucanus] in hoc opere principaliter
Pompeium et Cesarem et attributa personarum, quorum
XI enumerat Tullius [*sc. Inv.* 1.34–36, 2.28–31]: nomen,
fortuna, victus, natura, habitus, affectio, studia, consilia,
factum, casus, oratio. Ab his trahuntur argumenta, a nomine, ⟨yronice⟩[1] quod est derisorie, ut "iuste vocatus
Cecilius ⟨. . .⟩[2] et altera vice deceptus est a Greco;" . . .

[1] *add. Huygens*
[2] *lac. ind. Huygens*

*13 F 3 Quint. *Inst.* 9.3.43

Sed sensus quoque toti quem ad modum coeperant desinunt: "Venit ex Asia. Hoc ipsum quam novum! Tribunus
plebis venit ex Asia." In eadem tamen perihodo et verbum

**13 F 2 *Introductions to Authors*

In this work, he [sc. Lucan] has as his major subject matter Pompey and Caesar and the attributes of the individuals, of which Cicero enumerates eleven [sc. in *On Invention*]: the name, fortune, way of life, nature, bearing, disposition, enthusiasms, plans, action taken, circumstances, speech. Arguments are drawn from these, from the name ironically, that is, derisively, as "he was rightly called Caecilius, . . . and he was deceived by a Greek for the second time"; . . .[1]

[1] This citation in one version of a twelfth-century *Introduction* (*Accessus*) to Lucan was connected with our speech by Broscius 1988. If it is indeed a fragment from this speech (which is by no means certain; see above, xxvi and n. 41). Cicero may perhaps, as in *Against Piso*, have followed the exordium immediately with discussion of his adversary's family (cf. *Pis.* F ix–xi Nisbet). The orator implicitly derives the family name Caecilius from *caecus* (blind); this may have been what Nepos' brother Metellus Celer had in mind when he complained that he had been held up to derision by Cicero (*ludibrio laesum iri: Fam.* 5.2[2].1). Cicero pretends not to know what he is talking about. Steel 2013, 160n65, notes this incident as "an early example of Cicero's capacity to offend through his search for a laugh."

*13 F 3 Quintilian, *The Orator's Education*

But even entire sentences end as they began: "He came from Asia. What a novelty! A plebeian tribune came from Asia." In the same period the last word echoes the first;

ultimum primo refertur, tertium iam sequitur;[1] adiectum[2]
est enim: "Verumtamen venit."

[1] sequitur *D. C. Innes*: sermone *codd.*
[2] adiectum *edd.*: *abiectum* A

13 F 4 Gell. *NA* 18.7.7

"Contionem" autem tria significare: locum suggestumque
unde verba fierent, sicut M. Tullius in oratione quae in-
scripta est *Contra contionem Q. Metelli* "Escendi" inquit

the third occurrence soon follows, for he added: "Nonetheless he came."[1]

[1] Though this fragment is not expressly attested for our oration, Quintilian knew the speech (F 9), and other fragments (nos. 8, 10, and 11) are assigned to it on the basis of Quintilian's quotations. This is perhaps the beginning of the narrative. In order to campaign for tribune of the plebs, in the spring of 63 Q. Caecilius Metellus Nepos returned to Italy from Asia, where he had served under his brother-in-law Pompey both against the pirates and in the war with Mithridates (*MRR* 2:148, 160, 164). Cf. Plut. *Vit. Cat. Min.* 20, reporting that the sight of Nepos and his vast entourage returning to Rome caused Cato to decide to canvass for plebeian tribune (so that he could block any moves by Nepos). Cicero evidently seeks to exploit a Roman prejudice against Asia (as degenerate), as did Cato in his prosecution of Murena (*Mur.* 11, 31) or the prosecutors of Plancius when they criticized Cicero for spending time at Rhodes (*Planc.* 84). On Cicero's treatment of Asia and exploitation of anti-Asian prejudices in his speeches, cf. Arweiler 2008.

13 F 4 [= F 2] Aulus Gellius, *Attic Nights*

Contio, however, means three things:[1] the place, i.e., the raised platform from which one speaks, as M. Tullius says in the speech entitled *Against Q. Metellus' Speech in a Public Meeting*, "I climbed onto the platform, and people

[1] Gellius reports the contents of a book by Verrius Flaccus (*GRF* p. 522, fr. 31) in which *senatus*, *civitas*, *tribus*, and *decuriae* were cited as examples of words with multiple meanings.

"in contionem, concursus est populi factus"; item significare coetum populi adsistentis[1] . . . item orationem ipsam
quae ad populum diceretur.

[1] item . . . adsistentis *huc transp. Madvig: ante* item *seq. codd.*

13 F 5 Iul. Vict. *Ars rhet.* 36.15 Giomini-Celentano
(*RLM* 398.12)

Sed illa prior subtilius et limatius philosophicis disputatio-
nibus coartatur; at vero haec inferior oratoriis[1] actionibus
dilatatur, et magis descriptionibus et eiusmodi definitionibus explicatur quae ex pluribus speciebus rem notent, ut
Marcus Tullius Contra contionem Quinti Metelli: "Qui
animum hostilem habet et cuius facta hostilia sunt" et
cetera.

[1] orationis: *corr. Orelli*

gathered";[2] it likewise signifies the crowd of people standing by . . . likewise the speech itself that is given to the people.

[2] Evidently, a narrative of the events of December 29, when, though Cicero's valedictory speech was hindered by Metellus' veto, he was allowed to swear an oath that he had performed his duties under the laws but quick-wittedly changed the oath, swearing instead that the republic and the city had been saved by his sole effort (*Pis.* 6; cf. *Fam.* 5.2[2].7). *TLL* 4:731.43 and *OLD* s.v. *contio* claim that Gellius and Verrius Flaccus have misunderstood an idiom and that *escendere in contionem* means "rise to speak in an assembly." But *escendere* does not mean "rise"; it would hardly have been used unless the underlying picture were that of climbing the speaker's platform; and the phrase was evidently synonymous with *escendere in rostra* (*Off.* 3.80). For the semantic extension to an associated concrete thing, cf., e.g., *hora*, "hour," but also *horae* = "sundial": *OLD* s.v. 1, 2b.

13 F 5 [= F 4] Iulius Victor, *Handbook of Rhetoric*

The former [i.e., a definition based upon the general nature of the thing] is narrowed with fineness and polish in philosophical argumentation; but the latter [i.e., a definition based upon enumeration of parts] is expanded in an orator's speeches and is further unfolded by descriptions and definitions of the kind that identify the thing on the basis of several species, as Marcus Tullius does in *Against Quintus Metellus' Speech in a Public Meeting*: "He who has a hostile attitude and whose deeds are hostile," etc.[1]

[1] This seems to be a step toward designating Nepos as a "public enemy" (*hostis*), as he later would P. Clodius (14 F 20, *Mil.* 78) and Mark Antony (*Phil.* 3.6 etc.).

13 F 6 Prisc. *GL* 2.510.10

Quae vero in "vi" syllabam proferunt praeteritum perfectum mutant eam in "tum" et faciunt supinum, "requievi requietum," unde participium futuri fit "requieturus." Cicero Contra Metellum: "nisi eorum exitio non requieturam" . . .

13 F 7 Prisc. *GL* 2.487.7

Quaedam supina in "si" praeteritum terminantia "i" in "um" convertentia faciunt, sive secundae seu tertiae sint coniugationis; nam quartae in "tum" faciunt supinum, ut . . . "mulsi mulsum" et "mulctum" . . . unde Cicero in contionem Metelli: "permulsa atque recreata est."

*13 F 8 Quint. *Inst.* 9.3.49

Congeruntur et diversa . . . mixta quoque et idem et diversum significantia, quod et ipsum diallagen vocant: "Quaero ab inimicis, sintne haec investigata comperta [id est]¹ pa-

¹ *del. edd.*

258

13 F 6 [= F 5] Priscian, *Textbook of Grammar*

Verbs that express the perfect in *vi* change it to *tum* and form the supine, *requievi requietum*, from which is formed the future participle *requieturus*. Cicero, *Against Metellus*: "It was not going to come to rest (*requieturam*) except through their destruction."[1]

[1] The subject is perhaps the republic (*rem publicam*), and the people are the Catilinarian conspirators put to death under Cicero's supervision on December 5, 63.

13 F 7 [= F 6] Priscian, *Textbook of Grammar*

Verbs that end the perfect in *si* form some supines by changing *i* to *um*, whether they are of the second or third conjugation; for those of the fourth form the supine in *tum*, as for instance . . . *mulsi mulsum* and *mulctum* . . . Hence Cicero, *Against Metellus' Speech in a Public Meeting*, "was soothed and refreshed."[1]

[1] Another probable reference to the republic (*res publica*), perhaps a description of its condition after the execution of the conspirators held in custody; cf. *Dom.* 96: "If I perished along with the good citizens, the republic could by no means be refreshed" (*nullo modo posse <rem publicam> [Nägelsbach] recreari*).

*13 F 8 [= *F 7] Quintilian, *The Orator's Education*

Disparate things are also piled up . . . as are miscellaneous phrases and ones that bear identical and divergent meanings; this, too, is called *diallage*: "I ask my enemies: have these matters been investigated, discovered, revealed,

tefacta sublata [delata][2] extincta per me?" [Et "investigata
comperta id est patefacta" aliud ostendunt, "sublata delata
extincta" sunt inter se similia, sed non etiam prioribus.][3]
Et hoc autem exemplum et superius aliam quoque effi-
ciunt figuram, quae quia coniunctionibus caret dissolu-
tum[4] vocatur, apta cum quid instantius dicimus: nam et
singula inculcantur et quasi plura fiunt.

[2] *del. Halm*   [3] *del. Russell*
[4] dissolutio A: *corr. Russell*

13 F 9 Quint. *Inst.* 9.3.50

Ideoque utimur hac figura non ‹in›[1] singulis modo verbis,
sed sententiis etiam, ut Cicero dicit contra contionem
Metelli: "Qui indicabantur, eos vocari, custodiri, ad senatum adduci iussi: senatum [si][2] interposui," et totus hic
locus talis est.

[1] *add. Regius*
[2] *del. Becher: fort.* statim

*13 F 10 Quint. *Inst.* 9.3.40

Illa vero apud Ciceronem mira figurarum mixtura deprehenditur, in qua et primo verbo longum post interval-
lum redditum est ultimum, et media primis et mediis ultima congruunt: "Vestrum iam hic factum reprehenditur,[1]
patres conscripti, non meum, ac pulcherrimum quidem
factum, verum, ut dixi, non meum, sed vestrum."

[1] *Spalding:* deprehenditur *codd.*

---

[1] Evidently, referring to the execution of the conspirators held
in custody. He similarly emphasizes the senate's "deeds" (as re-

removed, and blotted out by me?"[1] This and the previous example also form a second figure, which is called "unbound," since it lacks conjunctions; it is fitting when we say something urgently, since individual points are driven home and become, as it were, more numerous.

[1] There is a similar list at *Cat.* 3.3: "Since these things have been brought to light in the senate, revealed, and discovered by me . . ."; cf. also *Mil.* 103: "What great crime did I commit . . . when I investigated, disclosed, brought to light, and blotted out those proofs of our common destruction?"

13 F 9 [= F 8] Quintilian, *The Orator's Education* (immediately after *F 8)

We therefore use this figure[1] not only as regards individual words but also sentences, as Cicero says in *Against Metellus' Speech in a Public Meeting*: "I ordered the incriminated persons to be summoned, kept under guard, brought before the senate; I brought the senate in"; and the entire passage is of this kind.

[1] Namely, "unbound"; see *13 F 8.

*13 F 10 [= *F 9] Quintilian, *The Orator's Education*

This remarkable mixture of figures is found in Cicero, in which the last word echoes the first after a long interval and the middle corresponds to the first and the last to the middle: "Your deed is being criticized here, gentlemen of the senate, not mine, and a very fine deed to be sure, but, as I said, not mine, but yours."[1]

gards Cicero's house) at *Har. resp.* 16: "I am not speaking of my deeds but of yours" (*non ego de meis sed de vestris factis loquor*).

*13 F 11 Quint. *Inst.* 9.3.45

Aliquando, sicut in geminatione verborum diximus, initia quoque et clausulae sententiarum aliis sed non alio tendentibus verbis inter se consonant. Initia hoc modo: "Dediderim periculis omnibus, optulerim insidiis, obiecerim invidiae." Rursus clausulae ibidem statim: "Vos enim statuistis, vos sententiam dixistis, vos iudicastis."

*13 F 11 [= *F 10] Quintilian, *The Orator's Education*

As I said regarding the doubling of words, the beginnings and endings of sentences, too, are sometimes in agreement with words that are different but of the same tenor. Beginnings in this fashion: "I would have subjected myself to all dangers, gone to meet plots, exposed myself to hatred." On the other hand, the endings immediately in the same passage: "You were the ones who made the decision, gave your opinions, pronounced judgment."[1]

[1] "You" (plural) are the senators; there is a similar emphasis on the senate's involvement at *Phil.* 2.11. Cf. Berry 2020, 179, who speaks of Cicero's "general policy of claiming the credit for saving Rome but shifting to the senate the blame for the action taken," with the examples cited ibid. 188–89; similarly Robinson 1994, esp. 50.

14 IN CLODIUM ET CURIONEM

This was an invective that Cicero composed, probably in the summer of 61, based on a speech delivered in the senate on May 15 (the "Ides of May": T 1), 61, in the aftermath of Clodius' acquittal on the charge of sacrilege (TLRR 236). Like the Second Philippic, *it is "staged" as a speech delivered in the senate, with direct address of the senators (F 1; cf. *F 33, an excerpt of the delivered speech). Cicero took pen in hand because Curio, who had been Clodius' advocate at the trial, had published a pamphlet attacking him. Cicero changed his mind about publishing it, however, and though he thought he had thoroughly suppressed the work, it somehow leaked to the public during his exile in 58 (had it perhaps been found among his papers when some of his houses were pillaged and demolished?). He feared in particular the repercussions of the attacks on Curio, whose support he wanted to have as he sought to procure his recall, and he considered trying to deny au-*

14 T 1 Cic. *Att.* 1.16[16].9 (. . . = *F 33)

Nam ut Idibus Maiis in senatum convenimus, rogatus ego sententiam multa dixi de summa re publica, atque ille locus inductus a me est divinitus, ne una plaga accepta

14 AGAINST CLODIUS AND CURIO
(SUMMER 61 BC)

thorship (T 2–3). Though the extant fragments include several references to Curio (F 7, 18, 20), the vast majority of them excoriate Clodius. As usual, Cicero is at pains to establish an ethos for himself as a temperate and serious statesman (F 1 and *33). The speech reflects banter with Clodius in the senate about Cicero's Arpinate origin but possession of a property at Baiae (F 19–20; cf. Att. 1.16[16].10; Malaspina 1997b, 136–37). The topics of invective include Clodius' impecuniousness both before and after the trial (F 6, 8–10, and possibly 32) and his general unreliability in financial dealings (F 16–17, 26), but above all his invasion of the rites of the Good Goddess, with emphasis on his feminine disguise (F 21–24) and his alleged goal, an affair with Caesar's wife Pompeia (F 27–28). See further Tatum 1991, 370; Higbie 2017, 159–60; on the subsequent fate of the speech, La Bua 2019, 87.

14 T 1 Cicero, *Letters to Atticus* (. . . = *F 33)

The senate being convened on the Ides of May, when called upon to express my opinion, I spoke at length about general affairs of state, and I deftly introduced the topic

patres conscripti conciderent, ne deficerent; vulnus esse
eius modi quod mihi nec dissimulandum nec pertimes-
cendum videretur, ne aut ignorando stultissimi ⟨aut me-
tuendo ignavissimi⟩[1] iudicaremur: bis absolutum esse
Lentulum, bis Catilinam, hunc tertium iam esse a iudicibus in rem publicam immissum . . . Sed quid ago? Paene
orationem in epistulam inclusi.

[1] *add. anon. apud Victorium*

14 T 2 Cic. *Att.* 3.12[57].2

Percussisti autem me etiam de oratione prolata. Cui
vulneri, ut scribis, medere, si quid potes. Scripsi equidem
olim iratus quod ille prior scripserat, sed ita compresse-
ram ut numquam emanaturam putarem. Quo modo exci-
derit nescio. Sed quia numquam accidit ut cum eo verbo
uno concertarem et quia scripta mihi videtur neglegentius
quam ceterae, puto ex se ⟨posse⟩[1] probari non esse meam.
Id, si putas me posse sanari, cures velim; sin plane perii,
minus laboro.

[1] *add. Shackleton Bailey*

14 T 3 Cic. *Att.* 3.15[60].3

In senatu rem probe scribis actam. Sed quid Curio? An
illam orationem non legit? Quae unde sit prolata nescio.
Sed Axius eiusdem diei scribens ad me acta non ita laudat

that the senate should not collapse upon receiving a single blow, should not lose heart. The wound is such that it seemed to me that it should neither be concealed nor greatly feared, lest we be judged stupid for being unaware of it or craven for fearing it. Lentulus was acquitted twice, as was Catiline.[1] The jurors have now set this third man [sc. Clodius] on the republic . . . But what am I doing? I have practically enclosed the speech in a letter.

[1] The acquittals of the Catilinarian conspirator P. Cornelius Lentulus Sura (pr. 63) were for embezzlement of public funds as quaestor in 81 and for bribery (*TLRR* 130, 219); Catiline's were for extortion as governor of Africa and for murder (*TLRR* 212, 217).

14 T 2 [= T 3] Cicero, *Letters to Atticus*

I was also shaken by your news about the publication of the speech. If you can, heal this wound, as you suggest. I formerly wrote in anger since he [sc. Curio] had written first, but I had suppressed it so thoroughly that I imagined it would never leak out. I have no idea how it got out. But since I was never in the slightest conflict with him, and since it seems to me to be written more carelessly than my other speeches, I think it can be argued on internal evidence that it is a forgery. If you think it can be remedied, please apply the cure; if the case is hopeless, I won't worry.

14 T 3 [= T 4] Cicero, *Letters to Atticus*

You write that the matter has been properly dealt with in the senate. But what of Curio? Has he not read that speech? I have no idea about the source of the leak. But

Curionem. At[1] potest ille aliquid praetermittere; tu, nisi quod erat, profecto non scripsisti.

[1] at *recentiores*: ac *codd.*

14 T 4 = 9 T 4

14 T 5 Schol. Bob. ad *Vat.* 148.23St

C. CURIONEM, PERPETUUM HOSTEM INPROBORUM (*Vat.* 24): Et hunc L. Vettius nominasse inter ceteros videbatur vel⟨ut⟩[1] mandatae in Pompeium caedis auctorem. Qui tamen Curio honorifice nunc a Tullio nominatur, cum vehementer et aspere laceratus sit ab eodem in oratione qua et ipsum et P. Clodium lacessivit.

[1] *post Mai suppl. Stangl*

in writing to me about what occurred the same day, Axius[1] does not praise Curio so much. But he may have omitted something; you certainly have not written anything except what was the case.

[1] Q. Axius, a senator and moneylender, was a friend of both Cicero and M. Terentius Varro, who included him as one of the interlocutors in his dialogue *On Agriculture* (3.2.1 etc.). Cicero's published correspondence with him comprised at least two books (ep. fr. X.4 S.B. = Non. 819L); cf. Klebs, *RE* s.v. Axius 4.

14 T 4 [= T 5] = 9 T 4

14 T 5 [= T 7] Bobbio Scholia

C. CURIO, CEASELESS ENEMY OF REPROBATES (*Vat.* 24): L. Vettius seemed also to have named him among others as a ringleader of the murder plot directed at Pompey.[1] This Curio is now accorded honorable mention by Tullius, even though he was vehemently and bitterly excoriated by him in the speech in which he attacked both him and P. Clodius.

[1] This incident occurred before the consular elections held October 18, 59 (*Att.* 2.20[40].6; Ramsey 2019, 219 and 257h). L. Vettius, an eques who had been a conspirator-turned-informer in the Catilinarian affair, now came forward to accuse leading optimates of plotting the murder of Pompey. He died in custody in mysterious circumstances; cf. Gundel, *RE* s.v. Vettius 6; Seager 1965; *OCD* s.v. Vettius, Lucius; Morstein-Marx 2021, 158–60.

14 T 6 Schol. Bob. ad *Clod. et Cur.* 85.3–17 (85.28–86.5St)

1. . . . apud Graecos . . . nominantur, continentia ferme laudes et vituperationes. Non enim rei postulantur a Tullio vel C. Curio vel P. Clodius, sed quoniam habuerant in senatu quandam iurgiosam decertationem, visum Ciceroni est hanc orationem conscribere plenam sine dubio et asperitatis et facetiarum, quibus mores utriusque proscindit et de singulorum vitiis quam potest acerbissime loquitur. Sed enim principium huius offensae fertur a P. Clodi reatu[1] descendisse. Nam visus est in domo pontificis maximi C. Caesaris eiusdemque praetoris incestum fecisse cum eius uxore Pompeia [cum][2] eo tempore quo per Vestales virgines et matronas honestissimas in operto Bonae Deae sacrificium viris omnibus inaccessum fiebat. Unde elapso tamen Clodio magna invidia percrebruit et infamia caerimoniarum, ut senatus decernere cogeretur omni[3] diligentia consulum pervestigandum, si quod esset publicis religionibus inlatum flagitium. Accedebat huc etiam praeiudicium quoddam C. Caesaris ipsius pontificis qui uxorem suam ilico repudiavit. Post quod reus de in-

[1] ratu: *corr. Orelli*
[2] *del. Mai*
[3] omnia: *corr. Beier*

---

[1] The beginning of the passage suffers from a lacuna that seems to cover some reference to display (epideictic) speeches.

[2] This crime previously covered sexual relations between blood relatives or unchastity of Vestal Virgins; cf. Mommsen 1899, 18–20, 682–88; on *incestum* in marriage, cf. Treggiari 1991, 37–39. The senate now redefined it (retroactively) to include Clo-

14 T 6 [= T 8] Bobbio Scholia

1. . . . they are called . . . among the Greeks, containing praise and blame.[1] In fact neither C. Curio nor P. Clodius was prosecuted by Tullius, but since they had had a contentious duel in the senate, Cicero decided to write up this speech, brimming with bitter mockery with which he excoriates the character of both men and speaks as bitingly as possible about each one's vices. But it is said that the origin of this animosity derived from P. Clodius' prosecution. For he seemed to have committed *incestum*[2] in the house of C. Caesar, the pontifex maximus and likewise praetor, with his wife Pompeia at the time when a sacrifice barred to all men was being offered in the secret shrine of the Good Goddess by the Vestal Virgins and honorable matrons.[3] Though Clodius escaped from the scene, great indignation spread, and a stigma attached to the ceremonies, so that the senate was compelled to decree that the consuls should investigate with utmost diligence whether an outrage had been visited upon public religious rites. Added to this was a certain adverse judgment passed by the pontifex C. Caesar himself, who immediately divorced his wife.[4] After this, P. Clodius was put

---

dius' sacrilege in intruding on the rites of the Bona Dea on December 4, 62: *LPPR* 385.

[3] On the Good Goddess (Bona Dea), a fertility divinity whose cult featured a festival of inversion comparable to the Athenian Thesmophoria, cf. Brouwer 1989, esp. 363–70; Mastrocinque 2014.

[4] Cf. *Att.* 1.13[13].3; Suet. *Iul.* 74.2; for Caesar's possible recourse and the attitude he adopted, see Moreau 1982, 26–50.

cesto factus est P. Clodius accusante L. Lentulo, defendente C. Curione patre . . . Verum ita res cecidit, ut in eum multi grave testimonium dicerent: quorum in numero Marcus ipse Tullius interrogatus ait ad se salutatum venisse ipsa die Clodium qua se ille contenderat Interamnae fuisse millibus passuum ferme LXXXX ab urbe disiunctus: quo scilicet videri volebat incesti Romae committendi facultatem non habuisse.

2. Et post haec ab iudicibus XXV damnatus est. Praevaluit tamen ad eius victoriam maior eorum numerus qui absolverunt, nam XXX et una pro eo sententiae latae sunt. Inde igitur capitalis inimcus in M. Tullium coepit efferri et, cum illo anno potestate quaestoria fungeretur, apud populum creberrimis eum contionibus lacessebat; minas quin immo praetendens ad familiam se plebeiam transiturum, ut tribunus pl. fieret, denuntiabat. Quibus minacissimis illius vocibus vehementi et acerrimo spiritu hac oratione Cicero respondet ⟨. . .⟩[4] duorum, tam ipsius quam Curionis.

[4] *lac. indic. edd.*

---

[5] *TLRR* 236: L. Cornelius Lentulus Crus (cos. 49, *FRLO* 157 F 3–4); C. Scribonius Curio (cos. 76, *FRLO* 86 F 8), so designated to distinguish from his homonymous son (tr. pl. suff. 50), who died in 49 campaigning in Africa, as narrated in Caes. *B Civ.* 2.

[6] The distance implies Interamna Lirenas, rather than the closer Interamna Nahars; cf. Lintott 2008, 158n37.

[7] Apparently based on a misunderstanding: Clodius took up his quaestorship in Sicily after the trial (*MRR* 2:180); his appearance in public meetings (*contiones*) occurred in the run-up to the

on trial for *incestum*, with L. Lentulus as prosecutor and C. Curio *père* as counsel for the defense[5] . . . The matter turned out in such a way that many pronounced weighty testimony against him, including Marcus Tullius himself, who under questioning declared that Clodius had come to pay his respects to him on the very day on which he claimed to have been at Interamna, approximately ninety miles away from the city;[6] by this claim he wanted it to appear that he had no ability to commit *incestum* at Rome.

2. Thereafter he was convicted by twenty-five jurors. Nevertheless, the majority of jurors, who acquitted him, lent the upper hand to his victory: thirty-one votes were cast in his favor. From then on, he began to be revealed as a deadly enemy to M. Tullius, and since in that year he was exercising the office of quaestor, he kept provoking him before the people in frequent meetings.[7] Moreover, he kept uttering threats, claiming that he would transfer to a plebeian family, in order to become a plebeian tribune. Cicero replies to these menacing words of his in this speech, with a vehement and bitter tone . . .[8] of the two, both [Clodius] himself and Curio.

trial and was presumably on invitation of magistrates who had the right to call such meetings (a quaestor did not; cf. Messalla fr. 2 Huschke *apud* Gell. 13.16.1); cf. on F 14 below. Contrast Moreau 1982, 121–22, and Pina Polo and Díaz Fernández 2019, 119 and n. 214, allowing the possibility that Clodius summoned the meetings himself.

[8] This lacuna, posited by editors, probably contained "with harsh criticism" (*acerba vituperatione*) or the like.

14 F 1 Schol. Bob. 86.7St

"Statueram, patres conscripti, quoad reus esset P. Clodius, nihil de illo neque apud vos neque alio ullo in loco dicere."

14 F 2 Schol. Bob. 86.14St

"Ac furiosis contionibus indixerat."

14 F 3 Schol. Bob. 86.17St

"Quod simul ab eo mihi et rei publicae denuntiabatur."

14 F 4 Schol. Bob. 86.21St

"Nihil me addere ad alterius periculum."

14 AGAINST CLODIUS AND CURIO

14 F 1 Bobbio Scholia

"I had decided, gentlemen of the senate, as long as P. Clodius was on trial, to say nothing about him either before you or in any other venue."[1]

[1] Under the provocation of Clodius' public speeches (see F 2 and 3), Cicero had spoken publicly against him (in other public meetings), but prior to the trial; cf. *Att.* 1.16[16].1; Pina Polo 2018, 114.

14 F 2 Bobbio Scholia

"And he had proclaimed in wild public meetings."[1]

[1] See T 6.2 with note.

14 F 3 Bobbio Scholia

"He was issuing this threat simultaneously to me and to the republic."[1]

[1] Namely, that he would seek to be adopted into a plebeian family and thus be eligible to canvass for tribune of the plebs; see T 6.2. For Cicero's self-identification with the Roman state, cf. MacKendrick 1995, General Index s.v. "*L'État c'est moi* syndrome."

14 F 4 Bobbio Scholia

"That I am adding nothing to another man's danger."[1]

[1] That is, merely testifying to the facts at Clodius' trial, rather than, e.g., joining the prosecution team. When on trial for treason (*maiestas*) in 54 (*TLRR* 296), A. Gabinius was grateful to Cicero for testifying against him (rather than prosecuting): *QFr.* 3.4[24].3.

14 F 5 Schol. Bob. 86.23St

"Sin esset iudicatum non videri virum venisse quo iste venisset."

14 F 6 Schol. Bob. 86.28St

"Ut ill⟨o⟩ e¹ iudicio tamquam e naufragio nudus emersit."

¹ illo e *Halm*: ille *codd.*

14 F 7 Quint. *Inst.* 5.10.92

Ex faciliore [*sc.* argumentum] in Clodium et Curionem: "Ac vide an facile fieri tu potueris, cum is factus non sit cui tu concessisti."

14 F 5 Bobbio Scholia

"But if the judgment had been that it did not appear that a man had come to the place where he came."[1]

[1] The question was referred to the pontiffs and the Vestal Virgins whether a breach in the rite of the Good Goddess, i.e., the intrusion of a man, had occurred (*Att.* 1.13[13].3), and when they ruled that it had, Clodius was put on trial for the offense. The scholiast explains (86.25–27St): "as if the jurors who acquitted him with their ballots made this pronouncement, not to claim that incest could not be proven, but to deny that he [Clodius] himself was a man"; cf. *Dom.* 139; *Mil.* 55; Leach 2001.

14 F 6 Bobbio Scholia

"When he emerged from that trial like a naked man from a shipwreck."[1]

[1] Suggesting that he was bankrupt after bribing the jury to secure his acquittal; cf. *Rosc. Am.* 147: "whom [sc. the defendant] you [sc. Chrysogonus] expelled from his patrimony naked as if from a shipwreck" (*quem tu e patrimonio tamquam e naufragio nudum expulisti*). Quintilian (*Inst.* 8.3.81), perhaps quoting from memory, offers a less plausible version: "From that trial he fled naked as if from a conflagration."

14 F 7 Quintilian, *The Orator's Education*

[An argument] from the easier, *Against Clodius and Curio*: "See whether you could easily have been elected when the man to whom you yielded failed to be elected."[1]

[1] A reference to Curio's stepping aside so as to allow Mam. Aemilius Lepidus Livianus to be elected consul for 77; the latter had been defeated in consular elections at some time before 78; cf. Cic. *Off.* 2.58; Sall. *Hist.* 1.75R; *MRR* 2:88; Ryan 2001, 413–14.

14 F 8 Schol. Bob. 86.32St

"Syriam sibi nos extra ordinem polliceri."

14 F 9 Schol. Bob. 87.4St

"Creditoribus suis spem ostentare provinciae videretur."

14 F 10 Schol. Bob. 87.7St

"Ingemuit gravius timidior quidam creditor."

14 F 11 Schol. Bob. 87.11St

"Confirmat se comitiis consularibus Romae futurum."

14 F 8 Bobbio Scholia

"That we promised him Syria by special assignment."[1]

[1] Quoting a claim of Clodius'; "we" will be the senators. This should be read in conjunction with the next fragment, Syria being a particularly lucrative province. "By special assignment," i.e., bypassing the usual lottery (see on F 12): the claim seems to have been that the consul M. Pupius Piso, who was scheduled to hold Syria, would request Clodius as his quaestor; for parallels, cf. Pina Polo and Díaz Fernández 2019, 131–32. However, not only was Clodius not given a "special assignment" as quaestor in Syria (see on F 12), but after Clodius' trial Cicero was able to persuade the senate to reassign the province to a different governor (*Att.* 1.16[16].8); cf. Tatum 1999, 87–88. See also on F 10.

14 F 9 Bobbio Scholia

"He seemed to be dangling the hope of a province before his creditors."

14 F 10 Bobbio Scholia

"A certain fearful creditor groaned deeply."[1]

[1] Presumably, when Clodius' claim about Syria was not fulfilled, and he was instead assigned Sicily as his quaestorian province; see *MRR* 2:180 and on F 8.

14 F 11 Bobbio Scholia

"He confirmed that he would be at Rome for the consular elections."[1]

[1] The scholiast (87.12–13St) connects this with Cicero's claims elsewhere in the speech that Clodius embezzled candidates' funds.

14 F 12 Schol. Bob. 87.14St

"Tanto prius ad aerarium venit, ut ibi ne scribam quidem quemquam offenderet."

14 F 13 Quint. *Inst.* 9.2.96 (qui . . . nosset ~ Schol. Bob. 87.20St)

Tertium est genus [*sc.* ironiae] in quo sola melius dicendi petitur occasio, ideoque id Cicero non putat esse positum in contentone. Tale est illud quo idem utitur in Clodium: "Quibus iste, qui omnia sacrificia nosset, facile ab se deos placari posse arbitrabatur."

14 F 12 Bobbio Scholia

"He came to the treasury so far ahead [sc. of the other newly elected quaestors] that he did not even encounter any clerk there."[1]

[1] Referring to December 5, 62, the date on which the newly elected quaestors presented themselves at the treasury to participate in the lottery for their assignments in the coming year; cf. Mommsen 1887–1888, 1:606 and n. 4; Kunkel and Wittmann 1995, 514 and n. 22; Pina Polo and Díaz Fernández 2019, ch. 4 and 133–37 (esp. 136n50). Clodius' haste shows his "excessive greed," as the scholiast points out (87.18St). Presumably his participation in the lottery shows that his claim about his "special assignment" to Syria (F 8) was false.

14 F 13 Quintilian, *The Orator's Education*

The third type [sc. of irony] is the one by which one merely seeks an opportunity for stylistic improvement, and Cicero therefore thinks it is not used in a dispute.[1] Such is the following example that he uses in *Against Clodius*: "By means of which he who knows all sacrifices thought he could easily placate the gods."[2]

[1] *De or.* 3.203.
[2] The reference to Clodius as "he who knows all sacrifices" glances at his intrusion on the rites of the Good Goddess. It is not clear by what means Clodius hoped to placate offended deities, possibly by donations to their cults; cf. *Leg.* 2.19 and 25, where Cicero is keen to remove the influence of wealth from the cult of the gods. In the aftermath of the trial, Clodius seems to have remarked that the goddess was good because she had forgiven him (*Har. resp.* 37).

14 F 14 Schol. Bob. 87.23St

"Cum se ad plebem transire velle diceret, sed misere fretum transire cuperet."

14 F 15 Schol. Bob. 87.30St

"Hanc loquacem Siciliam non despexit."

14 F 16 Schol. Bob. 88.1St

"Accesserunt ita pauci ut eum non ad contionem sed sponsum diceres advocasse."

14 F 14 Bobbio Scholia

"When he said he wanted to transfer to the plebs but was wretchedly hankering to cross the strait."[1]

[1] A play on *transire* in the literal and metaphorical sense. The reference is to crossing the strait of Messina, to take up his duties as quaestor in Sicily (cf. on F 10) and thus get out of Rome (cf. on F 15). As an elected magistrate, Clodius would normally have been exempt from prosecution while in office (Mommsen 1899, 352–53). However, the governor of Sicily to whom he had been assigned, C. Vergilius Balbus (*MRR* 2:180 and 181), may have banned him from the island pending his acquittal in the trial (cf. Mommsen 1887–1888, 1:262 and n. 6); alternatively, the senate may have suspended his exercise of office pending the outcome, just as in early 62 it had suspended the praetorship of Caesar and the plebeian tribunate of Metellus Nepos (*Fam.* 5.2[2].9; Suet. *Iul.* 16.1); cf. Mommsen 1887–1888, 3:1241n2. Morstein-Marx 2021, 107–8, is skeptical of Caesar's suspension, though he admits that the suspension of the praetorship of M. Caelius in 48 (*MRR* 2:273) is a possible parallel.

14 F 15 Bobbio Scholia

"He did not despise this gossipy Sicily."[1]

[1] Perhaps Clodius had said he was glad to get clear of the gossip and backbiting in Rome, to which Cicero alludes elsewhere (*Flac.* 68, *Cael.* 38). For Sicilian backbiting, cf., e.g., the puns on Verres' name that Cicero attributes to "the tongues of the vulgar": *Div. Caec.* 57, *Verr.* 2.1.121, 2.2.19 and 52, 2.4.53, 57, and 95.

14 F 16 Bobbio Scholia

"So few approached that you would have said that he had summoned people not to a public meeting but to stand surety."

14 F 17 Schol. Bob. 88.8St

"Cuius satisdationes semper [indicuntur] inducuntur."[1]

[1] indicūtur induci *codd.: corr. Madvig*

14 F 18 Turin palimpsest p. 115 Peyron

"‹Intel›lego[1] quam[2] in absentem[3] esse dicenda."

[1] *suppl. Peyron*
[2] *fort.* quam caute
[3] abgente *T: corr. Peyron*

14 F 19 Turin palimpsest p. 115 Peyron ("Primum . . . essent" ~ Schol. Bob. 88.13St; "per quem . . . servire" ~ Schol. Bob. 88.22St)

"Primum homo durus ac priscus invectus est in eos qui mense Aprili apud Baias essent et aquis calidis uterentur. Quid cum hoc homine nobis tam tristi ac severo? Non possunt hi mores ferre hunc tam austerum et tam vehementem magistrum, per quem hominibus maioribus natu ne in suis quidem praediis inpune tum,[1] cum Romae nihil agitur, liceat esse valetudinique servire. Verum tamen

[1] inpune tum *T:* tunc (*inpune* om.) *Schol. Bob.*

14 F 17 Bobbio Scholia

"His sureties are always annulled."[1]

   [1] Cf. F 9–10 and 16.

14 F 18 Turin Palimpsest

"I know how one should speak against a person who is absent."[1]

   [1] Evidently, a reference to Curio, since Clodius was present in the senate on the Ides of May: *Att.* 1.16[16].9.

14 F 19 Turin Palimpsest (in part ~ Bobbio Scholia)

"In the first place, this gentleman of unbending, old-time character railed against those who spent the month of April in Baiae enjoying the warm waters.[1] What do we have to do with this baleful and severe gentleman? Today's mores cannot endure this master, so austere and vehement.[2] As far as he is concerned, senior citizens do not have the right to be on their own estates and look after their health even when there is no business at Rome.[3]

   [1] It may be surprising to see Clodius taking on the role of a moralist, but this was, in fact, a persona that he regularly assumed; cf. Tatum 1999, 42–43.   [2] Cf. the characterization of L. Herennius Balbus at *Cael.* 25 *pertristis quidam patruus, censor, magister* (a gloomy uncle, censor, master), who is similarly dismissed as being at odds with current attitudes.

   [3] Cicero cites extenuating circumstances. In this context, he contrasted Clodius as one "dedicated to the desire for all pleasures" (*omnium libidinum cupiditatibus deditus*: 88.18–19St), possibly, as Butrica 2002, 515, suggested, a paraphrase or verbatim quotation from this speech.

ceteris ‹licitum sit ignoscere, ei vero qui praedium habeat›[2] in illo loco, nullo modo. 'Quid homini' inquit 'Arpinati cum Baiis, agresti ac rustico?'"

[2] *suppl. Beier, Schoell*

14 F 20 Turin palimpsest p. 115 Peyron ("ita . . . fuisset" ~ Schol. Bob. 88.31St; "illum . . . suae" ~ Schol. Bob. 89.3St)

"Quo loco ita fuit caecus ut facile appareret vidisse eum quod fas non fuisset. Nec enim respexit illum ipsum[1] patronum libidinis suae non modo apud Baias esse, verum eas ipsas aquas habere quae ‹e›[2] gustu tamen Arpinatis fuissent. Sed videte metuendam inimici et hostis bilem

[1] ipsum *om. Schol. Bob.*
[2] *add. Schoell*

Though others may be pardoned, this by no means applies to the man who has an estate in that place. 'What truck,' he asks, 'does a man from Arpinum, a bumpkin and rustic, have with Baiae?'"[4]

[4] The point was raised by Clodius in the rapid-fire debate (*altercatio*) in the senate that followed the trial (*Att.* 1.16[16].10). This posed a problem for Cicero, since, as the scholiast remarks, he wanted to avoid being considered "either arrogant or overrefined" (*vel superbus vel nimium delicatus*: 88.21St).

14 F 20 Turin Palimpsest (in part ~ Bobbio Scholia)

"On this topic he was so blind that it became readily apparent that he saw what it was not permitted to see.[1] He had no regard for the fact that the very patron of his lust was not only at Baiae but possessed the very waters that had been to the taste of an Arpinate.[2] But behold the fearsome unbridled spleen of a private and public enemy! He

[1] Blindness, as in the case of Tiresias, was believed to be the divine punishment for seeing forbidden sights; Cicero repeatedly plays on the idea with reference to Clodius: *Har. resp.* 26, 38, 48; *Dom.* 104, 129; *Sest.* 17.

[2] A reference to Curio as both Clodius' advocate (*patronus*) in the trial for sacrilege (see on T 6.1) and also purchaser of the estate of the Arpinate C. Marius near Baiae. The scholiast claims that Curio bought the property "on the basis of the Sullan proscription" (*de proscriptione Syllana*: 89.4St). However, Badian 1973 argues plausibly that the scholiast's assertion is a mere guess, that the property is the one attested for Marius at Misenum (not far from Baiae: Plut. *Vit. Mar.* 34.2; Plin. *HN* 18.32), and that it was bought by Sulla's daughter Cornelia, then by L. Lucullus, and finally by Curio; cf. also Hinard 1985, 199.

et licentiam. Is me dixit aedificare ubi nihil habeo, ‹ubi habeo›[3] ibi fuisse. Qu‹id ego› enim non ‹admirer in›pat‹i›entem[4] adversarium, qui id obiciat quod vel honeste confiteri vel manifesto redarguere possis?"

3 *add. Baiter*
4 quid . . . inpatientem *suppl., corr. Schoell*

14 F 21 Turin palimpsest pp. 115–16 Peyron ("Nam . . . tunicam" ~ Schol. Bob. 89.8St; "tu vero . . . ornatus" ~ Iul. Rufin. *RLM* 38.8; "tu elegans . . . potes" ~ Non. 745L)

"Nam rusticos ei nos videri minus est mirandum,[1] qui manicatam tunicam et mitram et purpureas fascias habere non possumus. Tu vero festivus, tu elegans, tu solus urbanus, quem decet muliebris[2] ornatus, quem incessus psaltriae, qui effeminare[3] vultum, attenuare[4] vocem, levare corpus potes. O singulare prodigium atque[5] monstrum! Nonne te huius templi, non urbis [non vitae],[6] non lucis pudet?"

1 est mirandum] mirandum est *Schol. Bob.*
2 muliebris *T, Iul. Ruf. (clausula suffragante)*: mulieris *Nonius*
3 levare *Nonius*
4 mollire *Nonius*
5 adq *T*: at o *Peyron: corr. Madvig (cf., e.g., Rosc. Am. 141)*
6 non vitae *secl. Dyck*

claimed that I am building where I have no property and where I have property was there.[3] Why should I not wonder at an impatient adversary who casts in my teeth what one can honorably admit or clearly refute?"

[3] Namely, at Arpinum. On Cicero's double identity as a Roman and an Arpinate and the rhetorical exploitation thereof, cf. Carlà-Uhink 2017.

14 F 21 Turin Palimpsest (in part ~ Bobbio Scholia, Iulius Rufinianus, Nonius Marcellus)

"It is no wonder that we strike him as rustics, we who cannot have a long-sleeved tunic, an oriental headdress, and purple puttees. But you alone are fine, elegant, urbane:[1] a woman's finery becomes you, a lute-girl's gait; you can put on makeup, raise the pitch of your voice, slim down your body.[2] O unparalleled horror and monstrosity! Do you feel no shame before this temple, the city, the light of day?"[3]

[1] The scholiast remarks that Cicero explains "rustic" and "urbane" with reference to himself and Clodius, contrasting his own "character of sober manhood" (*ingenium sobriae virtutis*) with "proofs of disreputableness and disgraceful acts" (*indicia foeditatis et dedecora*) in his adversary (89.11–12St).

[2] Details of Clodius' feminine disguise recur at F 23 and *Har. resp.* 44; cf. Geffcken 1973, 75–79; Leach 2001. Williams 1999, 160, remarks that "the arresting image of Clodius dressed as a woman . . . seems to have piqued the orator's imagination most, and he seems to have expected that it would have the same effect on his audience."

[3] The temple will be the site of the senate's meeting on May 15, 61 (which one is not specified at *Att.* 1.16[16].9). Cicero takes a similar approach to Catiline at *Cat.* 1.16–17.

14 F 22 Turin palimpsest p. 116 Peyron ("Tu . . . fueris" ~ Schol. Bob. 89.13St)

"Tu, qui indutus muliebri veste fueris, virilem vocem audes emittere, cuius inportunam libidinem et stuprum cum scelere coniunctum ne subornandi quidem mora retardavit."

14 F 23 Turin palimpsest p. 116 Peyron ("Tune . . . accommodaretur" ~ Non. 861L; "cum calautica . . . accommodaretur" ~ Schol. Bob. 89.17St; "cum strophio . . . praecingerere" ~ Non. 863L)

"Tune, cum vincirentur pedes fasciis, cum calautica capiti accommodaretur,[1] cum vix manicatam tunicam in lacertos induceres, cum strophio accurate praecingerere, in tam longo spatio numquam te Appi Claudi nepotem esse recordatus es? Nonne etiamsi omnem mentem libido averterat, tamen ex . . ."

[1] calautica . . . accommodaretur: calauticam . . . accommodares *Nonius*

14 F 24 Schol. Bob. 89.29St (~ Non. 535L, 700L)

"Sed[1] credo, postquam speculum tibi[2] adlatum est, longo te a pulchris abesse sensisti."

[1] *om. schol.*   [2] speculum tibi: tibi speculum *Non.*

---

[1] The scholiast comments that with the use of the mirror Cicero "uncovered his feminine character" (*mores femineos . . . detexit*: 89.31–32St); cf. also F 5 and 21–23. There is also a pun on Clodius' cognomen, Pulcher (beautiful), sometimes used in the

14 F 22 Turin Palimpsest (in part ~ Bobbio Scholia)

"You, who, though clothed in a woman's dress, dared to utter a masculine voice,[1] whose relentless lust for illicit sex was not even held back by a delay in supplying it."

[1] It was this that betrayed Clodius on the fatal night in Caesar's house: Plut. *Vit. Caes.* 10.3.

14 F 23 Turin Palimpsest (in part ~ Nonius Marcellus, Bobbio Scholia)

"When your feet were being bound with puttees, when the headdress was being fitted to your head, when you were struggling to put the long-sleeved tunic on your arms, when you were being carefully fitted with a brassiere, during this entire time did you never recall that you are the descendant of Appius Claudius?[1] Even though lust turned your entire attention away, did you nonetheless . . . ?"

[1] Appius Claudius Caecus (cens. 312, cos. II 296), the first distinct personality in Roman history: see Linke 1997; Humm 2005. Cicero likes contrasting the dour censor with his descendants, as also in *Cael.* 33–34.

14 F 24 Bobbio Scholia (~ Nonius Marcellus)

"But after the mirror was brought to you, you realized, I suppose, that you were far removed from the beautiful."[1]

diminutive form to identify him in correspondence: *Att.* 1.16[16].10, 2.1[21].4, 2.18[38].3, 2.22[42].1. In light of this passage, one might query the claim of Tatum 1999, 43, that Cicero "never suggests that Clodius is lacking in the good looks . . . that his name implies."

14 F 25 Schol. Bob. 90.9St

"'At sum' inquit 'absolutus!' Novo quidem hercle more, cui uni absoluto lites aestimatae sunt."

14 F 26 Schol. Bob. 90.17St

"Quasi ego non contentus sim, quod mihi quinque et XX iudices crediderunt, ⟨XXXI tibi nihil crediderunt,[1] qui ab senatu praesidium petierint⟩,[2] qui sequestres abs te locupletes acceperint."

[1] XXXI . . . crediderunt *add. Buecheler et R. Beck*
[2] qui . . . petierint *add. Leo*

14 F 27 Schol. Bob. 90.31St

"Divortium pontificis maximi."

14 F 28 Schol. Bob. 91.5St

"Stupro scelerato . . ."

---

[1] The scholiast relates these words to Clodius' rumored incest with his sister (91.6–7St), but in this context, dealing with the Bona Dea trial, Cicero seems more likely to refer to the alleged affair with Caesar's wife Pompeia; cf. Butrica 2002, 514. At 516,

14 F 25 Bobbio Scholia

"'But,' he says, 'I was acquitted!' By a newfangled custom, by God, he is the only acquitted defendant to whom damages were assessed."[1]

[1] Alluding to the practice in trials for extortion or peculation that conviction was followed by assessment of damages (*litis aestimatio*): Greenidge 1901, 502–4. Cicero wittily assimilates to such damages the bribes paid to the jurors.

14 F 26 Bobbio Scholia

"As if I were not contented that twenty-five jurors credited me, whereas thirty-one gave you no credit, since they petitioned the senate for a guard and received reliable bribery agents from you."[1]

[1] A pun on "credit" (*credo*) in the senses "believe" and "issue credit"; cf. *Att.* 1.16[16].5–6 and 10; Plut. *Vit. Cic.* 29.8 (a simplified version).

14 F 27 Bobbio Scholia

"The divorce of the pontifex maximus."[1]

[1] That is, Julius Caesar; cf. T 6.1 with note.

14 F 28 Bobbio Scholia

"An illicit affair . . ."[1]

Butrica suggests that, in view of *Cael.* 32, dated to the year 56, "the charge of sibling incest is a later escalation of Cicero's anti-Clodian rhetoric."

14 F 29 Quint. *Inst.* 8.6.56

Aliquando cum inrisu quodam contraria dicuntur iis quae intellegi volunt, quale est in Clodium: "Integritas tua te purgavit, mihi crede, pudor eripuit, vita ante acta servavit."

14 F 30 Schol. Bob. 91.8St

"Quattuor tibi sententias solas ad perniciem defuisse."

14 F 31 Schol. Bob. 91.12St

"Nam L. quidem Cotta."

14 F 32 Schol. Bob. 91.16St

"Ut posthac lege Aurelia iudex esse non possit."

14 F 29 Quintilian, *The Orator's Education*

Sometimes things are said with a certain mockery opposite to what the speaker wants to be understood, as in *Against Clodius*: "Your uprightness cleared you, assuredly, your modesty snatched you away, your previous life saved you."[1]

[1] A sarcastic explanation of Clodius' acquittal in the Bona Dea trial.

14 F 30 Bobbio Scholia

"You were only four votes short of ruin."[1]

[1] That is, if four of the thirty-one jurors who acquitted Clodius had changed their votes to conviction, he would have been condemned by a vote of twenty-nine to twenty-seven; see F 26.

14 F 31 Bobbio Scholia

"For L. Cotta."[1]

[1] As praetor in 70, L. Aurelius Cotta (cos. 65), sponsored the current law governing eligible jurors; see note on following fragment.

14 F 32 Bobbio Scholia

"So that hereafter he cannot be a juror under the Aurelian Law."[1]

[1] For the Aurelian Law, see on 5–6 T 11.6. The scholiast guesses, implausibly, that some of the jurors wanted to return their bribes but would thereby fall below the property qualification for jury service. Cicero perhaps refers rather to Clodius himself, pictured as so impoverished by payment of bribes to jurors that he falls below the property qualification; cf. F 6 and 25.

*14 F 33 Cic. *Att.* 1.16[16].9

"Erras, Clodi. Non te iudices urbi sed carceri reservarunt, neque te retinere in civitate sed exsilio privare voluerunt. Quam ob rem, patres conscripti, erigite animos, retinete vestram dignitatem. Manet illa in re publica bonorum consensio; dolor accessit bonis viris, virtus non est imminuta; nihil est damni factum novi, sed quod erat inventum est. In unius hominis perditi iudicio plures similes reperti sunt."

*14 F 33 Cicero, *Letters to Atticus*[1]

"You are mistaken, Clodius. The jurors have reserved you not for the city but the prison, nor did they want to keep you in the citizen body but deprive you of exile. Therefore, gentlemen of the senate, lift up your spirits, hold on to your dignity. The consensus of sound citizens abides in the state; the patriots have suffered an outrage, but their courage is undiminished. There has been no new loss, but a previous loss has been detected. In the trial of a single desperado many similar ones have been discovered."

[1] This is marked as a conjectural attribution because it is attested for the speech delivered in the senate on May 15, not the invective composed later. It would be surprising, however, if Cicero did not include this or something like it in the written version.

15 INTERROGATIO DE AERO
ALIENO MILONIS

*This speech is, as its title indicates, based on an "interroga-
tion" in the senate, i.e., an occasion when a senator who
has already spoken begs leave to challenge something said
by the current speaker (cf. T 1). The incident probably
occurred late in the year 53 (or possibly early in 52), and
the topic was the (postponed) elections of magistrates for
52, in which Milo was canvassing for consul, P. Clodius for
praetor. Clodius claimed that Milo's indebtedness stood
well above the six million sesterces he had declared and
warned that a person so mired in debt should not be a
candidate for consul since he could be expected to exploit
the office for his personal gain. The extant fragments show*

15 T 1 Schol. Bob. 169.14–170.2, 170.8–14St

. . . et Hypsaeus, quo anno etiam P. Clodius Pulcher, inimicus eius, in praeturae candidam venerat; idem cum
petitioni Milonis adversaretur et comitia multo et vario

15 INTERROGATION ABOUT MILO'S DEBT

(LATE 53/EARLY 52 BC)

Cicero not so much defending Milo as attacking Clodius (again). Besides the usual abuse of Clodius' character (F 2, 21), he highlights his use of violence or the threat of violence in procuring Cicero's exile (F 8, 11, 24) and confining Pompey to his house (F 4, 9–10) as well as an incident in which the two consuls were hit by thrown stones (F 13). He also taunts Clodius with his current political fecklessness (F 17–18, 22–23). The speech can be seen as a warmup exercise for the defense of Milo (for killing Clodius) on April 8, 52 (TLRR 309). We owe all of our twenty-five extant fragments to the Bobbio Scholia.

15 T 1 [= T 3] Bobbio Scholia

. . . and Hypsaeus,[1] the year in which P. Clodius Pulcher, his [i.e., Milo's] enemy, had also come to canvass, for the praetorship. When he was putting up opposition to Milo's

---

[1] Evidently, the end of a list of the candidates for the consulship of 52; cf. Asc. 30.8–9C: "T. Annius Milo, P. Plautius Hypsaeus, and Q. Metellus Scipio canvassed for the consulship."

ambitus genere turbaret, quo magis Hypsaeus et Scipio
consules designarentur, Milo autem repulsam ferret, per
hos dies senatus convocatus est. Apud quem P. Clodius
invectionem sibi non tantum contra Milonem verum
etiam contra ipsum M. Tullium contumeliosam simul atque asperam depoposcit, ut ambitum moveri ab eo diceret, quoniam multis erga rem publicam meritis praevale-
ret, vim moliri etiam per armatos homines criminaretur,
ad extremum longe minus quam haberet aeris alieni esse
professum: nam sestertium sexagies in aere alieno se habere professus Milo secundum veterem consuetudinem
fuerat. Cum igitur obnixe contenderet Clodius non oportere ‹consulatum petere›[1] qui magno aere alieno defae-
neratus praedae videretur habiturus esse rem publicam,
contradixit eius insectationi M. Cicero, qui familiaritate
praecipua Milonem diligebat ob id vel maxime meritum,
quod restitutionem suae dignitatis ab eodem tribuno pl.
meminerat adiutam. Quanto autem odio habuerit P. Clodium, iam compertum est ex orationibus illius aliis quibus
eius vitam moresque dilacerat. Ex iurgio itaque quod inter
se moverant oratio ista composita est; cuius inscriptionis
titulum, priusquam commentari adgrediar, explanandum
puto, non ab re existimans futurum [non][2] lectoribus, si
orationis titulum non indocte perspexerint. Quippe inscri-

[1] *add. Madvig*
[2] *del. Orelli*

candidacy and was throwing the elections into turmoil with much illegal conduct of various kinds in order that Hypsaeus and Scipio might be elected consuls and Milo be defeated, during that time the senate was convened. Before the senate, P. Clodius undertook an insulting and bitter harangue not only against Milo but even against M. Tullius [Cicero] himself, claiming that he [Milo] was responsible for violations of electoral law since he [Clodius] was prevailing in view of his many services to the state; he also charged that violence was being engineered by means of armed men; finally, that he [Milo] had declared far less debt than he had; for by ancient custom Milo had declared that he had a debt of six million sesterces.[2] Clodius, therefore, raised a vigorous claim that one who was mired in huge debt and seemed likely to pillage the state ought not to stand for the consulship.[3] M. Cicero spoke in opposition to his [Clodius'] attack. Cicero had a special fondness for his friend Milo above all because of this service: he recalled that as plebeian tribune, he had aided in the restoration of his [Cicero's] public standing. On the other hand, how intensely he loathed P. Clodius is already clear from his other speeches, in which he excoriated his life and character. This speech, then, arose from the quarrel they were involved in. Before I begin the commentary, I suppose I should explain its title, since I think it will be pertinent for readers to engage in a learned investigation of the title of the speech. It is in fact entitled

[2] Corrupt figures in the MSS of *QFr.* 3.7[27].2 and Plin. *HN* 36.104 prevent us from knowing the exact amount of Milo's alleged indebtedness; cf. Shatzman 1975, 294 and n. 41.

[3] On Milo's munificence, see Tatum 1999, 325n117. On debt as a political liability, see Frederiksen 1966.

bitur *Interrogatio de aere alieno Milonis.* Interrogationis
autem non una species erat, sed variae . . . Tertia haec est
interrogandi species, ut Sinnio Capitoni videtur, pertinens
ad officium et consuetudinem senatoriam: quando enim
aliqui[3] sententiam loco suo iam dixerat et alius postea
interrogatus quaedam videbatur ita locutus ut refutari
posse[4] iustissime viderentur, postulabat ille qui iam sententiam dixerat ut sibi liceret interrogare, hoc est illum
redarguere cuius sententia in multis quasi mendax et ca-
lumniosa redargui posset. Quoniam ergo dixerat Clodius
et minus professum aeris alieni Milonem . . .

   [3] aliquid: *corr. Stangl*
   [4] posse *edd.*: posset *codd.*

15 F 1 Schol. Bob. 170.16St

" . . . ⟨velut Cim⟩ber,[1] animose confidens."

   [1] *suppl. Stangl*

15 F 2 Schol. Bob. 170.20St

"Non pudet? Sed quid pudeat hominem non modo sine
rubore, verum omnino sine ore?"

---

   [1] "To have a face" is to have a sense of shame; Cicero puns on
the literal and figurative senses of *os*. Cf. the similar pun at Sen.
Dial. 5.38.2: Lentulus, the Catilinarian conspirator, spat upon
Cato, who wiped his face and commented, "I will assert to one

Interrogation about Milo's Debt. There is, however, not a single type of interrogation, but several . . . The third is this type of interrogation, as Sinnius Capito thinks, that pertains to senatorial duty and custom. When someone had already expounded his opinion in his proper place, but another called upon afterward appeared to say things that seemed to be cogently refutable, the man who had already given his view would beg permission to "interrogate," i.e., to refute, the man whose view could be refuted at many points as mendacious and slanderous.[4] Therefore, since Clodius had said both that Milo had declared less debt . . .

[4] The scholar Sinnius Capito was a younger contemporary of Varro; *GRF* p. 460 F 6, cf. *OCD* s.v.

15 F 1 Bobbio Scholia

"‹. . . like a Cim›brian with high confidence."[1]

[1] Describing Clodius' manner. If the restored text is correct, Cicero compares Clodius' behavior to that of the Cimbri, a Germanic tribe whose attempted invasion of Italy was thwarted by a Roman victory won near Vercellae in the Po Valley in 101; see further *OCD* s.v. Cimbri; Timpe 2006, 63–113. Such displays of self-confidence by foreign peoples offended the Romans; cf. Cicero's remarks on the manner of the Gauls who came to Rome to testify against Fonteius (*Font.* 33).

15 F 2 Bobbio Scholia

"Is he not ashamed? But what would shame a fellow who not only lacks a blush but has no face at all?"[1]

and all, Lentulus, that they are mistaken who claim that you have no mouth" (*adfirmabo omnibus, Lentule, falli eos qui te negant os habere*).

15 F 3 Schol. Bob. 170.25St

"Sic enim homines egentes et turbarum cupidi loquebantur: 'O virum versutum!'"[1]

   [1] versutum *vel* astutum *vel* vafrum *Stangl*: usuum *codd.*

15 F 4 Schol. Bob. 170.30St

"Male dicere autem? Immo vero domo principem civem vi et metu continere."

15 F 5 Schol. Bob. 171.5St

"Ut quas haberet in vestibulo tabulas refigeret."

15 F 3 Bobbio Scholia

"The poor and those eager for disorder were saying this: 'O clever man!'"[1]

[1] Cicero's characterization of Clodius' followers; cf. *Dom.* 25, 45, 47, 58, 79, 90, 116; *Planc.* 86; *Mil.* 36.

15 F 4 Bobbio Scholia

"To deal out insults? On the contrary, to confine the leading citizen[1] to his house with violence and intimidation."

[1] That is, Pompey, confined to his house by fears of Clodius' violence in the latter part of 58; cf. F 9 as well as Asc. 46.21–25C; Cic. *Dom.* 67, 129; *Sest.* 69; *Har. resp.* 49; *Pis.* 28; and *Mil.* 18. Cf. also Plut. *Vit. Pomp.* 49.2; Tatum 1999, 174. Marshall 1987 argues that Pompey's alleged fear of assassination was calculated, designed to leverage political benefits for himself as Rome's "indispensable man." Seager 2002, 180, doubts, however, that Pompey, so attentive to his public image, would have "courted such a crushing loss of face."

15 F 5 Bobbio Scholia

"In order to revise the tablets he had in his forecourt."[1]

[1] According to the scholiast (171.5–10St), the reference is to tablets recording Cicero's alleged crimes that Clodius posted in the vestibule of his house after Cicero departed into exile, not to the laws that Clodius was preparing in his house according to *Mil.* 33 and 87.

15 F 6 Schol. Bob. 171.11St

"Etenim tria, ut opinor, haec in Milonis personam questus es: de aere alieno, ⟨de⟩[1] vi, de ambitu; duo praeteristi: nihil de religionibus violatis, nihil de incestis stupris questus es."

[1] *add. Mai*

15 F 7 Schol. Bob. 171.18St

". . .[1] adversarii."

[1] *desunt 4 paginae*

15 F 8 Schol. Bob. 171.22, 27St

"Eiciundus est ex urbe civis, auctor et custos[1] salutis otii dignitatis fidei."[2]

[1] et custos *om. 171.22*   [2] otii dignitatis fidei *om. 171.22*

---

[1] A tendentious paraphrase of Clodius' Law on the Life of a Roman Citizen (*de capite civis Romani* [the name is modern]: *LPPR* 394–95), the enactment of which by plebiscite precipitated

15 F 6 Bobbio Scholia

"These, I think, are the three complaints you have lodged against the individual Milo: concerning debt, concerning violence, concerning corrupt electioneering. You have omitted two complaints: you raised none about the violation of religious rites, none about incest."[1]

[1] Cicero adds the two crimes attributed to Clodius himself. "Incest" could refer to Clodius' *incestum* at the rite of the Bona Dea (cf. 14 T 6.1 with note) and/or his alleged incest with one or more of his three sisters. On the latter point, cf. Tatum 1999, 42; Kaster 2006, 409–11; Günther 2000, 235, claiming that politically motivated contacts were tendentiously assimilated to sexual ones. Similarly, Harders 2008, 230–48, argues in detail that Cicero found defamation on grounds of incest effective because of the close (asexual) relation of Clodius and his sisters; cf. also Thurn 2018, 123–26. The violation of family ties is also part of Cicero's depiction of Clodius as a monster; cf. Lévy 1998, 149 and 156.

15 F 7 Bobbio Scholia

". . . opponents."

15 F 8 Bobbio Scholia

"A citizen must be cast out of the city, a man who promoted and guarded its security, peace, standing, and honor."[1]

Cicero's exile in March 58. As the scholiast remarks (171.26–29St), the presentation of these qualities in the third person reduces somewhat the potentially offensive self-praise. There is a similar third-person description of himself in reference to Clodius' law at *Red. sen.* 8: "a citizen who had served the republic very well"; similarly *Har. resp.* 58, *Sest.* 53 and 83.

15 F 9 Schol. Bob. 172.1St

"Includendus intra parietes."

15 F 10 Schol. Bob. 172.4St

"Qui populi Romani imperium non terrarum regionibus sed caeli partibus terminavit."

15 F 11 Schol. Bob. 172.9St

"Nec vero tum timendum fuit cum cessimus."

15 F 12 Schol. Bob. 172.13St

"Eosdem ad caedem civium de Apennino deduxisti."

15 F 9 Bobbio Scholia

"He must be confined within his walls."[1]

[1] See on F 4.

15 F 10 Bobbio Scholia

"Who bounded the empire of the Roman people not by the regions of the earth but the heights of heaven."[1]

[1] That is, Pompey; similar encomium at *Cat.* 3.26; cf. also *Balb.* 13. This continues the sentence begun in F 9. Lévy 2020, 24, remarks that in this passage "he portrays Rome as approaching the realm of immortality," albeit this picture remains "within the boundaries of rhetoric."

15 F 11 Bobbio Scholia

"And there was no need to fear when I withdrew."[1]

[1] Cicero uses the verb "withdraw" (*cedo*) as a euphemism for going into exile, as elsewhere (*Red. sen.* 4; *Dom.* 56, 58, 68, 99; *Sest.* 36, 53). The scholiast remarks (172.11–12St) that the point is to show that he withdrew not out of fear or a bad conscience but to spare the bloodshed that would have been entailed by armed conflict, a point emphasized at *Red. sen.* 33; *Red. pop.* 13; *Dom.* 63, 96, 98, and 144; *Sest.* 46, 49.

15 F 12 Bobbio Scholia

"You led the same men down from the Apennines to murder citizens."[1]

[1] "The same men" implies that Clodius' use of these ruffians was previously described, probably in connection with the devastation of public forests and of Etruria generally, mentioned at *Mil.* 26; contrast the usual view that "Clodius' popular base . . . was almost wholly urban" (Tatum 1999, 144).

15 F 13 Schol. Bob. 172.16St

"Lapidibus duo consules ceciderunt."

15 F 14 Schol. Bob. 172.21St

"Qui multis inspectantibus caput feriebas, femina plangebas."

15 F 15 Schol. Bob. 172.25St

"Est enim, quocumque venit, et reorum crimen et iudicum."

15 INTERROGATION ABOUT MILO'S DEBT

15 F 13 Bobbio Scholia

"They [sc. the Clodiani] struck two consuls with stones."[1]

[1] Namely, when the consuls of 53, Cn. Domitius Calvinus and M. Valerius Messalla Rufus, attempted to hold elections of magistrates for the following year: *MRR* 2:227–28.

15 F 14 Bobbio Scholia

"In full view of many people you kept striking your head, hitting your thighs."[1]

[1] Gestures of astonishment or lamentation; cf., e.g., *Att.* 1.1[10].1, Sen. *Tro.* 119 (Hecuba in mourning). On this trait of Clodius (according to Cicero), see Berno 2007, 78–87. Such public displays of emotion, generally disapproved, especially by a member of the political class, lend color to Cicero's characterization of Clodius as a "madman" (*furibundus*): *Sest.* 15, 117; cf. *Har. resp.* 38–39.

15 F 15 Bobbio Scholia

"Wherever he goes, there is a charge against both defendants and jurors."[1]

[1] According to the Bobbio Scholia, "By speaking badly he brought them into danger of conviction" (*inutiliter loquens adfert illis periculum damnationis*: 172.26–27St). However, Clodius would also accuse the jurors of being bribed to cover up his own acceptance of payoffs (ibid. 172.27–30); the bribery at the Bona Dea trial may also be implied (cf. F 20 and 14 F 6, 25, and 26).

15 F 16 Schol. Bob. 172.31St

"Tuamque[1] praeturam non tuo more differas."

¹ quamque *codd.*: *corr. edd.*

15 F 17 Schol. Bob. 173.1St

"Nec suffragia dabis quibus ostentas."

15 F 18 Schol. Bob. 173.6St

"Nec vero illam nefariam libertatem."

---

[1] This may continue the sentence begun in the previous fragment, as is argued by Loposzko 1978–1979, 158–59; 1980, 91–92. Here he turns from the proposal on suffrage to another plan by Clodius as praetor to recognize the legal validity of freedom informally granted by masters to slaves, as was later accomplished by a *lex Iunia* (*LPPR* 463–64). The possibility was raised (after

15 F 16 Bobbio Scholia

". . . (that) you do not postpone your praetorship, as is your wont."[1]

[1] The scholiast paraphrases (172.35St): "Everyone is amazed that he does not also postpone his candidacy in the current year, as he did once already." At *Mil.* 24 Cicero remarks that Clodius abandoned his intention to seek the praetorship of 53 (his first year of eligibility for that office), choosing instead to stand for the praetorship of 52, because the delayed elections for 53 resulted in a shortened term (and less scope for wickedness, Cicero adds). In our speech this claim is raised, as Lintott 1974, 66n60, emphasizes, during Clodius' lifetime; hence, the attempt of Badian 1964, 150, to explain the claim in *On Behalf of Milo* as a lawyer's trick is unconvincing. Cf. also Morrell 2023.

15 F 17 Bobbio Scholia

"Nor will you grant suffrage to those before whom you are dangling it."[1]

[1] As the scholiast remarks (173.3–5St; cf. Asc. 52.18–21C), this seems to refer to a plan to distribute freedmen, so far confined to the four urban tribes, to rural tribes as well; see further Tatum 1999, 236–38.

15 F 18 Bobbio Scholia

"Nor that wicked freedom."[1]

Peyron and Mommsen) by Loposzko 1978–1979, 162–63; 1980, 97–98, and reinforced by Benner 1987, 130–33; cf. also Tatum 1999, 238–39. It is in this context that the Bobbio scholiast cites 16 F 1, probably a reference to the same plan. Cf. also *Mil.* 87, "laws that would assign us in bondage to our slaves," and 89, "by a new law he . . . would have made our slaves his freedmen."

15 F 19 Schol. Bob. 173.11St

"Quis non meminerit pueritiam tuam?"

15 F 20 Schol. Bob. 173.16St

"Iterum a piratis redem⟨ptum⟩:[1] quo enim nomine appellem eos qui te pretio . . . accepto liberaverunt?"

[1] *lac. suppl. Mai*

15 F 21 Schol. Bob. 174.2St

"Nisi vero liniamentis hominis nomen et figuris positum, non naturis putes."[1]

[1] putas: *corr. Dyck*

15 INTERROGATION ABOUT MILO'S DEBT

15 F 19 Bobbio Scholia

"Who fails to remember your boyhood?"[1]

¹ Cicero dilates on the subject at *Har. resp.* 42 (cf. also *Cael.* 36). Corruption in youth was a standard topic of invective; cf. Nisbet 1961, 194.

15 F 20 Bobbio Scholia

"Ransomed from pirates a second time; for by what name should I call those who freed you upon receiving payment?"[1]

¹ Clodius was captured by pirates in 67 when commanding a fleet under his brother-in-law Q. Marcius Rex, proconsul of Cilicia (*MRR* 2:146). Cicero provides the incident with a malicious interpretation at *Har. resp.* 42; cf. Tatum 1999, 50. Here he describes the jurors in Clodius' trial for sacrilege as a second set of pirates, since they were believed to have been bribed to acquit him; cf. 14 F 6, 25, and 26; *Mil.* 87: "He openly ransomed himself from the jurors by bribery."

15 F 21 Bobbio Scholia

"Unless you think that the name [sc. man] has been given to the outlines and forms but not the properties of a man."[1]

¹ Probably explaining why he designates Clodius as a beast (*belua*; see on F 22), as he had already done at *Sest.* 16 and *Pis.* 21 and would do repeatedly in *Mil.* (32, 40, 85); cf. May 1996; Lévy 1998. The sentence transmitted out of place at *Off.* 3.82 might perhaps come from this context (perhaps preceding our fragment): "For what difference does it make whether someone changes from a man to a beast or bears the monstrousness of a beast in human form?" (*Quid enim interest utrum ex homine se convertat quis in beluam an hominis figura immanitatem gerat beluae?*).

15 F 22 Schol. Bob. 174.6St

"Tum habuisti quasdam formidines, ‹quae›¹ quasi cornua quaedam exciderunt impleta."

¹ *add. Mai*

15 F 23 Schol. Bob. 174.11St

"Non enim viderunt, quos ipsi exturbarant, eos in civitatem restitutos."

15 F 24 Schol. Bob. 174.18St

"Qui armis cessissem vel t‹uis urb›anis¹ vel, ut opinio tum erat, alienis."

¹ *suppl. Mai*

15 F 25 Schol. Bob. 174.23St

. . . invigilavit Tullius ut eum "virum cautissimum" diceret . . .

---

¹ According to the scholiast (174.21–25St), Cicero thus explains why Pompey reconciled with Clodius, not because he trusted him or regarded him as innocent but to ensure his own personal safety.

15 F 22 Bobbio Scholia

"At that time[1] you incited certain fears that fell off, like horns after they had filled out."[2]

[1] That is, in the year 58, when Clodius was plebeian tribune; cf. *Har. resp.* 2. The point is that, as it turned out, Clodius was more to be despised than feared.   [2] The scholiast points out the implication that Cicero assimilates Clodius to a wild beast (174.8St); see on F 21.

15 F 23 Bobbio Scholia

"They did not see those whom they themselves had expelled restored to citizenship."[1]

[1] "They" refers to other plebeian tribunes, e.g., C. Gracchus and Saturninus, who, unlike Clodius, were killed and so did not see the restoration of those whom they had sent into exile, respectively, P. Popilius Laenas (cos. 132), exiled in 123, and Q. Caecilius Metellus Numidicus (cos. 109), exiled in 100: *TLRR* 25; *MRR* 1:575–76. The point that he returned during Clodius' lifetime was already made at *Dom.* 87.

15 F 24 Bobbio Scholia

"I who yielded to arms, whether your urban ones, or, as people then thought, those of others."[1]

[1] That is, the arms of Caesar, who was outside the city gate with his army (*Sest.* 41). Compare *Prov. cons.* 41–47, where Cicero downplays his differences with Caesar.

15 F 25 Bobbio Scholia

Tullius took pains to call him [sc. Pompey] "a very cautious man."[1]

16 PRO MILONE
(EXCEPTA ORATIO)

This is the speech that was delivered at Milo's trial for the murder of P. Clodius on January 18, 52, on the Appian Way near Bovillae. The trial took place on April 4–8, 52, in a shortened format imposed by Pompey's recent legislation; see LPPR 410; TLRR 309. As sole speaker for the defense, Cicero delivered his speech on the last day of the trial; cf. Keeline 2021, 15n70 and 336. According to Asconius, the speech was taken down (excepta) in performance and circulated (T 1).[1] Quintilian's use of the diminutive oratiuncula *(little speech) with reference to it (T 2) suggests that it was short. Dio claimed that Cicero, "having uttered with difficulty a brief speech that all but died on his lips, was glad to retire" (T 3; similarly 50.54.3 and T 4). But Cicero is unlikely to have cited the situation of this speech as demanding an impassioned style (Opt. gen. 10), if he had utterly failed to fulfill the requirements.[2] It seems*

[1] Cf. Dyck 2002.
[2] Cf. Keeline 2021, 16n74.

16 ON BEHALF OF MILO
(SPEECH TAKEN DOWN, APRIL 8, 52)

likely that the accounts of Cicero's total breakdown in per-
formance were invented in order to explain Milo's convic-
tion in spite of the excellence of Cicero's published speech.
Even if that is so, however, it may not be necessary to
conclude that the "delivered speech" was fabricated by
Cicero's enemies.[3] *The roughness, choppiness, and lack of*
polish (T 4, F 1) are just what one might expect from a
speech taken down in performance.[4] *The one fragment is*
quoted by two authors, one offering a bit more at the be-
ginning, the other a bit more at the end.[5]

[3] As argued by Settle 1963, revived by Fotheringham 2013,
6n4. Cf. La Bua 2014, and 2019, 51–54; Morrell 2018: 170n41.

[4] So Keeline 2021, 40.

[5] Cf. Loposzko 1978–1979, 160; 1980, 93. The Bobbio scholiast cites that fragment as "from the speech that was delivered on
Milo's behalf and ‹taken down by scribes›" (the bracketed words
supplied by Rau after T 1); Quintilian quotes the fragment without attribution (F 1).

16 T 1 Asc. 41.24C (37.14St)

Cicero cum inciperet dicere, exceptus ⟨est⟩[1] acclamatione Clodianorum, qui se continere ne metu quidem circumstantium militum potuerunt. Itaque non ea qua solitus erat constantia dixit. Manet autem illa quoque excepta eius oratio; scripsit vero hanc quam legimus ita perfecte ut iure prima haberi possit.

[1] *add. ed. Ald.*

16 T 2 Quint. *Inst.* 4.3.17

Unde Ciceroni quoque in prohoemio, cum diceret pro Milone, degredi fuit necesse, ut ipsa oratiuncula qua usus est patet.

16 T 3 Cass. Dio 40.54.2

Ὁ γὰρ ῥήτωρ ἐκεῖνος τόν τε Πομπήιον καὶ τοὺς στρατιώτας ἐν τῶι δικαστηρίωι παρὰ τὸ καθεστηκὸς ἰδὼν ἐξεπλάγη καὶ κατέδεισεν, ὥστε τῶν μὲν παρεσκευασμένων μηδὲν εἰπεῖν, βραχὺ δέ τι καὶ τεθνηκὸς χαλεπῶς φθεγξάμενος ἀγαπητῶς μεταστῆναι. Τοῦτον γὰρ τὸν λόγον τὸν νῦν φερόμενον ὡς καὶ ὑπὲρ τοῦ Μίλωνος τότε λεχθέντα χρόνωι ποθ᾽ ὕστερον καὶ κατὰ σχολὴν ἀναθαρσήσας ἔγραψε ... Ὁ Μίλων τῶι λόγωι πεμφθέντι οἱ ὑπ᾽ αὐτοῦ ἐντυχών (ἐπεφυγάδευτο γάρ) ἀντεπέστειλε λέγων ὅτι ἐν τύχηι αὐτῶι ἐγένετο τὸ μὴ ταῦθ᾽ οὕτω καὶ ἐν τῶι δικαστηρίωι λεχθῆναι· οὐ γὰρ ἂν τοιαύτας ἐν τῆι Μασσαλίαι (ἐν ἧι κατὰ τὴν φυγὴν ἦν) τρίγλας ἐσθίειν, εἴπερ τι τοιοῦτον ἀπελελόγητο.

16 T 1 Asconius

When Cicero began to speak, he was greeted by a shout of Clodius' followers, who could not even restrain themselves out of fear of the surrounding soldiers. Therefore, he did not speak with his accustomed steadiness. However, the speech that was taken down also survives. But he composed this speech that we read with such perfection that it can rightly be considered the best.

16 T 2 Quintilian, *The Orator's Education*

Hence Cicero, too, had to digress in the exordium when he spoke on behalf of Milo, as is clear from the little speech that he delivered.

16 T 3 Cassius Dio, *Roman History*

Upon seeing Pompey and the soldiers contrary to custom in the court, the orator was dumbfounded and took fright, so that he delivered none of his prepared remarks, but having uttered with difficulty a brief speech that all but died on his lips, he was glad to retire. Some time later, when he had recovered his nerve, he wrote up this speech at his leisure that is now in circulation as the one then given on Milo's behalf . . . Upon reading the speech that had been sent to him by Cicero (for he had gone into exile), Milo wrote back saying that it was fortunate for him that he had not so spoken in court; for he would not be feasting on such fine mullets in Massilia (where he was in his exile) if he had offered such a defense.

16 T 4 Schol. Bob. 112.7St

Sed quoniam et turbulenta res erat et confessa caedes et ad seditionem populus inflammatus et circumpositi iudicio milites et non longe praesidens consul ipse Pompeius obnixe studens in damnationem Milonis, perferri defensio ista non potuit: nam metu consternatus et ipse Tullius pedem rettulit. Et exstat[1] alius praeterea liber actorum pro Milone, in quo omnia interrupta et inpolita et rudia, plena denique maximi terroris agnoscas.

[1] exsistat: *corr. Halm*

16 F 1 Quint. *Inst.* 9.2.54 ("An huius . . . dicere"), Schol. Bob. 173.6St ("De nostrum . . . reprehensio est")

"An huius ille legis, quam Cloelius[1] a se inventam gloriatur, mentionem facere ausus esset vivo Milone, non dicam consule? De nostrum omnium—non audeo totum dicere: videte quid exitii lex habitura fuerit cuius periculosa etiam reprehensio est."[2]

[1] Clodius: *corr. Dyck*
[2] sit *Hedicke*

16 T 4 Bobbio Scholia

But since the affair was disorderly, the murder admitted, the populace fired up for insurrection, soldiers posted round about the court and Pompey himself, as consul, exerting control nearby and resolutely striving for Milo's conviction, the defense could not be sustained: for Cicero himself was unsettled by fear and withdrew. And in addition, another book of pleadings on behalf of Milo is extant, in which one may discern that everything is choppy, unpolished, and rough, in fine that it is filled with utter terror.

16 F 1 Quintilian, *The Orator's Education*, Bobbio Scholia

"Would he have ventured to mention this law, which Cloelius boasts of having devised, with Milo alive, not to say as consul? Concerning all of our—I dare not say the whole plan: see what ruin the law would have entailed, when it is even dangerous to criticize it."[1]

[1] Here "he" is surely Clodius. This will be an argument corresponding to *Mil.* 32–33 that Milo was the chief obstacle to Clodius' plans. The reference is evidently to Clodius' law granting full liberty to slaves freed informally by their masters; see further on 15 F 18. Transmitted "Clodius" in this passage is surely a mistake for "Cloelius," a common error. For Sextus Cloelius as the author of Clodius' legislation, cf. *Dom.* 47, 83, 129; *Har. resp.* 11; *Sest.* 133; *Mil.* 33; Shackleton Bailey 1992 s.v. Cloelius, Sex.

FRAGMENTA INCERTAE SEDIS

F 1 Rutil. Lup. *Schem. lex.*, *RLM* 4.31 (~ Charis. 4 = 370.18 Barw., *GL* 1.282.2; Diom. *GL* 1.446.2; Sacerd. *GL* 6.458.21, all of whom attribute the fragment to Cicero)

Παρονομασία. Hoc aut addenda aut demenda aut mutanda aut porrigenda aut contrahenda littera aut syllaba fieri consuevit. Id est huius modi . . . item: "At[1] huius sceleratissimi opera, qui fuit lucus religiosissimus[2] ‹nunc est locus desertissimus:›[3] nimirum quoniam[4] traditam sibi publicorum custodiam sacrorum non honori sed oneri[5] esse existimavit."

[1] ad: *corr. Ruhnken*
[2] locus disertissimus *Plotius Sacerdos*
[3] *suppl. Ruhnken ex Charisio et Diomede (qui* erit, non *est, praebent)*
[4] quom: *corr. Ruhnken*
[5] honori sed oneri *Stephanus*: honoris sed oneris *C*

UNPLACED FRAGMENTS

F 1 [= F 26] Rutilius Lupus, *Figures of Diction* (~ Charisius, Diomedes, Plotius Sacerdos)

Paronomasia. This generally occurs by either adding or removing or changing or lengthening or contracting a letter or syllable. For instance, . . . likewise: "But by the effort of this wicked man what was a most sacred grove is now a deserted place: no wonder, since he regarded the charge of sacred public property entrusted to him not as an honor but a burden."[1]

---

[1] The destruction of sacred groves was among the crimes Cicero laid to the charge of P. Clodius (*Mil.* 85, with Keeline 2021, 309: "The sacred groves seem to have provided construction material [sc. for his new home on the Alban Mount]"), so this passage could derive either from no. 14 or 15. Cicero's client C. Rabirius had been charged with destruction of sacred groves by C. Licinius Macer (*FRLO* 110 F 4 = *Rab. perd.* 7), but if our passage is from that speech, the grammarians are mistaken in assigning it to Cicero. The (untranslatable) puns are on *lucus* (grove) and *locus* (place) and *honos* (honor) and *onus* (burden); cf. Varro, *Ling.* 5.73, etymologizing *honos* from *onus*.

*F 2 Quint. *Inst.* 5.13.26

Quod autem posui, referre quo quidque accusator modo dixerit, huc pertinet, ut . . . si acri et vehementi fuerit usus oratione, eandem rem nostris verbis mitioribus proferamus . . . [5 F 31] et protinus cum quadam defensione, ut, si pro luxurioso dicendum sit: "Obiecta est paulo liberalior vita."

F 3 Quint. *Inst.* 8.3.21

Vim rebus aliquando verborum ipsa humilitas adfert . . . Cicero . . . Et alibi: "Caput opponis cum eo coruscans."[1]

  [1] *Freund*: conificans A

F 4 Quint. *Inst.* 8.6.47

Habet usum talis allegoriae frequenter oratio, sed raro totius, plerumque apertis permixtum est. Tota apud Ciceronem talis est: "Hoc miror, hoc queror, quemquam hominem ita pessumdare alterum velle ut etiam navem perforet in qua ipse naviget."

---

  [1] Possibly a reference to Clodius' challenge, in the summer of 58, to the validity of Caesar's legislation, even though its invalidation *en bloc* would have rescinded Clodius' adoption into a plebeian family and thus have made his own plebeian tribunate (and

*F 2 [= F 1] Quintilian, *The Orator's Education*

The point of my statement that it makes a difference how the prosecutor said each thing is this: . . . if he used sharp and forceful language, we should express the same thing in our own milder words . . . [5 F 31] and immediately follow with some defense, as for instance, if we must defend a debauchee: "He has been reproached with a somewhat liberal lifestyle."[1]

---

[1] This would fit, e.g., C. Antonius, Cicero's former colleague, whom he defended on extortion charges in 59 (*TLRR* 241); for moral charges raised against him by M. Caelius, see *FRLO* 162 F 17 (= Quint. *Inst.* 4.2.123–24). There is no other indication, however, that Cicero published this defense; cf. Crawford 1984, 126–27.

F 3 [= F 2] Quintilian, *The Orator's Education*

Sometimes the very lowliness of the words lends power to the content . . . Cicero . . . And elsewhere: "You place your head opposite and shake it."

F 4 [= F 3] Quintilian, *The Orator's Education*

Oratory frequently has a use for such allegory, but rarely in its pure form, and for the most part it is thoroughly combined with literal words. This is an example of the pure form in Cicero: "What I marvel at and complain of is that any man should so wish to destroy another that he would even bore through the ship in which he himself is sailing."[1]

its legislation) illegal; cf. Tatum 1999, 172–74. If that is right, the fragment might come from no. 14 or 15.

F 5 Quint. *Inst.* 9.2.18 (~ Rufin. *Fig.*, *RLM* 42.30, where the fragment is explicitly attributed)

Verborum quoque vis ac proprietas confirmatur [vel] praesumptione ⟨aut correctione:⟩[1] "Quamquam[2] illa non poena sed prohibitio sceleris fuit" . . .

[1] [vel] praesumptione ⟨aut correctione⟩ *Russell post Winterbottom*   [2] *ante* quamquam *hab.* Ruf. *Tullius*

***F 6–7** Quint. *Inst.* 9.2.60

Sunt et illa iucunda et ad commendationem cum varietate tum etiam ipsa natura plurimum prosunt, quae simplicem quandam et non praeparatam ostendendo orationem minus nos suspectos iudici faciunt. Hinc est . . . cum quaerere nos quid dicamus fingimus: . . . "Num quid omisi?" et . . . "Aliud ex alio succurrit mihi" . . .

F 8 Quint. *Inst.* 9.3.21

Et de nobis loquimur tamquam de aliis: "Dicit Servius,[1] negat Tullius."

[1] *fort.* Servilius

---

[1] Crawford 1994, 297n3 (similarly Russell 2001, 4:112n47) suggests a connection with *On Behalf of Murena*, in which Cicero spoke in opposition to Servius Sulpicius Rufus, but that speech is not lacunose, and it seems doubtful that Cicero would have con-

UNPLACED FRAGMENTS

F 5 [= F 4] Quintilian, *The Orator's Education*

Anticipation or correction strengthens the force and propriety of words: "And yet that was not a punishment but a prevention of crime" . . .[1]

[1] A reference to the execution of the captured Catilinarians? If so, this could be assigned to no. 13.

*F 6–7 [= F 9–10] Quintilian, *The Orator's Education*

Those points are agreeable and effective at gaining approval both on grounds of variety and per se which, by showing a simple and unpremeditated style of speaking, make us less suspect to the juror. Of this type is . . . when we pretend that we are asking what to say: . . . "Have I forgotten something?" and . . . "One thing after another comes to my mind."[1]

[1] *Plin. Pan.* 18.1 has a similar expression, perhaps imitating Cicero: "One thing after another occurs to me" (*aliud ex alio mihi occurrit*).

F 8 [= F 11] Quintilian, *The Orator's Education*

We speak of ourselves in the third person: "Servius claims it, Tullius says no."[1]

tradicted his friend so brusquely. If this instead refers to the "young Servius" whose charges were abridged at *Mur.* 57, it might be a fragment of the unabridged speech (if that version was published). Alternatively, *Servius* might be a mistake for *Servilius*, with reference to Cicero's dispute with P. Servilius Isauricus in one of the lost *Philippics*; cf. *Ad Brut.* 2.2[3].3; *Fam.* 10.12[377].3–4.

F 9 Quint. *Inst.* 9.3.42

Hanc frequentiorem repetitionem πλοκήν vocant, quae fit . . . in isdem sententiis crebrioribus mutata declinationibus iteratione verborum, ut . . . apud Ciceronem: "Neque enim poterat ⟨non damnari⟩[1] indicio et his damnatis qui indicarant."[2]

[1] *add. Schoell*
[2] *Winterbottom*: indicabantur *A*

*F 10 Quint. *Inst.* 9.4.100

Ex iis quae supra probavi apparet molosson quoque clausulae convenire, dum habeat ex quocumque pede ante se brevem: "Illud scimus, ubicumque sunt esse pro nobis."

F 11 Schemata Dianoeas, *RLM* 73.12

Ὑπεξαίρεσις[1] est latine exceptio, quando aliquid a generali complexione distinguimus, qualis est illa exceptio Ciceronis: "Minus me commovit hominis summa auctoritas in hoc uno genere dumtaxat, nam in ceteris egregie commovit."

[1] afexairesis *cod.*: *corr. Eckstein*

F 9 [= F 12] Quintilian, *The Orator's Education*

They [sc. the Greeks] call this more frequent repetition *plokē*; this is produced . . . within the same sentence by repetition of words varied by frequent changes of inflection, as for instance . . . in Cicero: "Nor could he fail to be convicted on the evidence and by the conviction of those who had offered it."[1]

[1] Perhaps a reference to one of the Catilinarian conspirators tried and convicted in 62: *TLRR* 228–33.

*F 10 [= *F 13] Quintilian, *The Orator's Education*

On the basis of the examples I previously approved, it is clear that the molossus,[1] too, is appropriate for a clausula provided that it have before it a short [sc. syllable] from any foot at all: "We know this, that wherever they are, they are on our side."[2]

[1] A molossus is a foot consisting of three long syllables.
[2] A reference to Brutus and Cassius from one of the lost *Philippics*? Cf. *Phil.* 10.14: "and above all, Brutus is ours and ours forever" (*maximeque noster est Brutus semperque noster*).

F 11 [= F 27] *Figures of Thought*

Hypexairesis is "exception" in Latin, when we are distinguishing something from a general mass, as the following exception of Cicero's: "I have been less influenced by the man's supreme authority in this one category, since in all the others he has exercised outstanding influence."[1]

[1] If he means Pompey, this might be a reference to *Corn. I*; cf. 5–6 T 13.

F 12 Aq. Rom. *Fig*. 9.8 Elice (*RLM* 23.10)

Προδιόρθωσις, praecedens correctio. Haec figura, ubi aliquid necessarium dictu, sed[1] insuave audientibus aut odiosum nobis dicturi sumus, praemunit. Exemplum apud Ciceronem frequens: "Quamquam sentio quanta hoc cum offensione dicturus sim, dicendum est."

[1] et: *corr. Halm*

F 13 Aq. Rom. *Fig*. 37.5 Elice (*RLM* 30.2 ~ Mart. Cap. 5.531)

Ἀντίθετον, oppositum[1] ex contrariis. Haec figura constat ex eo, quod verba pugnantia inter se[2] paria paribus opponuntur. Cuius modi brevissimum est illud Ciceronis . . . aut[3] si dicas: "In pace ad vexandos cives acerrimus, in bello ad oppugnandos[4] hostes inertissimus."

[1] oppositum *Aquila*: compositum *Capella*
[2] *post* inter se *hab. Capella* paribus vocibus colliduntur vel
[3] ut *corr. Ruhnken*
[4] expugnandos α

F 12 [= F 14] Aquila of Rome, *On Figures*

Prodiorthōsis, correction in advance. This figure provides advance fortification when we are going to say something that, though it must be said, is unpleasant to the audience or stirs ill-well toward us. A frequent example in Cicero: "Although I know what great offense will be given by what I am about to say, it must be said."[1]

---

[1] Possibly from no. 12, where Cicero was speaking against the view of many that the Sullan restrictions on the sons of the proscribed should be lifted, since he spoke of having taken on personal ill will in that matter (12 T 2). Cf. *Phil.* 7.8: "Although it will be bitter to hear, please accept without offense what I am about to say" (*etsi erit vel acerbum auditu . . . accipiatis sine offensione quod dixero*).

F 13 [= F 15] Aquila of Rome, *On Figures* (~ Martianus Capella, *On the Marriage of Philology and Mercury*)

Antitheton, an opposition of contraries. This figure consists of opposing words that are set against each other like to like. The following passage of Cicero's is a brief example of this type . . . or if one were to say: "In peace he was ferocious in harassing his fellow citizens; in war, supine in attacking the enemy."[1]

---

[1] This could apply to P. Clodius, in which case it might be from no. 14 or 15. For his role in stirring mutiny in Lucullus' army at Nisibis, cf. Tatum 1999, 44–49.

*F 14 Aq. Rom. *Fig.* 43.3 Elice (*RLM* 31.8 ~ Mart. Cap. 5.532)

Πλοκή, copulatio. Ea figura elocutionis in qua idem verbum aut nomen bis[1] continuo positum diversa significat, ut est illud: "Sed tamen ad illam[2] diem Memmius erat Memmius."

[1] *om. Capella*
[2] illum *a*

*F 15 Aq. Rom. *Fig.* 63.11 Elice (*RLM* 36.17 ~ Mart. Cap. 5.537)

Ἐπεζευγμένον,[1] iniunctum.[2] Hoc genus enuntiationis[3] diversam habet vim a figura superiore [*sc.* διεζευγμένον]: ibi enim copia verborum iactatur, hic brevitas. Nam ut in superiore singulis membris singula diversa reddimus, ita hic plura in uno coniungimus. Quale est hoc: "Quorum ordo ab humili fortuna, a sordida natura, a turpi ratione[4] abhorret."

[1] *ante* ἐπεζευγμένον *hab. codd.* διεζευγμένον *sive vel sim., del. Ald.*
[2] *ante* iniunctum *hab. codd.* disiunctum *sive, del. Ald.*
[3] E: enumerationis *rell.*
[4] E: oratione *rell.*

*F 14 [= *F 16] Aquila of Rome, *On Figures* (~ Martianus Capella, *On the Marriage of Philology and Mercury*)

Plokē, combination. This is a figure of speech in which the same verb or noun, used twice in a row, means different things, as the following: "But nevertheless down to that day Memmius was Memmius."[1]

---

[1] Possibly a reference to C. Memmius, who divorced Fausta, whereupon she married Milo toward the end of the year 55 (*Att.* 4.13[87].1); if so, this point may have figured in speech no. 15.

*F 15 [= *F 17] Aquila of Rome, *On Figures* (~ Martianus Capella, *On the Marriage of Philology and Mercury*)

Epezeugmenon, conjoined. This type of expression has a different force from the preceding figure [sc. *diezeugmenon*]: in that case an abundance of words is flaunted, in this case brevity. As in the previous one we make individual points different by means of individual units, so here we conjoin several points in a single unit. For instance: "Their order is far removed from humble fortune, from a sordid nature, from a base scheme."[1]

---

[1] This may be a description of the equestrian order (*ordo equestris*). If so, it was possibly taken from one of two senatorial speeches in 61 in which Cicero defended the interests of the equites. In one speech, he argued against making equites liable for misconduct as jurors; in the other, he advocated remitting a portion of the contract to farm taxes in Asia Minor (cf. Crawford 1984, 111–14). There is no other evidence, however, that either speech was published. If the context was a senatorial speech, "order" (*ordo*) is unlikely to have referred to the senate because it would have been more natural for Cicero to speak of "your order" (*vester ordo*).

F 16, 17 Iul. Rufin. *Fig.*, *RLM* 39.8

Χλευασμός sive ἐπικερτόμησις. Haec figura risum exci-
tat et severe proposita vafre excutit, eludens personarum
aut rerum comparatione, ut . . . apud Ciceronem: "Quasi
vero ego de facie tua, catamite, dixerim." Vel alias:
"Potuisti⟨ne⟩[1] contumeliosius facere, si tibi hoc Parmeno
per aliquem[2] ac non ipse Parmeno nuntiasset?"

[1] *suppl. Halm*
[2] per aliquem *R. Stephanus*: alloqui *B*

F 18 Iul. Rufin. *Fig.*, *RLM* 39.12

Χαριεντισμός sive σκῶμμα. Hac figura fit festiva dictio,
cum amoenitate mordax, ut apud Ciceronem: "Infirmo
corpore atque aegro, colore, ut ipsi iudicare[1] potestis,
vario."[2]

[1] ipse indicare *ed. princ.*: *corr. Halm*
[2] vario *Dyck*: u. *ed. princ.*

F 16, 17 [= F 23, 24] Iulius Rufinianus, *On Figures*

Chleuasmos [irony] or *epikertomēsis* [sarcasm]. This figure raises a laugh and, when used with a severe tone, cleverly provokes it by mockery with a comparison of persons or things, as . . . in Cicero: "As if I were talking about your appearance, catamite."[1] Or elsewhere: "Could you have acted more insultingly if Parmeno had made this announcement using an agent rather than in person?"[2]

[1] Perhaps a pun on Clodius' cognomen Pulcher (beautiful); cf. 14 F 24; the fragment might therefore be from either no. 14 or 15. For the term of abuse, cf. *Phil.* 2.77 (addressing Antony): "Therefore, when the woman looked at you, a catamite . ." (*ergo, ut te catamitum . . . mulier aspiceret . . .*).

[2] Ruhnken assigned the fragment to *On Behalf of Fundanius*; cf. 8 F 2, where *Parmeno* might perhaps be read instead of *Meno*.

F 18 [= F 25] Iulius Rufinianus, *On Figures*

Charientismos [wit] or *skōmma* [jibe]. By means of this figure language brightens, becomes biting, but not unpleasantly, as in Cicero: "Of a weak and sickly constitution, and, as you yourselves can judge, a motley complexion."[1]

[1] Raillery directed at the young man who unbound his wound in court? Cf. 1 T 2.

*F 19 Ar. Mess. *Elocut.* 85.13 Di Stefano (*GL* 7.504.17)

Quae, malum, ista ratio est? "⟨Quae, malum, est⟩[1] igitur ista ratio, cum statueras eripere, ad iniuriam eripiendi fraudem sceleris adiungere?"

[1] quae malum *add. Schoell*, est *add. Dyck*

F 20 Iul. Vict. *Ars rhet.* 35.4 Giomini-Celentano (*RLM* 395.21, 397.8–11)

De artificiali argumentatione . . . A modo in fine, ut Marcus Tullius dolum circa servos Publii Fabii definivit ex eo quod insidiati sint. Et idem: "Non esse detrectationem[1] circa pacem, cum non clam nec furtim profectus sit, sed palam."

[1] detractionem: *corr. Mai*

*F 19 Arusianus Messius, *Examples of Expressions*

What, confound it, is the reason: "What, then, confound it, is the reason, when you had decided to snatch it, for adding the crime of wickedness to the injury of snatching?"[1]

[1] The words "What, confound it, is the reason" also occur at *Scaur.* F 45d Olechowska, and *Phil.* 10.18; this makes it plausible that the fragment comes from Cicero. For the type of argument, cf. also *Nat. D.* 3.84: "He (sc. Dionysius I of Syracuse) thus added injury to humans to impiety toward the gods" (*ita ad impietatem in deos in homines adiunxit iniuriam*). Possibly the fragment derives from *On King Ptolemy* (see on 7 F 1).

F 20 [= F 30] Iulius Victor, *Handbook of Rhetoric*

On artificial argumentation . . . From the means regarding the goal, as Marcus Tullius defined treachery as regards Publius Fabius' slaves from the fact that they lay in ambush. And the same author: "It is not an evasion regarding peace, since he did not set out in secret or clandestinely but openly."[1]

[1] For P. Fabius' slaves, see Cic. *Tul.* 34. Huschke 1826, 181, suggested that our fragment may also derive from that speech. But in *On Behalf of Tullius* the action that gave rise to the suit was the setting out of Fabius' slaves not openly but by night (sc. to attack M. Tullius' slaves: *Tul.* 21). Following Drumann's suggestion, Schoell 1918, 470, refers the fragment to no. 11 (*On Otho*). But it might more plausibly be connected with *On Behalf of L. Varenus*, since in that case Varenus' journey was at issue (1 F 7 and 8).

*F 21 Iul. Sev. *Praec. rhet.* 13, p. 93.16 Castelli Montanari (*RLM* 361.24)

In coniecturalibus causis hinc argumenta sumuntur . . . a causa: "Satisne igitur cernitis quibus ille mercedibus, quibus emolumentis, quibus praemiis incitatus . . ."

F 22 Iul. Sev. *Praec. rhet.* 18, p. 107.19 Castelli Montanari (*RLM* 365.15; "Hic . . . ingredi" = Grill. *Comm. in Cic. rhet.* 20.126 Jakobi)

Moralis argumentatio de natura hominum vel morum consuetudine ducitur, ut Cicero: "Hic ego[1] dubitem in eam disputationem ingredi quae ducatur ex natura hominum atque omnium sensibus?"

[1] ego *P²Grilli*: ergo *codd. Grilli*

*F 21 [= *F 28] Iulius Severianus, *Precepts on the Art of Rhetoric*

In conjectural cases,[1] the arguments are drawn from these sources . . . from the motive: "Do you see clearly enough by what wages, payments, and rewards urged on, he . . .?"[2]

[1] See on *5 F 30.
[2] A standard argument for discrediting witnesses (cf. *Part. or.* 49), deployed by Cicero at *Font.* 25 and *Scaur.* 36; he harps on the greed (*cupiditas*) of both the prosecutor and the witnesses at *Flac.* F Mediol. 13 and 66.

F 22 [= F 29] Iulius Severianus, *Precepts on the Art of Rhetoric* (~ [in part] Grillius, *Commentary on Cicero's* Rhetorica)

Moral argumentation derives from the nature of human beings or the habit of their character, as Cicero says: "In this connection, should I hesitate to enter upon an argument that derives from the nature of human beings and the feelings of all?"[1]

[1] Possibly from the exordium of one of the speeches *On Behalf of Cornelius*, where he shows similar hesitancy; cf. 5 F 3, 6 F 1.

APPENDIX

Outline of *On Behalf of Cornelius I*

Part of Speech	Frag. No.	Content
I. Exordium		
	1–2	Prayer
	3	Where to start?
	4	Cicero's dilemma
II. Clearing away prejudice (*praemunitio*)[1]		
	5	Prosecution of Manilius leads to second prosecution of Cornelius
	6–10	Cornelius' first trial
	11, 12	Aftermath of the trial; Cominius' options
	13–17	The prosecution's attempt to link Cornelius and Manilius
III. Division	18	The charges against Cornelius

[1] Treated first, according to 5–6 T 25.

Part of Speech	Frag. No.	Content
IV. Argumentation/Refutation		
A. "Bad law"	19–26	Examples of admirable statesmen enacting bad laws, having their laws repealed; senate's powers of repealing, amending laws
B. Flouting of veto	27–32	The procedure for veto; the definition of *maiestas*; comparison with A. Gabinius' action
	33–42	Defense of revised law on exemptions, law on praetors abiding by their edicts, and bill on electoral misconduct
C. Claim of Sedition	43–46	Cornelius disbanded the assembly at the first sign of violence; no evidence connects him with the unrest
Digression	47–58	The tribunate: its history promoting Roman liberty and continuing utility
Digression within digression	48	Praise of Pompey, Cornelius' commander

Part of Speech	Frag. No.	Content
V. Peroration	59	Appeal for pity
(Unplaced)	60–64	

CONCORDANCES

Crawford 1994 → Crawford-Dyck

Crawford 1994	Crawford-Dyck
1. *On Behalf of Varenus*	
T 1	T 8
T 2	T 7
T 3	T 5
T 4	T 4
T 5	T 1
T 6	T 6
T 7	T 3
T 8	T 2
3. *On Behalf of Oppius*	
T 1	T 10
T 2	T 8
T 3	T 1
T 4	T 2
T 5	T 3
T 6	T 4
T 7	T 5
T 8	T 6
T 9	T 7
T 10	T 11
T 11	T 9

Crawford 1994	Crawford-Dyck
4. On Manilius	
T 1	T 2
T 2	T 3
T 3	T 4
T 4	T 5
T 5	T 6
T 6	T 7
T 7	T 1
5–6. On Behalf of Cornelius I–II	
T 1	T 3
T 2	T 4
T 3	T 8
T 4	T 25
T 5	T 12
T 6	T 9
T 7	T 5
T 8	T 6
T 9	T 20
T 10	T 7
T 11	T 21
T 12	T 1
T 13	T 2
T 14	T 19
T 15	T 17
T 16	T 16
T 17	T 18
T 18	T 15
T 19	= 6 F 9b
T 20	T 10

Crawford 1994	Crawford-Dyck
T 21	T 11
T 22	—
5. *On Behalf of Cornelius I*	
F 1	F 1
F 2	F 2
F 3	F 3
F 4	F 4
F 5 (p. 78, n. 16)	F 29
*F 6	*F 30
F 7	F 5
F 8	F 11
F 9	F 8
F 10	F 9
*F 11	F 10
F 12	F 6
F 13	F 12
F 14	F 13
F 15	F 14
F 16	F 15
F 17	F 16
F 18	F 17
*F 19	F 18
F 20	F 19
F 21	F 20
F 22	F 21
F 23	F 22
F 24	F 23
F 25	F 24
F 26	F 25

CONCORDANCES

Crawford 1994	Crawford-Dyck
F 27	F 26
F 28	F 27
*F 29	F 31
F 30	F 28
F 31	F 32
F 32	F 33
F 33	F 34
F 34	F 35
F 35	F 36
F 36	F 37
F 37	F 38
F 38	F 39
F 39	F 40
F 40	F 41
F 41	F 42
F 42	F 43
*F 43	F 44
F 44	F 45
F 45	F 46
F 46	F 48
F 47	F 47
F 48	F 50
F 49	F 52
F 50	F 53
*F 51	F 54
F 52	F 55
F 53	F 57
F 54	F 58
F 55	F 59

Crawford 1994	Crawford-Dyck
F 56	F 60
F 57	F 61
*F 58	F 62
F 59	F 63
F 60	F 56
F 61	F 7
F 62	F 64

6. *On Behalf of Cornelius II*

F 1	F 1
F 2	F 2
F 3	F 3
*F 4	*Corn. I* F 49
F 5	F 4
F 6	F 5
F 7	F 6
F 8	F 7
F 9	F 8
F 10	F 10
F 11	F 11
F 12	F 12
*F 13	F 13
F 14	F 14
F 15	F 15
F 16	F 16
*F 17	F 17
F 18	F 18

7. *On the Alexandrian King*

T 1	T 2
T 2	T 3

Crawford 1994	Crawford-Dyck
T inc. 1	—
T inc. 2	T 4
T inc. 3	*T 1
8. *On Behalf of Fundanius*	
T 1	T 1
T 2	T 5
T 3	T 4
T 4	T 2
T 5	*T 3
9. *In a White Toga*	
T 5	T 5 (new content)
F 1	F 1
F 2	F 2
F 3	F 3
F 4	F 4
F 5	F 5
F 6	F 6
F 7	F 7
F 8	F 8
F 9	F 9
F 10	F 22
F 11	F 11
F 12	F 12
F 13	F 13
F 14	F 15
F 15	F 16
F 16	F 18
F 17	F 19
F 18	F 20
F 19	F 21

Crawford 1994	Crawford-Dyck
F 20	F 23
F 21	F 24
F 22	F 10
F 23	F 25
F 24	F 26
F 25	F 27
F 26	F 28
F 27	F 29

10. *On Behalf of Q. Gallius*

T 2	T 3
T 3	T 2
T 4	T 4 (new content)
T 5	T 5
F 1a	F 1c
F 1b	—
F 1c	F 1a
F 1d	F 1b
F 2	F 2
F 3	F 3
F 4	F 5
F 5	F 4
F 6	F 6
F 7	—

12. *On the Sons of the Proscribed*

T 4	—

13. *Against the Assembly Speech of Metellus Nepos*

T 1	T 1
T 2	T 3
T 3	T 2
F 2	F 4

Crawford 1994	Crawford-Dyck
*F 3	*F 3
F 4	F 5
F 5	F 6
F 6	F 7
F 7	F 8
F 8	F 9
*F 9	*F 10
*F 10	*F 11
14. *Against Clodius and Curio*	
T 1	T 1 (shortened)
T 2	—
T 3	T 2
T 4	T 3
T 5	T 4
T 6	—
T 7	T 5
T 8	T 6 (shortened)
F 6a	F 6
F 6b	—
15. *Interrogation on Milo's Debt*	
T 1	—
T 2	—
T 3	T 1 (shortened)
On Behalf of P. Servilius Isauricus	
T 1–2, F 1	— (see xxviii–xxix)
Unplaced Fragments	
F 1	F 2
F 2	F 3
F 3	F 4
F 4	F 5

Crawford 1994	Crawford-Dyck
F 5, 6, 7, 8	—
*F 9	*F 6
*F 10	*F 7
F 11	F 8
F 12	F 9
*F 13	*F 10
F 14	F 12
F 15	F 13
*F 16	*F 14
*F 17	*F 15
F 18	—
*F 19	*F 19
F 20	—
F 21	—
F 22	—
F 23	F 16
F 24	F 17
F 25	F 18
F 26	F 1
F 27	F 11
*F 28	*F 21
F 29	F 22
F 30	F 20
F 31	—

Crawford-Dyck → Crawford 1994

Crawford-Dyck	Crawford 1994
1 *On Behalf of L. Varenus*	
T 1	T 5
T 2	T 8
T 3	T 7
T 4	T 4
T 5	T 3
T 6	T 6
T 7	T 2
T 8	T 1
3 *On Behalf of P. Oppius*	
T 1	T 3
T 2	T 4
T 3	T 5
T 4	T 6
T 5	T 7
T 6	T 8
T 7	T 9
T 8	T 2
T 9	T 11
T 10	T 1
T 11	T 10
4 *On C. Manilius*	
T 1	T 7
T 2	T 1
T 3	T 2
T 4	T 3
T 5	T 4
T 6	T 5
T 7	T 6

Crawford-Dyck	Crawford 1994
5–6 *On Behalf of Cornelius I–II*	
T 1	T 12
T 2	T 13
T 3	T 1
T 4	T 2
T 5	T 7
T 6	T 8
T 7	T 10
T 8	T 3
T 9	T 6
T 10	T 20
T 11	T 21
T 12	T 5
T 13	—
T 14	—
T 15	T 18
T 16	T 16
T 17	T 15
T 18	T 17
T 19	T 14
T 20	T 9
T 21	T 11
T 22	—
T 23	—
T 24	—
T 25	T 4
5 *On Behalf of Cornelius I*	
F 1	F 1
F 2	F 2
F 3	F 3
F 4	F 4

CONCORDANCES

Crawford-Dyck	Crawford 1994
F 5	F 7
F 6	F 12
F 7	F 61
F 8	F 9
F 9	F 10
F 10	*F 11
F 11	F 8
F 12	F 13
F 13	F 14
F 14	F 15
F 15	F 16
F 16	F 17
F 17	F 18
F 18	F 19
F 19	F 20
F 20	F 21
F 21	F 22
F 22	F 23
F 23	F 24
F 24	F 25
F 25	F 26
F 26	F 27
F 27	F 28
F 28	F 30
F 29	p. 78, n. 16
*F 30	*F 6
F 31	*F 29
F 32	F 31
F 33	F 32
F 34	F 33

Crawford-Dyck	Crawford 1994
F 35	F 34
F 36	F 35
F 37	F 36
F 38	F 37
F 39	F 38
F 40	F 39
F 41	F 40
F 42	F 41
F 43	F 42
F 44	F 43
F 45	F 44
F 46	F 45
F 47	F 47
F 48	F 46
F 49	6 *F 4
F 50	F 48
F 51	—
F 52	F 49
F 53	F 50
F 54	*F 51
F 55	F 52
F 56	F 60
F 57	F 53
F 58	F 54
F 59	F 55
F 60	F 56
F 61	F 57
F 62	*F 58
F 63	F 59
F 64	F 62

Crawford-Dyck	Crawford 1994
6 *On Behalf of Cornelius II*	
F 1	F 1
F 2	F 2
F 3	F 3
F 4	F 5
F 5	F 6
F 6	F 7
F 7	F 8
F 8	F 9
F 9a	5–6 T 21.83
F 9b	5–6 T 19
F 10	F 10
F 11	F 11
F 12	F 12
F 13	*F 13
F 14	F 14
F 15	F 15
F 16	F 16
F 17	*F 17
F 18	F 18
7 *On King Ptolemy*	
*T 1	T inc. 3
T 2	T 1
T 3	T 2
T 4	T inc. 2
8 *On Behalf of C. Fundanius*	
T 1	T 1
T 2	T 4
*T 3	T 5

Crawford-Dyck	Crawford 1994
T 4	T 3
T 5	T 2
9 *In a White Toga*	
T 5	—
F 1	F 1
F 2	F 2
F 3	F 3
F 4	F 4
F 5	F 5
F 6	F 6
F 7	F 7
F 8	F 8
F 9	F 9
F 10	F 22
F 11	F 11
F 12	F 12
F 13	F 13
F 14	—
F 15	F 14
F 16	F 15
F 17	—
F 18	F 16
F 19	F 17
F 20	F 18
F 21	F 19
F 22	F 10
F 23	F 20a–b
F 24	F 21
F 25	F 23

Crawford-Dyck	Crawford 1994
F 26	F 24
F 27	F 25
F 28	F 26
F 29	F 27

10 *On Behalf of Q. Gallius*

T 1	T 1
T 2	T 3
T 3	T 2
T 4	—
T 5	T 5
F 1a	*F 1c
F 1b	*F 1d
F 1c	F 1a

13 *Against Q. Metellus' Speech in a Public Meeting*

T 1	T 1
T 2	T 3
T 3	T 2
F 1	F 1
**F 2	—
*F 3	*F 3
F 4	F 2
F 5	F 4
F 6	F 5
F 7	F 6
*F 8	*F 7
F 9	F 8
*F 10	*F 9
*F 11	*F 10

Crawford-Dyck	Crawford 1994
14 *Against Clodius and Curio*	
T 1 (shortened)	T 1
T 2	T 3
T 3	T 4
T 4	T 5
T 5	T 7
T 6 (shortened)	T 8
F 6	F 6a
15 *Interrogation about Milo's Debt*	
T 1 (shortened)	T 3
16 *On Behalf of Milo* (speech taken down)	
T 1–3, F 1	—
Unplaced Fragments	
F 1	F 26
*F 2	F 1
F 3	F 2
F 4	F 3
F 5	F 4
*F 6	*F 9
*F 7	*F 10
F 8	F 11
F 9	F 12
*F 10	*F 13
*F 11	F 27
F 12	F 14
F 13	F 15
*F 14	*F 16
*F 15	*F 17
F 16	F 23

CONCORDANCES

Crawford-Dyck	Crawford 1994
F 17	F 24
F 18	F 25
*F 19	*F 19
F 20	F 30
*F 21	*F 28
F 22	F 29

Schoell → Crawford-Dyck

Schoell	Crawford-Dyck
When He Departed Lilybaeum as Quaestor	
I T 1	2 T 1
I F 1	2 F 1
On Behalf of Varenus	
II F 1, 2	1 F 1, 2
II F 3, 4	1 F 3, 4
II F 5	1 F 7
II F 6	1 F 5
II F 7	1 T 5
II F 8	1 F 9
II F 9	1 T 4
II F 10	1 F 10
II F 11	1 F 6
II F 12	1 T 1
II F 13	1 T 6
II F 14	1 F 8
II F 15	1 F 11
II F 16	1 T 7
II F 17	1 T 2
II F 18	1 T 8
II F 19	1 T 3
On Behalf of Oppius	
III T 1	3 T 1
III T 2	3 T 8
III F 1	3 F 1
III F 2	3 F 2
III F 3	3 F 3
III F 4	3 F 4

CONCORDANCES

Schoell	Crawford-Dyck
III F 5	3 F 5
III F 6	3 F 6
III F 7a	3 T 3
III F 7b	3 T 4
III F 7c	3 T 5
III F 8	3 T 6
III F 9	3 T 7
III F 10	3 T 11
III F 11	3 T 9
III F 12	3 F 7
On Manilius	
IV T 1	4 T 2, 3, 5 F 47
IV T 2	4 T 5
IV T 3	4 T 6
IV T 4	4 T 7
IV T 5	4 T 1
IV F 1	4 F 1
On Behalf of Fundanius	
V T 1	8 T 1
V F 1	8 F 1
V F 2	8 F 2
V F 3	8 T 5
V F 4	8 F 3
V F 5	8 F 4
V F 6	8 F 5
V F 7	8 T 2
On Behalf of Gallius	
VI F 1	10 F 1c
VI F 2	10 F 2
VI F 3	10 F 4
VI F 4a	10 T 2

Schoell	Crawford-Dyck
VI F 4	10 F 6
VI F 5	10 F 3
VI F 6	10 F 5
10 F 7	10 T 5
On Behalf of Cornelius I	
VII T 1	5–6 T 3
VII T 2	5–6 T 4
VII T 3	5–6 T 8
VII T 4	5–6 T 25
VII T 5	5–6 T 12
VII T 6	5–6 T 5, 6
VII T 7	5–6 T 20
VII T 8	5–6 T 7
VII T 9	5–6 T 1, 2
VII T 10	5–6 T 19
VII T 11	5–6 T 17
VII T 12	5–6 T 16
VII T 13	5–6 T 18
VII T 14	5–6 T 10
VII T 15	5–6 T 9
VII T 16	5–6 T 11
VII T 17	6 F 9b
VII F 1	5 F 1
VII F 2	5 F 2
VII F 3	5 F 5
VII F 4	5 F 11
VII F 5	5 F 18
VII F 6	*5 F 30
VII F 7	5 F 3
VII F 8	5 F 4
VII F 9	5 F 13

Schoell	Crawford-Dyck
VII F 10	5 F 14
VII F 11	5 F 15
VII F 12	5 F 8
VII F 13	5 F 9
VII F 14	5 F 10
VII F 15	5 F 6
VII F 16	5 F 12
VII F 17	5 F 16
VII F 18	5 F 17
VII F 19, 20	5 F 19, 20
VII F 21	5 F 21
VII F 22	5 F 22
VII F 23	5 F 23
VII F 24	5 F 25
VII F 25	5 F 24
VII F 26	5 F 26
VII F 27	5 F 29
VII F 28	5 F 27
VII F 29	5 F 31
VII F 30	5 F 28
VII F 31	5 F 32
VII F 32	5 F 33
VII F 33	5 F 34
VII F 34	5 F 35
VII F 35	5 F 54
VII F 36	5 F 36
VII F 37	5 F 37
VII F 38	5 F 38
VII F 39	5 F 39
VII F 40	5 F 40

Schoell	Crawford-Dyck
VII F 41, 42	5 F 41, 42
VII F 43	5 F 43
VII F 44	5 F 44
VII F 45	5 F 45
VII F 46	5 F 46
VII F 47	5 F 48
VII F 48	5 F 47
VII F 49	5 F 50
VII F 49b	5 F 51
VII F 50	5 F 52
VII F 51	5 F 53
VII F 52	5 F 55
VII F 53	5 F 57
VII F 54	5 F 58
VII F 55	5 F 59
VII F 56	5 F 60
VII F 57	5 F 61
VII F 58	5 F 62
VII F 59	5 F 63
VII F 60	5 F 56
VII F 61	5 F 7
VII F 62	5 F 64
On Behalf of Cornelius II	
VIII F 1	6 F 1
VIII F 2	6 F 2
VIII F 3	6 F 3
VIII F 4	5 F 49
VIII F 5	6 F 4
VIII F 6	6 F 5
VIII F 7	6 F 6

Schoell	Crawford-Dyck
VIII F 8	6 F 7
VIII F 9	6 F 8
VIII F 10	6 F 17
VIII F 11	6 F 10
VIII F 12	6 F 11
VIII F 13	6 F 12
VIII F 14	6 F 13
VIII F 15	6 F 14
VIII F 16	6 F 15
VIII F 17	6 F 18
VIII F 18	6 F 16
VII–VIII inc. 1	5–6 T 23
VII–VIII inc. 2	5–6 T 14
VII–VIII inc. 3	5–6 T 16
In a White Toga	
IX T 1	9 T 4
IX T 2	9 T 1
IX T 3	9 T 2
IX T 4	9 T 3
IX T 5	—
IX F 1	9 F 1
IX F 2	9 F 2
IX F 3	9 F 3
IX F 4	9 F 4
IX F 5	9 F 26
IX F 6	9 F 27
IX F 7	9 F 22
IX F 8	9 F 23
IX F 9	9 F 5
IX F 10	9 F 6
IX F 11	9 F 7

Schoell	Crawford-Dyck
IX F 12	9 F 8
IX F 13	9 F 9
IX F 14	9 F 10
IX F 15	9 F 11
IX F 16	9 F 12
IX F 17	9 F 13
IX F 18	9 F 15
IX F 19	9 F 16
IX F 20	9 F 18
IX F 21	9 F 19
IX F 22	9 F 20
IX F 23	9 F 21
IX F 24	9 F 23
IX F 25	9 F 24
IX F 26	9 F 25
IX F 27	9 F 28
IX F 28	9 F 29

On Otho

X T 1	11 T 1
X T 2	11 T 2
X T 3	11 T 3
X F 1	11 F 1
X F 2	11 T 4

On the Sons of the Proscribed

XI T 1	12 T 1, 3
XI T 2	12 T 2
XI T 3	—
XI F 1	12 F 1

Against Metellus' Speech in a Public Meeting

XII T 1	13 T 1
XII T 2	13 T 3

Schoell	Crawford-Dyck
XII T 3	13 T 2
XII F 1	13 F 1
XII F 2	13 F 7
XII F 3	13 F 6
XII F 4	13 F 4
XII F 5	*13 F 10
XII F 6	* 13 F 3
XII F 7	*13 F 11
XII F 8	*13 F 8
XII F 9	13 F 9
XII F 10	13 F 5
Against Clodius and Curio	
XIV T 1	14 T 1
XIV T 2	—
XIV T 3	—
XIV T 4	14 T 2
XIV T 5	14 T 3
XIV T 6	14 T 4
XIV T 7	14 T 5
XIV T 8	14 T 6
XIV F 1	14 F 1
XIV F 2	14 F 2
XIV F 3	14 F 3
XIV F 4	14 F 4
XIV F 5	14 F 5
XIV F 6	14 F 6
XIV F 7	14 F 7
XIV F 8	14 F 8
XIV F 9, 10	14 F 9
XIV F 11	14 F 10

Schoell	Crawford-Dyck
XIV F 12	14 F 11
XIV F 13	14 F 12
XIV F 14	14 F 13
XIV F 15	14 F 14
XIV F 16	14 F 15
XIV F 17	14 F 16
XIV F 18	14 F 17
XIV F 19	14 F 18
XIV F 20	14 F 19
XIV F 21	14 F 20
XIV F 22	14 F 21
XIV F 23	14 F 22
XIV F 24	14 F 23
XIV F 25	14 F 24
XIV F 26	14 F 25
XIV F 27	14 F 26
XIV F 28	14 F 27
XIV F 28b	14 F 28
XIV F 29	14 F 29
XIV F 30	14 F 30
XIV F 31	14 F 31
XIV F 32	14 F 32
XIV F 33	14 T 1, *F 33
Interrogation on Milo's Debt	
XV T 1	—
XV T 2	—
XV T 3	15 T 1
XV F 1	15 F 1
XV F 2	15 F 2
XV F 3	15 F 3

Schoell	Crawford-Dyck
XV F 4	15 F 4
XV F 5	15 F 5
XV F 6	15 F 6
XV F 7	15 F 7
XV F 8	15 F 8
XV F 9	15 F 9
XV F 10	15 F 10
XV F 11	15 F 11
XV F 12	15 F 12
XV F 13	15 F 13
XV F 14	15 F 14
XV F 15	15 F 15
XV F 16	15 F 16
XV F 17	15 F 17
XV F 18	15 F 18
XV F 19	15 F 19
XV F 20	15 F 20
XV F 21	15 F 21
XV F 22	15 F 22
XV F 23	15 F 23
XV F 24	15 F 24
XV F 25	15 F 25
On King Ptolemy	
XVI T 1	—
XVI T 2	—
XVI T 3	—
XVI T 4	—
XVI T 5	—
XVI T 6	—
XVI T 7	7 T 2

SCHOELL TO CRAWFORD-DYCK

Schoell	Crawford-Dyck
XVI T 8	7 T 4
XVI F 1	7 F 1
XVI F 2	7 F 2
XVI F 3	7 F 3
XVI F 4	7 F 4
XVI F 5	7 F 5
XVI F 6	7 F 6
XVI F 7	7 F 8
XVI F 8	7 F 9
XVI F 9	7 F 10
XVI F 10	7 F 7
XVI F 11	*7 F 11
XVI F 13	*7 T 1
Unplaced Fragments	
1	1
2	5
3	—
4	9
5, 6	—
7	—
8–9	*6–7
10	*10
11	12
12	18
13	4
14	—
15	13
16	*14
17	*15
18	11

CONCORDANCES

Schoell	Crawford-Dyck
19	8
20	3
21	22
22	20
23	*2
24	—
25	—
26	—
27	*21
28	—
29	16
30	17
31	—
32	—
33	*19

Crawford-Dyck → Schoell

Crawford-Dyck	Schoell
1 *On Behalf of L. Varenus*	
1 T 1	II F 12
1 T 2	II F 17
1 T 3	II F 19
1 T 4	II F 9
1 T 5	II F 7
1 T 6	II F 13
1 T 7	II F 16
1 T 8	II F 18
1 F 1, 2	II F 1, 2
1 F 3, 4	II F 3, 4
1 F 5	II F 6
1 F 6	II F 11
1 F 7	II F 5
1 F 8	II F 14
1 F 9	II F 8
1 F 10	II F 10
1 F 11	II F 15
2 *When He Departed Lilybaeum as Quaestor*	
2 T 1	I T 1
2 F 1	I F 1
3 *On Behalf of P. Oppius*	
3 T 1	III T 1
3 T 2	—
3 T 3	III F 7a
3 T 4	III F 7b
3 T 5	III F 7c
3 T 6	III F 8

Crawford-Dyck	Schoell
3 T 7	III F 9
3 T 8	III T 2
3 T 9	III F 11
3 T 10	—
3 T 11	III F 10
3 F 1	III F 1
3 F 2	III F 2
3 F 3	III F 3
3 F 4	III F 4
3 F 5	III F 5
3 F 6	III F 6
3 F 7	III F 12
4 *On Manilius*	
4 T 1	IV T 5
4 T 2	IV T 1
4 T 3	—
4 T 4	IV T 1
4 T 5	IV T 2
4 T 6	IV T 3
4 T 7	IV T 4
4 F 1	IV F 1
5–6 *On Behalf of Cornelius I–II*	
5–6 T 1	VII T 9
5–6 T 2	—
5–6 T 3	VII T 1
5–6 T 4	VII T 2
5–6 T 5	VII T 6
5–6 T 6	VII T 6
5–6 T 7	VII T 8
5–6 T 8	VII T 3

Crawford-Dyck	Schoell
5–6 T 9	VII T 15
5–6 T 10	VII T 14
5–6 T 11	VII T 16
5–6 T 12	VII T 5
5–6 T 13	—
5–6 T 14	VII F inc. 2
5–6 T 15	—
5–6 T 16	VII F inc. 3
5–6 T 17	VII T 11
5–6 T 18	VII T 13
5–6 T 19	VII T 10
5–6 T 20	VII T 7
5–6 T 21	VII T 9
5–6 T 22	—
5–6 T 23	VII F inc. 1
5–6 T 24	—
5–6 T 25	VII T 4
5 *On Behalf of Cornelius I*	
5 F 1	VII F 1
5 F 2	VII F 2
5 F 3	VII F 7
5 F 4	VII F 8
5 F 5	VII F 3
5 F 6	VII F 15
5 F 7	VII F 61
5 F 8	VII F12
5 F 9	VII F 13
5 F 10	VII F 14
5 F 11	VII F 4
5 F 12	VII F 16

CONCORDANCES

Crawford-Dyck	Schoell
5 F 13	VII F 9
5 F 14	VII F 10
5 F 15	VII F 11
5 F 16	VII F 17
5 F 17	VII F 18
5 F 18	VII F 5
5 F 19, 20, 21	VII F 19, 20, 21
5 F 22	VII F 22
5 F 23	VII F 23
5 F 24	VII F 25
5 F 25	VII F 24
5 F 26	VII F 26
5 F 27	VII F 28
5 F 28	VII F 30
5 F 29	VII F 27
*5 F 30	VII F 6
5 F 31	VII F 29
5 F 32	VII F 31
5 F 33	VII F 32
5 F 34	VII F 33
5 F 35	VII F 34
5 F 36	VII F 36
5 F 37	VII F 37
5 F 38	VII F 38
5 F 39	VII F 39
5 F 40	VII F 40
5 F 41, 42	VII F 41, 42
5 F 43	VII F 43
5 F 44	VII F 44
5 F 45	VII F 45

Crawford-Dyck	Schoell
5 F 46	VII F 46
5 F 47	VII F 48
5 F 48	VII F 47
5 F 49	VIII F 4
5 F 50	VII F 49
5 F 51	VII F 49b
5 F 52	VII F 50
5 F 53	VII F 51
5 F 54	VII F 35
5 F 55	VII F 52
5 F 56	VII F 60
5 F 57	VII F 53
5 F 58	VII F 54
5 F 59	VII F 55
5 F 60	VII F 56
5 F 61	VII F 57
5 F 62	VII F 58
5 F 63	VII F 59
5 F 64	VII F 62
6 *On Behalf of Cornelius II*	
6 F 1	VIII F 1
6 F 2	VIII F 2
6 F 3	VIII F 3
6 F 4	VIII F 5
6 F 5	VIII F 6
6 F 6	VIII F 7
6 F 7	VIII F 8
6 F 8	VIII F 9
6 F 9a	—
6 F 9b	VII T 17

Crawford-Dyck	Schoell
6 F 10	VIII F 11
6 F 11	VIII F 12
6 F 12	VIII F 13
6 F 13	VIII F 14
6 F 14	VIII F 15
6 F 15	VIII F 16
6 F 16	VIII F 18
6 F 17	VIII F 10
6 F 18	VIII F 17
7 *On King Ptolemy*	
*7 T 1	XVI F 13
7 T 2	XVI T 7
7 T 3	XVI F 12
7 T 4	XVI T 8
7 F 1	XVI F 1
7 F 2	XVI F 2
7 F 3	XVI F 3
7 F 4	XVI F 4
7 F 5	XVI F 5
7 F 6	XVI F 6
7 F 7	XVI F 10
7 F 8	XVI F 7
7 F 9	XVI F 8
7 F 10	XVI F 9
*7 F 11	XVI F 11
8 *On Behalf of C. Fundanius*	
8 T 1	V T 1
8 T 2	V F 7
*8 T 3	—

Crawford-Dyck	Schoell
8 T 4	p. 398 adn. ad V F 3
8 T 5	V F 3
8 F 1	V F 1
8 F 2	V F 2
8 F 3	V F 4
8 F 4	V F 5
8 F 5	V F 6
9 *In a White Toga*	
9 T 1	IX T 2
9 T 2	IX T 3
9 T 3	IX T 4
9 T 4	IX T 1
9 T 5	—
9 F 1	IX F 1
9 F 2	IX F 2
9 F 3	IX F 3
9 F 4	IX F 4
9 F 5	IX F 9
9 F 6	IX F 10
9 F 7	IX F 11
9 F 8	IX F 12
9 F 9	IX F 13
9 F 10	IX F 14
9 F 11	IX F 15
9 F 12	IX F 16
9 F 13	IX F 17
9 F 14	—
9 F 15	IX F 18
9 F 16	IX F 19

Crawford-Dyck	Schoell
9 F 17	—
9 F 18	IX F 20
9 F 19	IX F 21
9 F 20	IX F 22
9 F 21	IX F 23
9 F 22	IX F 7
9 F 23	IX F 8, 24
9 F 24	IX F 25
9 F 25	IX F 26
9 F 26	IX F 5
9 F 27	IX F 6
9 F 28	IX F 27
9 F 29	IX F 28
10 *On Behalf of Q. Gallius*	
10 T 1	p. 398
10 T 2	VI F 4a
10 T 3	p. 429 adn. ad 18–21
10 T 4	—
10 T 5	VI F 7
10 F 1	VI F 1
10 F 2	VI F 2
10 F 3	VI F 5
10 F 4	VI F 3
10 F 5	VI F 6
10 F 6	VI F 4
11 *On Otho*	
11 T 1	X T 1
11 T 2	X T 2
11 T 3	X T 3

Crawford-Dyck	Schoell
11 T 4	X F 2
11 F 1	X F 1
12 *On the Sons of the Proscribed*	
12 T 1	XI T 1
12 T 2	XI T 1
12 T 3	XI T 2
12 F 1	XI F 1
13 *Against Q. Metellus' Speech in a Public Meeting*	
13 T 1	XII T 1
13 T 2	XII T 3
13 T 3	XII T 2
13 F 1	XII F 1
**13 F 2	—
*13 F 3	XII F 6
13 F 4	XII F 4
13 F 5	XII F 10
13 F 6	XII F 3
13 F 7	XII F 2
*13 F 8	XII F 8
13 F 9	XII F 9
*13 F 10	XII F 5
*13 F 11	XII F 7
14 *Against Clodius and Curio*	
14 T 1	XIV T 1, F 33
14 T 2	XIV T 4
14 T 3	XIV T 5
14 T 4	XIV T 6
14 T 5	XIV T 7

CONCORDANCES

Crawford-Dyck	Schoell
14 T 6	XIV T 8
14 F 1	XIV F 1
14 F 2	XIV F 2
14 F 3	XIV F 3
14 F 4	XIV F 4
14 F 5	XIV F 5
14 F 6	XIV F 6
14 F 7	XIV F 7
14 F 8	XIV F 8
14 F 9	XIV F 9, 10
14 F 10	XIV F 11
14 F 11	XIV F 12
14 F 12	XIV F 13
14 F 13	XIV F 14
14 F 14	XIV F 15
14 F 15	XIV F 16
14 F 16	XIV F 17
14 F 17	XIV F 18
14 F 18	XIV F 19
14 F 19	XIV F 20
14 F 20	XIV F 21
14 F 21	XIV F 22
14 F 22	XIV F 23
14 F 23	XIV F 24
14 F 24	XIV F 25
14 F 25	XIV F 26
14 F 26	XIV F 27
14 F 27	XIV F 28
14 F 28	XIV F 28b
14 F 29	XIV F 29
14 F 30	XIV F 30

Crawford-Dyck	Schoell
14 F 31	XIV F 31
14 F 32	XIV F 32
*14 F 33	XIV F 33
15 *Interrogation about Milo's Debt*	
15 T 1	XV T 3
15 F 1	XV F 1
15 F 2	XV F 2
15 F 3	XV F 3
15 F 4	XV F 4
15 F 5	XV F 5
15 F 6	XV F 6
15 F 7	XV F 7
15 F 8	XV F 8
15 F 9	XV F 9
15 F 10	XV F 10
15 F 11	XV F 11
15 F 12	XV F 12
15 F 13	XV F 13
15 F 14	XV F 14
15 F 15	XV F 15
15 F 16	XV F 16
15 F 17	XV F 17
15 F 18	XV F 18
15 F 19	XV F 19
15 F 20	XV F 20
15 F 21	XV F 21
15 F 22	XV F 22
15 F 23	XV F 23
15 F 24	XV F 24
15 F 25	XV F 25

Crawford-Dyck	Schoell
16 *On Behalf of Milo* (speech taken down)	
16 T 1	—
16 T 2	—
16 T 3	—
16 T 4	—
16 F 1	—
Unplaced Fragments	
F 1	F 1
*F 2	F 23
F 3	F 20
F 4	F 13
F 5	F 2
*F 6–7	F 8–9
F 8	F 19
F 9	F 4
*F 10	F 10
F 11	F 18
F 12	F 11
F 13	F 15
*F 14	F 16
*F 15	F 17
F 16	F 29
F 17	F 30
F 18	F 12
*F 19	F 33
F 20	F 22
*F 21	F 27
F 22	F 21

Puccioni → Crawford-Dyck

Puccioni	Crawford-Dyck
On Behalf of Varenus	
F 1, 2	1 F 1, 2
F 3	1 T 8
F 4	1 F 9
F 5, 6	1 F 3, 4
F 7	1 F 5
F 8	1 T 7
F 9	1 F 6
F 10	1 T 5
F 11	1 F 8
F 12	1 F 7
F 13	1 T 4
F 14	1 T 1
F 15	1 T 6
F 16	1 T 3
F 17	1 F 10
F 18	1 F 11
F 19	1 T 2
When He Departed Lilybaeum as Quaestor	
T 1	2 T 1
F 1	2 F 1
On Behalf of Oppius	
T 1	3 T 1
T 2	3 T 8
F 1	3 F 1
F 2	3 F 2
F 3	3 F 3
F 4a	3 T 3

Puccioni	Crawford-Dyck
F 4b	3 T 4
F 4c	3 T 5
F 5	3 F 4
F 6	3 F 5
F 7	3 F 6
F 8	3 T 6
F 9	3 T 7
F 10	3 T 11
F 11	3 T 9
F 12	3 F 7
On Behalf of Q. Gallius	
F 1	10 F 1c
F 2	10 F 2
F 3	10 F 4
F 4a	10 T 2
F 4	10 F 6
F 5	10 T 5
F 6	10 F 3
F 7	10 F 5
On Behalf of C. Manilius	
T 1–2	4 T 2, 5 F 47
T 2	4 T 5
T 3	4 T 6
T 4	4 T 7
T 5	4 T 1
F 1	4 F 1
On Behalf of C. Fundanius	
T 1	8 T 1
F 1	8 F 2
F 2	8 F 1
F 3	8 T 5

Puccioni	Crawford-Dyck
F 4	8 F 5
F 5	8 F 3
F 6	8 F 4
F 7	8 T 2

On Behalf of Cornelius I

T 1	5–6 T 3
T 2	5–6 T 4
T 3	5–6 T 8
T 4	5–6 T 25
T 5	5–6 T 12
T 6	5–6 T 5
T 7	5–6 T 20
T 8	5–6 T 7
T 9	5–6 T 21
T 10	5–6 T 19
T 11	*5 F 30
T 12	5–6 T 17
T 13	5–6 T 16
T 14	5–6 T 18
T 15	5–6 T 10
T 16	5–6 T 9
T 17	5–6 T 11
T 18	6 F 9b
F 1	5 F 1
F 2	5 F 2
F 3	5 F 3
F 4	5 F 4
F 5	5 F 18
F 6	5 F 29
F 7	*5 F 30
F 8	5 F 5

CONCORDANCES

Puccioni	Crawford-Dyck
F 9	5 F 11
F 10	5 F 13
F 11	5 F 14
F 12	5 F 15
F 13	5 F 8
F 14	5 F 9
F 15	5 F 10
F 16	5 F 6
F 17	5 F 12
F 18	5 F 16
F 19	5 F 17
F 20–21	5 F 19–20
F 22	5 F 21
F 23	5 F 22
F 24	5 F 23
F 25	5 F 25
F 26	5 F 24
F 27	5 F 26
F 28	5 F 27
F 29	5 F 31
F 30	5 F 28
F 31	5 F 32
F 32	5 F 33
F 33	5 F 34
F 34	5 F 35
F 35	5 F 54
F 36	5 F 36
F 37	5 F 37
F 38	5 F 38
F 39	5 F 39

Puccioni	Crawford-Dyck
F 40	5 F 40
F 41, 42	5 F 41, 42
F 43	5 F 43
F 44	5 F 44
F 45	5 F 45
F 46	5 F 46
F 47	5 F 48
F 48	5 F 47
F 49	5 F 50
F 49b	5 F 51
F 50	5 F 52
F 51	5 F 53
F 52	5 F 55
F 53	5 F 57
F 54	5 F 58
F 55	5 F 59
F 56	5 F 60
F 57	5 F 61
F 58	5 F 62
F 59	5 F 63
F 60	5 F 56
F 61	5 F 7
F 62	5 F 64

On Behalf of Cornelius II

F 1	6 F 1
F 2	6 F 2
F 3	6 F 3
F 4	5 F 49
F 5	6 F 4
F 6	6 F 5

CONCORDANCES

Puccioni	Crawford-Dyck
F 7	6 F 6
F 8	6 F 7
F 9	6 F 8
F 10	6 F 17
F 11	6 F 10
F 12	6 F 11
F 13	6 F 12
F 14	6 F 13
F 15	6 F 14
F 16	6 F 15
F 17	6 F 18
F 18	6 F 16
Inc. 1	5–6 T 23
Inc. 2	5–6 T 14
Inc. 3	5–6 T 16
On King Ptolemy	
T 1	—
T 2	7 T 2
T 3	7 T 4
F 1	7 F 1
F 2	7 F 2
F 3	7 F 3
F 4	7 F 4
F 5	7 F 5
F 6	7 F 6
F 7	7 F 8
F 8	7 F 9
F 9	7 F 10
F 10	7 F 7

Puccioni	Crawford-Dyck
F 11	*7 F 11
F 12	7 T 3
F 13	*7 T 1
In a White Toga	
T 1	9 T 4
T 2	9 T 1
T 3	9 T 2
T 4	9 T 3
T 5	—
F 1	9 F 1
F 2	9 F 2
F 3	9 F 3
F 4	9 F 4
F 5	9 F 26
F 6	9 F 27
F 7	9 F 22
F 8	9 F 23
F 9	9 F 16
F 10	9 F 5
F 11	9 F 6
F 12	9 F 7
F 13	9 F 8
F 14	9 F 9
F 15	9 F 10
F 16	9 F 11–13, 15
F 17	9 F 18
F 18	9 F 19
F 19	9 F 20
F 20	9 F 21

CONCORDANCES

Puccioni	Crawford-Dyck
F 21	9 F 23
F 22	9 F 24
F 23	9 F 25
F 24	9 F 28
F 25	9 F 29

When He Called a Public Assembly Away from the Games

T 1	11 T 1
T 2	11 T 2
T 3	11 T 3
F 1	11 F 1
F 2	11 T 4

On the Sons of the Proscribed

T 1	12 T 1, 3
T 2	12 T 2
T 3	—
F 1	12 F 1

Against the Assembly Speech of Q. Metellus

T 1	13 T 1
T 2	13 T 3
T 3	13 T 2
F 1	13 F 1
F 2	13 F 4
F 3	13 F 9
F 4	13 F 5
F 5	13 F 7
F 6	13 F 6
F 7 (inc.)	*13 F 10
F 8 (inc.)	*13 F 11
F 9 (inc.)	*13 F 8

Puccioni	Crawford-Dyck
Against Clodius and Curio	
T 1	14 T 1 (part)
T 2	—
T 3	—
T 4	14 T 2
T 5	14 T 3
T 6	14 T 4
T 7	14 T 5
T 8	14 T 6 (part)
F 1	14 F 1
F 2	14 F 2
F 3	14 F 3
F 4	14 F 4
F 5	14 F 5
F 6	14 F 6
F 7	14 F 7
F 8	14 F 8
F 9	14 F 9
F 10	14 F 10
F 11	14 F 11
F 12	14 F 12
F 13	14 F 13
F 14	14 F 14
F 15	14 F 15
F 16	14 F 16
F 17	14 F 17
F 18	14 F 18
F 19	14 F 19
F 20	14 F 20
F 21	14 F 21

Puccioni	Crawford-Dyck
F 22	14 F 22
F 23	14 F 23
F 24	14 F 24
F 25	14 F 25
F 26	14 F 26
F 27	14 F 27
F 27b	14 F 28
F 28	14 F 29
F 29	14 F 30
F 30	14 F 31
F 31	14 F 32
F 32	14 T 1 (part)
F 32b	*14 F 33

Interrogation on Milo's Debt

T 1	—
T 2	—
T 3	T 1 (part)
F 1	15 F 1
F 2	15 F 2
F 3	15 F 3
F 4	15 F 4
F 5	15 F 5
F 6	15 F 6
F 7	15 F 7
F 8	15 F 8
F 9	15 F 9
F 10	15 F 10
F 11	15 F 11
F 12	15 F 12
F 13	15 F 13

Puccioni	Crawford-Dyck
F 14	15 F 14
F 15	15 F 15
F 16	15 F 16
F 17	15 F 17
F 18	15 F 18
F 19	15 F 19
F 20	15 F 20
F 21	15 F 21
F 22	15 F 22
F 23	15 F 23
F 24	15 F 24
F 25	15 F 25
Fragments of	Unplaced
Uncertain Speeches	Fragments
F 1	F 9
F 2	F 8
F 3	F 20
F 4	F 1
F 5	F 5
F 6	—
F 7	*F 6
F 8	*F 7
F 9	F 12
F 10	F 18
F 11	F 4
F 12	—
F 13	F 13
F 14	F 11
F 15	F 3
F 16	F 22

CONCORDANCES

Puccioni	Crawford-Dyck
F 17	*F 2
F 18	—
F 19	—
F 20	F 16
F 21	F 17
F 22	—
F 23	—
F 24	*13 F 3
F 25	*F 10
F 26–27	—
F 28	*F 14
F 29	*F 15
F 30	*F 21
F 31	*F 19

Crawford-Dyck → Puccioni

Crawford-Dyck	Puccioni
1 *On Behalf of L. Varenus*	
1 T 1	I F 14
1 T 2	I F 19
1 T 3	I F 16
1 T 4	I F 13
1 T 5	I F 10
1 T 6	I F 15
1 T 7	I F 8
1 T 8	I F 3
1 F 1, 2	I F 1, 2
1 F 3, 4	I F 5, 6
1 F 5	I F 7
1 F 6	I F 9
1 F 7	I F 12
1 F 8	I F 11
1 F 9	I F 4
1 F 10	I F 17
1 F 11	I F 18
2 *When He Departed Lilybaeum as Quaestor*	
2 T 1	II T 1
2 F 1	II F 1
3 *On Behalf of P. Oppius*	
3 T 1	III T 1
3 T 2	—
3 T 3	III F 4a
3 T 4	III F 4b
3 T 5	III F 4c
3 T 6	III F 8

CONCORDANCES

Crawford-Dyck	Puccioni
3 T 7	III F 9
3 T 8	III T 2
3 T 9	III F 11
3 T 10	—
3 T 11	III F 10
3 F 1	III F 1
3 F 2	III F 2
3 F 3	III F 3
3 F 4	III F 5
3 F 5	III F 6
3 F 6	III F 7
3 F 7	III F 12
4 *On C. Manilius*	
4 T 1	V T 5
4 T 2	p. 38.27
4 T 3	—
4 T 4	V T 1
4 T 5	V T 2
4 T 6	V T 3
4 T 7	V T 4
4 F 1	V F 1
5–6 *On Behalf of Cornelius I–II*	
5–6 T 1	—
5–6 T 2	V T 5
5–6 T 3	VII T 1
5–6 T 4	VII T 2
5–6 T 5	VII T 6
5–6 T 6	VII T 6
5–6 T 7	VII T 8
5–6 T 8	VII T 3

Crawford-Dyck	Puccioni
5–6 T 9	VII T 16
5–6 T 10	VII T 15
5–6 T 11	VII T 17
5–6 T 12	VII T 5
5–6 T 13	—
5–6 T 14	VIII F 2 inc.
5–6 T 15	—
5–6 T 16	—
5–6 T 17	VII T 12
5–6 T 18	VII T 14
5–6 T 19	VII T 10
5–6 T 20	VII T 7
5–6 T 21	VII T 9
5–6 T 22	—
5–6 T 23	VIII F 1 inc.
5–6 T 24	—
5–6 T 25	VII T 4
5 *On Behalf of Cornelius I*	
5 F 1	VII F 1
5 F 2	VII F 2
5 F 3	VII F 3
5 F 4	VII F 4
5 F 5	VII F 8
5 F 6	VII F 16
5 F 7	VII F 61
5 F 8	VII F 13
5 F 9	VII F 14
5 F 10	VII F 15
5 F 11	VII F 9
5 F 12	VII F 17

CONCORDANCES

Crawford-Dyck	Puccioni
5 F 13	VII F 10
5 F 14	VII F 11
5 F 15	VII F 12
5 F 16	VII F 18
5 F 17	V T 1
5 F 18	VII F 5
5 F 19, 20	VII F 20, 21
5 F 21	VII F 22
5 F 22	VII F 23
5 F 23	VII F 24
5 F 24	VII F 26
5 F 25	VII F 25
5 F 26	VII F 27
5 F 27	VII F 28
5 F 28	VII F 30
5 F 29	—
*5 F 30	VII T 11
5 F 31	VII F 29
5 F 32	VII F 31
5 F 33	VII F 32
5 F 34	VII F 33
5 F 35	VII F 34
5 F 36	VII F 36
5 F 37	VII F 37
5 F 38	VII F 38
5 F 39	VII F 39
5 F 40	VII F 40
5 F 41	VII F 41
5 F 42	VII F 42
5 F 43	VII F 43

Crawford-Dyck	Puccioni
5 F 44	VII F 44
5 F 45	VII F 45
5 F 46	VII F 46
5 F 47	VII F 48
5 F 48	VII F 47
5 F 49	VIII F 4
5 F 50	VII F 49
5 F 51	VII F 49b
5 F 52	VII F 50
5 F 53	VII F 51
5 F 54	VII F 35
5 F 55	VII F 52
5 F 56	VII F 60
5 F 57	VII F 53
5 F 58	VII F 54
5 F 59	VII F 55
5 F 60	VII F 56
5 F 61	VII F 57
5 F 62	VII F 58
5 F 63	VII F 59
5 F 64	VII F 62
6 *On Behalf of Cornelius II*	
6 F 1	VIII F 1
6 F 2	VIII F 2
6 F 3	VIII F 3
6 F 4	VIII F 5
6 F 5	VIII F 6
6 F 6	VIII F 7
6 F 7	VIII F 8
6 F 8	VIII F 9

Crawford-Dyck	Puccioni
6 F 9a	p. 41.1
6 F 9b	VII T 18
6 F 10	VIII F 11
6 F 11	VIII F 12
6 F 12	VIII F 13
6 F 13	VIII F 14
6 F 14	VIII F 15
6 F 15	VIII F 16
6 F 16	VIII F 18
6 F 17	VIII F 10
6 F 18	VIII F 17
7 *On King Ptolemy*	
*7 T 1	IX F 13
7 T 2	IX T 2
7 T 3	IX F 12
7 T 4	IX T 3
7 F 1	IX F 1
7 F 2	IX F 2
7 F 3	IX F 3
7 F 4	IX F 4
7 F 5	IX F 5
7 F 6	IX F 6
7 F 7	IX F 10
7 F 8	IX F 7
7 F 9	IX F 8
7 F 10	IX F 9
*7 F 11	IX F 11
8 *On Behalf of C. Fundanius*	
8 T 1	VI T 1
8 T 2	VI F 7

Crawford-Dyck	Puccioni
*8 T 3	—
8 T 4	VI F 3n.
8 T 5	VI F 3
8 F 1	VI F 2
8 F 2	VI F 1
8 F 3	VI F 5
8 F 4	VI F 6
8 F 5	VI F 4
9 *In a White Toga*	
9 T 1	X T 2
9 T 2	X T 3
9 T 3	X T 4
9 T 4	X T 1
9 T 5	—
9 F 1	X F 1
9 F 2	X F 2
9 F 3	X F 3
9 F 4	X F 4
9 F 5	X F 10
9 F 6	X F 11
9 F 7	X F 12
9 F 8	X F 13
9 F 9	X F 14
9 F 10	X F 15
9 F 11	X F 16
9 F 12	X F 16
9 F 13	X F 16
9 F 14	—
9 F 15	X F 16
9 F 16	X F 9

Crawford-Dyck	Puccioni
9 F 17	—
9 F 18	X F 17
9 F 19	X F 18
9 F 20	X F 19
9 F 21	X F 20
9 F 22	X F 7
9 F 23	X F 8
9 F 24	X F 22
9 F 25	X F 23
9 F 26	X F 5
9 F 27	X F 6
9 F 28	X F 24
9 F 29	X F 25
10 *On Behalf of Q. Gallius*	
10 T 1	VI T 1
10 T 2	IV F 4a
10 T 3	—
10 T 4	—
10 T 5	IV F 5
10 F 1	IV F 1
10 F 2	IV F 2
10 F 3	IV F 6
10 F 4	IV F 3
10 F 5	IV F 7
10 F 6	IV F 4
11 *On Otho*	
11 T 1	XI T 1
11 T 2	XI T 2
11 T 3	XI T 3

Crawford-Dyck	Puccioni
11 T 4	XI F 2
11 F 1	XI F 1
12 *On the Sons of the Proscribed*	
12 T 1	XII T 1
12 T 2	XII T 2
12 T 3	XII T 1
12 F 1	XII F 1
13 *Against Q. Metellus' Speech in a Public Meeting*	
13 T 1	XIII T 1
13 T 2	XIII T 3
13 T 3	XIII T 2
13 F 1	XIII F 1
*13 F 2	—
*13 F 3	inc. or. fr. 24
13 F 4	XIII F 2
13 F 5	XIII F 4
13 F 6	XIII F 6
13 F 7	XIII F 5
*13 F 8	XIII F 9
13 F 9	XIII F 3
*13 F 10	XIII F 7
*13 F 11	XIII F 8
14 *Against Clodius and Curio*	
14 T 1	XV T 1, F 32
14 T 2	XV T 4
14 T 3	XV T 5
14 T 4	XV T 6
14 T 5	XV T 7

CONCORDANCES

Crawford-Dyck	Puccioni
14 T 6	XV T 8
14 F 1	XV F 1
14 F 2	XV F 2
14 F 3	XV F 3
14 F 4	XV F 4
14 F 5	XV F 5
14 F 6	XV F 6
14 F 7	XV F 7
14 F 8	XV F 8
14 F 9	XV F 9
14 F 10	XV F 10
14 F 11	XV F 11
14 F 12	XV F 12
14 F 13	XV F 13
14 F 14	XV F 14
14 F 15	XV F 15
14 F 16	XV F 16
14 F 17	XV F 17
14 F 18	XV F 18
14 F 19	XV F 19
14 F 20	XV F 20
14 F 21	XV F 21
14 F 22	XV F 22
14 F 23	XV F 23
14 F 24	XV F 24
14 F 25	XV F 25
14 F 26	XV F 26
14 F 27	XV F 27
14 F 28	XV F 27b

Crawford-Dyck	Puccioni
14 F 29	XV F 28
14 F 30	XV F 29
14 F 31	XV F 30
14 F 32	XV F 31
*14 F 33	XV F 32b
15 *Interrogation about Milo's Debt*	
15 T 1	XVII T 3
15 F 1	XVII F 1
15 F 2	XVII F 2
15 F 3	XVII F 3
15 F 4	XVII F 4
15 F 5	XVII F 5
15 F 6	XVII F 6
15 F 7	XVII F 7
15 F 8	XVII F 8
15 F 9	XVII F 9
15 F 10	XVII F 10
15 F 11	XVII F 11
15 F 12	XVII F 12
15 F 13	XVII F 13
15 F 14	XVII F 14
15 F 15	XVII F 15
15 F 16	XVII F 16
15 F 17	XVII F 17
15 F 18	XVII F 18
15 F 19	XVII F 19
15 F 20	XVII F 20
15 F 21	XVII F 21
15 F 22	XVII F 22

Crawford-Dyck	Puccioni
15 F 23	XVII F 23
15 F 24	XVII F 24
15 F 25	XVII F 25
16 *On Behalf of Milo* (speech taken down)	
16 T 1	—
16 T 2	—
16 T 3	—
16 T 4	—
16 F 1	—
Unplaced Fragments	
F 1	F 4
*F 2	F 17
F 3	F 15
F 4	F 11
F 5	F 5
*F 6–7	F 7–8
F 8	F 2
F 9	F 1
*F 10	F 25
F 11	F 14
F 12	F 9
F 13	F 13
*F 14	F 28
*F 15	F 29
F 16, 17	F 20, 21
F 18	F 10
*F 19	F 31
F 20	F 3
*F 21	F 30
F 22	F 16

INDEX OF SOURCES

INDEX OF SOURCES

GENERAL INDEX

Items in repeated passages (indicated by "=" in the text) are cited only for a text that is written out. The introduction (printed in italics) to the given speech is cited as "intro." Notes are cited as "n." Where possible and necessary, brief identification of individuals is provided in parentheses. If an entry occurs in the text of a fragment, discussion in an attached note is not separately referenced.

GENERAL INDEX

15 F 8. *See also* laws allegedly planned by Clodius

Clodius Pulcher, P. (tr. pl. 58; aed. cur. 56), 3 T 10n, F 1n; 5–6 T 11.5n; 5 F 10n, 11n, 13n, 26n; 9 F 4n, 23n, 28n; 13 F 5n; 14 intro., T 1, 5, 6 and FF *passim*; 15 intro., T 1, FF *passim*; 16 intro., T 1, F 1n; Unpl. 1n, 13n, 16n; as a moralist, 14 F 19

Cloelius, Sextus, 5 F 13n; 16 F 1

Cluentius Habitus, A. (of Larinum; Cicero's client), 3 F 1n; 5–6 T 5; 6 F 9b

Coelius Caldus, C. (cos. 94), 5–6 T 11.1

coitio (electoral alliance), 9 T 2n

Cominii brothers (i.e., C. and P.), 5–6 T 11.4; 5 intro., F 9n, 44n, 47n

Cominius, C. (eques, assistant prosecutor of C. Cornelius), 5–6 T 11.5n; 5 intro.

Cominius, P. (eques, prosecutor of C. Cornelius), 5–6 T 4, 11.5, 11.7; 5 intro., F 5, 7n, 10, *30n, 31n, 48; 6 F 17n

comparison(s), 1 T 4, 5; 5 F 32; Unpl. 16–17. *See also* simile

Compitalia (festival), 5 F 14n

conjectural case (in forensic rhetoric), *5 F 30; Unpl. 21

contio, senses of, 13 T 2, F 4; right to call, 14 T 6.2n

Cornelia (daughter of Sulla), 14 F 20n

Cornelian Law on Electoral Malfeasance, 5 F 25n

Cornelian Law on Treason (*lex Cornelia de maiestate*), 4 T 5n; 5–6 T 11.4n, 12; 5 intro. n.

Cornelian Law on Tribunician Power, 5–6 T 11.6n; 5 F 55n

Cornelii, 5 F 45

Cornelius (owner of the slave Phileros), 5 F 45

Cornelius, C. (tr. pl. 67), 3 T 6; 4 T 1; 5–6 *passim*; 9 T 1; 10 intro.

Cornelius, Cn., 5 F 38

Cornelius Celsus, A. (encyclopedist under Tiberius), 5 F 48

Cornelius Chrysogonus, L. (freedman of Sulla), 14 F 6n

Cornelius Dolabella, Cn. (cos. 81), 5 F 37n

Cornelius Dolabella, Cn. (pr. 81), 5 F 37n

Cornelius Lentulus Crus, L. (cos. 49), 14 T 6.1

Cornelius Lentulus Sura, P. (pr. 63; Catilinarian), 14 T 1

Cornelius Nepos, 5–6 T 7

Cornelius Scipio Africanus, P. (cos. II 194), 5 F 26, 46n

Cornelius Scipio Africanus Aemilianus, P. (cos. II 134), 5 F 49; 6 F 8

Cornelius Scipio Nasica Serapio, P. (cos. 138), 5 F 46n